CURZON'S
PERSIA

TO THOSE OFFICIALS CIVIL AND MILITARY, IN INDIA
WHOSE HANDS UPHOLD
THE NOBLEST FABRIC YET REARED
BY THE GENIUS OF A CONQUERING NATION

Since his two visits to England in 1873 and 1889 the personality and many of the idiosyncrasies of the Shah have become familiar to the British public. Nasr-ed-Din (Defender of the Faith) was the eldest son of Mohammed Shah, and was born on 17 July, 1831. Consequently, he is now just sixty years of age.

From these noble heights let us return once more to earth to the route followed by Curzon on his travels. His plan was to keep to the main routes, and to the most frequented cities—Mashhad to Teheran, Kum and Isfahan to Shiraz, and Bushire to Baghdad. He entered Persia via Transcaspia (the story of the rail journey through that region was given in *Russia in Central Asia*, his earlier book, published just before he set out for Persia).

As on his earlier journey, he failed to obtain from the Russian authorities the necessary franchise for crossing the frontier, and once again, taking the high hand, he started without authority and got through. As the story (here edited) opens, Curzon is riding his horse toward Kuchan, expecting to be met by its Khan, whose emissary he had encountered on the previous day at the village of Imam Kuli. Now read on.

From Ashkabad to Kuchan

Wild warriors of the turquoise hills.

T. MOORE, *Veiled Prophet of Khorasan.*

IT was a little past noon when I arrived. For three-quarters of an hour beforehand I had seen the town and its orchards and vineyards lying far below in the midst of a broad valley, like a footprint of red mould upon a sandy floor. The limits of the highly cultivated ground around the town were distinctly marked; and it was as though some giant, stepping over the earth, had planted one big foot in this desolate hollow of the world's surface, which had straightway burgeoned and blossomed under the magic touch. On the north and south the valley was confined by rolling ranges which stretched away towards Shirwan in the west and eastwards in the direction of Meshed. Within about two miles of the town, and at the last swell of the hill before descending into the plain, I struck the main road again, and galloped briskly towards the walls. About a mile therefrom a bridge with a single high arch and no attempt at a parapet spanned the then waterless channel of the Atrek. A flock of goats was standing in the dried-up bed, and sipping the little remaining moisture in a few stagnant pools. A few dusty poplars fringed the banks of the vanished stream. On the other side vegetation was general and even prolific. Orchards of peaches, mulberry, apricot, and pomegranate were yellowing under the fall of the year. The enclosures were thickly planted with vines straggling in irregular double rows with broad deep irrigation trenches for the water between, and presenting an appearance very unlike the trim precision of the

Russia can afford to leave this portion of her Asiatic frontier absolutely unguarded, aggression from Persia being out of the question, and none but Russians or natives going the other way. This is the Persian Baj Girha, where there is a Custom-house at which dues are levied on caravans from Ashkabad.

N. E. KHORASAN.

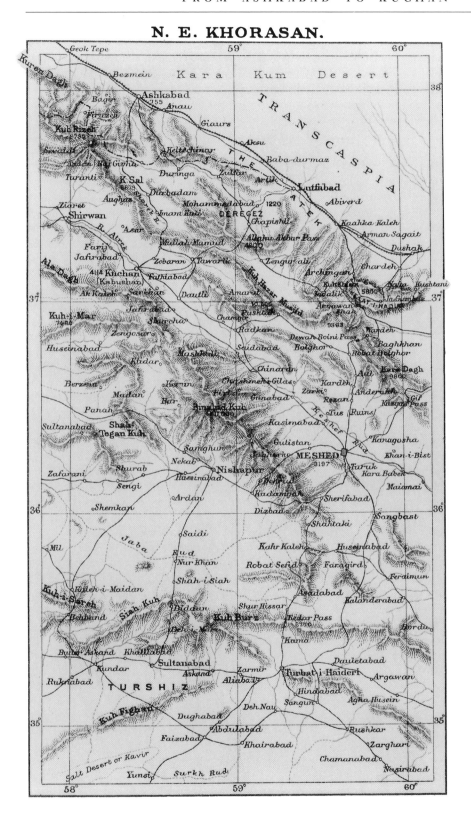

vineyards of Bordeaux. The industrial energy of Kuchan seems to be specially devoted to the manufacture of wine, and in a scarcely less degree to its consumption, a genial immunity which the Shiah Mahometans have never been slow to claim for themselves from the stern asceticism of the Sunni dogma.

By this time I was much surprised to have met no carriage or deputation from the Khan, in view of the recognised reception given to strangers at Persian seats of government, and of the preparations of the previous day. I remembered that when Colonel Baker[1] came to Kuchan in 1873, in the time of the same Ilkhani, he was treated with a similar scant ceremony on his arrival, the reason being that the Khan was sleeping off the effects of a heavy debauch the night before. As these orgies were said to be of constant occurrence, it was extremely likely that the same plea might be forthcoming for the failure to receive me now. However, I was sufficiently versed in Oriental etiquette to know that in matters of ceremony a foreigner is taken at his own estimation, and that any failure to vindicate his titular importance is ascribed not to modesty but to weakness.[2] Accordingly I halted outside the walls of the town, which I declined to enter under such auspices, and sent on my Afghan sergeant and one of the Turkoman *sowars* to the house of the Khan, to say that I had arrived at the hour agreed upon, and was surprised at the indignity of being compelled to halt in a caravanserai outside the walls. In about ten minutes there was a clatter of hoofs; eight or ten horsemen galloped up; and a somewhat dilapidated single brougham, drawn by two grey steeds, on one of which was mounted a postilion, rumbled up to the door. The leader explained that the Khan was very much distressed at my legitimate annoyance; that he had intended to meet me as arranged, but that the messenger from Imam Kuli, the old fellow with the skewbald beard, had named one o'clock as the hour of my arrival. He begged I would forgive the mistake and accept a house which he had prepared for me. My wounded dignity having received this balsam, I mounted the vehicle; my horse was led before; my escort came behind; and the Khan's cavaliers galloped in front, clearing a way through the streets and bazaars with astonishing rapidity.

Entering the town by a low gateway with the earthen towers in the earthen wall, we jolted along a number of narrow and tortuous lanes, and at length pulled up at a house which, I was informed, the Khan had furnished and placed at my disposal. Three excellent rooms, carpeted and with whitewashed walls, relieved by shallow niches, looked out on a little open court, in the centre of which was a circular basin and fountain, surrounded by flower-beds—the normal interior of every Persian mansion. A Russian *samovar* simmered on the table, and some cane-bottomed chairs (which a Persian nobleman invariably keeps for European visitors) stood around. The entire garden wall of the principal room was one large window frame, filled, according to the prevailing Persian fashion, with little pieces of stained glass prettily set in a species of wooden lattice. The second apartment, intended as a bedroom, contained a small iron stove of Persian manufacture; and the niches in the walls were completely covered with Russian pictures of a character that we associate either with tradesmen's advertisements at Christmas time or with the special issues of illustrated newspapers—viz. brilliantly coloured pictures of the Russian Royal Family, and fanciful portraits of black-haired houris with gorgeous necklaces and bare necks and arms. There were no less than four large pictures of the Czar and Czarina, and a coloured print of the principal sovereigns of the world, with the Czar, quite double the size of the rest, in the centre; and the old Emperor of Germany and the Emperor of Austria, of size No. 2, on his right and left. Queen Victoria, in a red silk dress, occupied the central position in a row of the third dimension. Along with these embellishments were nailed up a number of brightly coloured and gilded chromos of religious subjects, such as the Virgin Mary, Christ, and different saints of the Greek calendar, contrasting curiously with the uniformed royalties and the smiling coquettes. The decorations of the room sufficiently indicated the foreign influences to which the Khan is most amenable, and must originally have been devised for guests of another nationality than my own. Huge trays laden with pink and white sweetmeats now arrived from the Khan, who renewed his apologies, asked when I would come to see him, and inquired whether I would be willing to remit the punishment of the red-bearded emissary from Imam Kuli on the ground that, being a Kurd, he had imperfectly understood the explanations of my interpreter. I named five o'clock as the hour of meeting, and gladly acquiesced in the pardon of the offender.

And now, having arrived at Kuchan, let me, before proceeding further, give some idea of the character and inhabitants of this important frontier province, and of the personality of the Kurdish chieftain whose guest I was, and whom I was about to interview.

Three hundred years ago the north-eastern border of Persia was as subject to Tartar inroads as, till ten years ago, it was to the *alamans* of the Akhal Tekkes. Collecting in the desert on the north, they burst through the mountain gorges and defiled, burnt, harried, massacred, plundered, and retired with as much swiftness and as great impunity as they had come. It was characteristic of the dispositions of a great monarch that, recognising the inability of so timid a people as the Persians successfully to resist the invaders themselves, Shah Abbas looked elsewhere for his frontier garrison. Just as he transported an entire Armenian community from his north-west provinces to Isfahan, in order to teach trade and attract prosperity to his newly founded capital, so he now transferred an entire community of warlike Kurdish tribesmen from the same quarter, and planted them in the mountainous glens and uplands of Khorasan. By this judicious act he served a double purpose; for he both fortified his position in the east and relieved himself of the insecurity arising from the bloody feuds and divisions of the Kurdish clans in the west. The expatriated tribes were the Shahdillu, Zaferanlu, Kaiwanlu, and Amanlu; and it is said that while the transplantation of 40,000 families was originally contemplated by Abbas, the resistance of several of the chieftains reduced the number actually moved to 15,000 families. Settled in the mountains and valleys between Astrabad and Chinaran, they held their new territories free from revenue or tribute, on the feudal ground of military service, being responsible for the safety of the frontier and for the provision of mounted troops to the army of the King. The great richness of Kuchan accounted for a money tribute being subsequently demanded from its ruler as well. Bujnurd, as a poorer district, was not mulcted in more than a nominal annual present from its chief to the sovereign. The independent position, no less than the hereditary instincts of the new-comers, soon led to the acquisition by their chieftains of great power and much importance. Of these, Kuchan from an early date acquired the superiority, and the title of Ilkhani (i.e. Lord of the Ils or Clans) was bestowed upon its ruler, either in recognition of his pre-eminence or, as some say, in order to make him personally answerable to the central authority for the good behaviour of the whole. Nevertheless, the Kurdish settlers were constantly either in veiled or open rebellion; and although Nadir Shah attempted to conciliate them by marrying a daughter of the Ilkhani, they took advantage of his absence in India again to assert their independence. At this he was so infuriated that, vowing their complete extermination, he marched against Kuchan, and was already outside its walls when, in 1747, he was murdered in his tent. Again in the present century Kuchan was in open rebellion against Fath Ali Shah; and when Burnes was there in 1832 the town had just fallen, after a protracted siege, to the army of Abbas Mirza, the heir apparent, whose artillery was directed by British officers. The experiences of the present Ilkhani, which I shall presently relate, have shown that under the reigning Shah rebellion is a more precarious experiment; and during the last twenty years and more, especially since the advent of the Russians on the north, and the consequent disappearance of the particular necessity to which the Kurds owed both their position and their power, the strength of the latter and the authority of their chieftains have very sensibly declined.

Of the five Kurdish states originally settled in Khorasan, three alone—Kuchan, Bujnurd, and Deregez—now remain. Of a simple, if rude and independent, character when first they entered the country, their turbulent existence and the opportunities of plunder which they enjoyed soon exercised a deteriorating influence upon the *morale* of the colonists; and travellers who visited them during the days of Turkoman border warfare, and saw both parties at work, reported that there was very little to choose between the methods of the two. Both raided, pillaged, and massacred whenever they had a chance. A Turkoman was always fair game to a Kurd, and a Kurd to a Turkoman; and if we have heard more of the awful results of the Tekkes' devastations in Persia than of the return compliments paid by the Kurds to the Atek, it is probably

A Turkoman was always fair game to a Kurd, and a Kurd to a Turkoman; in appearance the Kurds are easily distinguishable from the Persians, both in physiognomy and dress. They are a fine masculine race, with open countenances, strongly marked and well-shaped features, sometimes fair complexions, and untrimmed beards and hair.

because no curious stranger ever dared to penetrate the Turkoman desert, while a hundred eyes have witnessed the desolated villages and hamlets of Khorasan. In appearance the Kurds are easily distinguishable from the Persians, both in physiognomy and dress. They are a fine masculine race, with open countenances, strongly marked and well-shaped features, sometimes fair complexions, and untrimmed beards and hair. They have adopted the principal articles of Persian costume, but they wear rough sheepskin bonnets (instead of the snug *kolah* or the small egg-shell felt cap) and long sheepskin coats or *poshtins*. Until quite recently they were distinguished for their tribal cohesion and attachment to their chiefs, whom they were ready to support at any time in an insurrection against the central power.

The title of Ilkhani has always been hereditary in one family, though nominally subject to the ratification of the Shah. The Persian Government has, on occasions, tried the experiment of appointing its own officials; but this has invariably led to rebellion and the compulsory withdrawal of the intruder. Till the accession, or rather till the assertion in the last twenty-five years of the authority of the present Shah, the Kurds have uniformly regarded the Kajar dynasty as an alien usurpation. They were the subjects of their own rulers, but not of the Persian monarch. The Ilkhanis dispensed law and justice in their own name, without reference to Teheran, and even wielded the power of life and death. An incident, however, which had occurred just before my arrival in Kuchan will better indicate than any words the change that has taken place. The Vizier or Deputy-Governor of Kuchan, one Ramzan Khan, had been shot by a would-be assassin in pursuit of personal revenge. Though the injured man had not died, the Ilkhani, without any reference to Teheran, put the attempted murderer to death, it was said with horrible tortures. This was regarded by the Shah as an unwarrantable encroachment upon his own prerogative; and I have no doubt that the old Ilkhani did not escape without paying a substantial indemnity.

The pedigree of the Ilkhani's family is as follows: The first chief of whom I find record was Mohammed Husein Khan, who resided at Shirwan towards the close of the last century. His son, Amir Gunah Khan, moved to Kuchan in the early years of this century, and was engaged in frequent conflict with the Turkomans. About 1815 he was deposed by his son, Reza Kuli Khan, who must have ruled for the greater part of fifty years. He was Ilkhani when Fraser visited Kuchan (which he called Kabushan or Cochoon, Kuchan being a contraction of the longer name) in 1822, and was described by him as a man of good and honourable character, but of no great courage or talents, although he succeeded for long in remaining more or less independent of the sovereign power. Taking advantage of his absence upon one occasion, Fath Ali Shah, who was as ambitious of military aggrandisement as he was personally timid and unwarlike, advanced against Kuchan, but failed to take the town, and was obliged to conclude a truce and withdraw. Later, as I have shown, the place was successfully captured by Abbas Mirza, and Reza Kuli Khan was compelled to acknowledge his subjection. Sent as a prisoner first to Teheran and afterwards to Tabriz, he died of chagrin on the way at Mianeh. His son, Sam Khan, was made ruler in his place. The present Ilkhani was a younger son, and told me that he succeeded his elder brother twenty-four years ago.

Amir Husein Khan, my host, who also bears the grandiloquent titles of Amir el Omrah (i.e. Lord of Lords) and Shuja-ed-Dowleh (i.e. Boldness of the Empire, a title conferred upon him by the Shah), has, during his life of over sixty years, enjoyed a somewhat checkered existence. In early days he took part in the campaign against Herat in 1856-7, and in the Persian expedition against Merv that had such disastrous consequences in 1860. Vain, ambitious, and inordinately proud, he was unwise enough, after succeeding to the chieftainship, to incur the enmity of the Governor-General of

Khorasan. Summoned to Meshed to render account, he declined to obey, and held out till a Persian army, sent to chastise him, arrived within sight of Kuchan, when a compromise was arrived at, and the Ilkhani was left in possession on payment of a fine to the Shah which I have heard variously named as 3,000*l*. and 7,000*l*. Again, however, he was either guilty or was suspected of rebellion, and on this second occasion was summoned to Teheran, deposed and imprisoned, his son being made Ilkhani in his stead. After a short time, probably in return for a second and larger ransom, he was released and reinstated, and has since remained in undisturbed possession, having learnt quite enough of the present Shah to find that rebellion, even on the part of a Warden of the Marches, no longer pays. Though the deterioration of his Kurdish clansmen, arising from a long period of peace, and the weakening of his own position consequent upon the strength of the present Shah, and upon the centralisation introduced in all parts of the kingdom by the electric telegraph, have shorn the Khan of much of his ancient prestige, he is still one of the most powerful vassals of the Persian crown, and, apart from his own personality, is interesting as perhaps the last survival of a vanishing order.

With his eldest son, Abul Hasan Khan, now about thirty-six years of age, he has long been upon the worst of terms. The latter was once Governor of Shirwan, the second town of the principality, but was deposed and imprisoned by his father. He now resides at Chinaran, where he enjoys a fixed revenue by order of the Shah, and had lately married a daughter of the Vizier of Khorasan. It is not certain, however, whether he will succeed the old Ilkhani, as he is subject to fits of madness, in one of which he was said to have beaten his former wife, a Turkoman woman, to death; and, moreover, he inherits in full measure the parental addiction to drink.

It is, I fear, as a drunkard that the old chief is best known to English readers and has been commemorated by English writers. During the past twenty years he has been visited and interviewed by several Englishmen: by Colonel Valentine Baker in 1873, Captain Napier in 1874, Sir C. MacGregor in 1875, and Edmund O'Donovan in 1880; and by most of these authorities was found either drinking or drunk, or slowly recovering from the effects of drink. Kuchan being noted for its white wine, and the Khan having a partiality besides for brandy, arrack, and any spirit that is sufficiently potent. General Grodekoff, who was despatched to Khorasan in disguise in 1880 by General Skobeleff, with the knowledge of the Shah, in order to purchase supplies for the Russian army then operating against the Tekke Turkomans in Transcaspia, was well aware beforehand of the propensities of the Kurdish chieftain, and in his official account of the mission entrusted to him very candidly avows the steps by which he sought to ingratiate himself with his too convivial host:—

Knowing that he was fond of liquor, we placed several bottles of wine, liqueurs, and *vodka* before him; and in a very short time the Shuja had drunk several glasses of different wines, and then called in his singers and musicians. The men who came with him, his surgeon, and his favourites, Vali Khan and Ramzan Khan, drank themselves stupid, and a regular orgy began. Next day I went to see the Amir, and presented my documents to him. Bottles were already standing before him, and he explained that he was recovering from his intoxication. During our conversation he repeatedly partook of brandy, opium, *hashish*, and wine, and by noon was quite drunk. In the evening of the same day he invited us to a European supper, and again got intoxicated to the last degree.

In the negotiations that followed, General Grodekoff was alternately impressed by the astuteness of the Ilkhani and disgusted by his habits. Once his editor writes:—

A three days' sojourn in his society showed Colonel Grodekoff that the Amir was very much in possession of all his faculties; that he was not to be deceived by our giving ourselves out as commission agents; and that, although he was a drunkard, still he saw and remembered everything.

But on another occasion:—

To carry on business with him was more than difficult. One had to drink with him, to listen to his drunken speeches, to be present at his orgies, and still to be on one's guard not to show signs of disgust, which would at once have called forth the anger of the barbarian. Truly the world has produced few such brutes, as Colonel Grodekoff expressed himself in a telegram to General Skobeleff.

It would appear, however, that the Khan has only perpetuated himself, and bequeathed to the estimable son whom I have before named, a taste which he had himself inherited from his father; for when Fraser was the guest of Reza Kuli Khan in 1822 he relates that he saw 'the Khan and the whole court dead drunk'. There is a certain fine continuity, therefore, in the family proceedings.

It may be imagined that, knowing as much as I did about Amir Husein Khan, my familiarity with whose antecedents would probably have caused a severe shock to the old gentleman had he been aware of it, I looked forward with some anxiety to my interview. Donning my frock coat, which I confess looked somewhat incongruous beneath a Terai hat, and my goloshes, and attended by as large a retinue of my own servants as I could muster,[3] I followed the escort of six persons who had been sent by the Khan to conduct me to his palace hard by. The façade over the entrance gateway was in the form of a triple arch filled with elegant bas-reliefs in white plaster, made after the fashion of an Italian villa, behind which a neat little kiosque rose above the roof. Passing through the gateway, which was filled with guards, I was conducted to the left into a large open court, about twice as long as it was broad, the lower end of which was divided into flower-beds, while above the middle was a *hauz*, one of those large tanks common to every Persian house of any pretensions, and so cunningly constructed that the water just laps over the stone brim and trickles down into a channel outside. On the pavement beyond were standing some thirty individuals with their backs turned to the tank and their faces towards the upper end, where I could see into an elevated *aiwan* or reception chamber, separated from the court by a latticed window, the central panels of which were thrown open. Entering a small room in the right-hand corner, I left my goloshes, and was ushered into the central apartment of the daïs, which contained only two inlaid tables down the middle, positively laden with coloured glass candelabra, vases, and curios, and an iron bedstead with a mattress in the corner. The glass baubles represent an incomprehensible but very widely spread taste among the Persians of the upper classes, while the bedstead was doubtless introduced as a crowning evidence of successfully assimilated civilisation. In the centre of this audience chamber at the back was a recessed apartment, where the Khan was seated at a table, and whence he rose to welcome me. While he was dictating to the interpreter the customary opening civilities, and during our subsequent interviews, which lasted fully two hours, I had abundant opportunity to become acquainted with his features and deportment.

In appearance the Shuja is striking, but the reverse of handsome. There was a photograph of him hanging in the house where he entertained me, which I subsequently begged of him, and a reproduction of which adorns the margin of the page. He was careful to explain that, having been taken by a Persian artist, the likeness entirely failed to do him justice, a criticism which I am bound to endorse, as, though an ugly, he was

Having been taken by a Persian artist, the likeness entirely failed to do him justice, a criticism which I am bound to endorse, as, though an ugly, he was in no sense a forbidding-looking man, but wore an air both of authority and of intelligence.

in no sense a forbidding-looking man, but wore an air both of authority and of intelligence. Though over sixty years of age, his beard and hair were jet black, the result, I imagine, of dye. He had strongly marked features and a very sallow complexion. He was dressed in a black cloth coat and trousers, with diamond buckles, and a diamond-hilted sword, a black sheepskin *kolah* or hat pressed low down on to his ears,[4] white cotton gloves and stockings, and patent leather shoes. Being very short-sighted, he wore colossal blue spectacles over his eyes. When speaking, his manner and locution were those of one habituated to command. In parleying with the interpreter he showed great animation, and when calling for his *kalian* (the Persian water-pipe or *narghileh*), or issuing an order, his utterance was an imperious growl. At his left hand sat a Seyid (i.e. descendant of the Prophet) in a green turban and prodigious *khelat* of dark blue colour, who occasionally interpolated remarks when appealed to, and generally acted the part of an echo to his master. One of the younger sons of the Khan, a boy of fourteen, was also present, and a *mirza* or secretary was afterwards called in, who understood a few words of French. A group of attendants stood at a little distance, and ran to and fro with *kalians*, tea, coffee, and ices.

In the two conversations which I enjoyed with the Khan—for he returned my visit early on the following morning—he said many quaint and characteristic things which I shall not here repeat at full length, but the bulk of which may advisably be condensed. I soon found that I was dealing with a man who, whatever his common delinquencies, was in full possession of his faculties upon the present occasion, and who had an acute and questioning mind. He occasionally displayed an ignorance that in a European would be puerile; but this mixture of childishness and sagacity is characteristic of the Oriental intelligence, and is natural to a state of life where mental development is crushed by restricted surroundings and by a total lack of general experience.

In reply to my question, he could not tell me how many subjects he possessed, because they were never counted. But there were 40,000 houses under his rule (I am afraid a great exaggeration), and each house paid one *toman* (six shillings) in taxation (a greater still), and each house supplied an armed soldier (the greatest of all). They were very good soldiers, and would fight anybody. This gave me the opportunity I desired of sounding the old gentleman about Russia and his Russian proclivities. I observed that Khorasan was a very rich country, and that it was sometimes said that the Russians wanted to take it.

'How should they take it?' he said.

'In the same way that they have already taken Akhal Tekke,' I replied.

'No, that is out of the question! The people will fight for it. They will all gather together and fight for Meshed. They are good soldiers. We are not sour milk that the Russians should swallow us down.[5] We have a wall of men; a wall of men is stronger than a wall of stones.'

While treating this asseveration with becoming respect, I fear that I was uncharitable enough at this juncture to remember not only the mural decorations of the house which I had so recently quitted, but a certain passage that occurred in a letter written by this same vehement old patriot to the Russian, Grodekoff, only ten years before, in which he had remarked: 'There is only one Jesus on whom were poured out all divine blessings, so that he should come from heaven and create such a people as the Russians.' Changing the subject, I inquired what the Khan thought about railways in Persia. Though he had never seen a railroad in his life, he surprised me by advocating their introduction everywhere into the country, and wondered why they were not begun. He was aware that Queen Victoria had reigned over fifty years and had recently celebrated her jubilee. He could not understand the niggardly policy of the Amir of

Afghanistan in refusing to allow strangers to enter his dominions, and was unwilling to believe that it was more difficult to penetrate to Herat than to Kuchan. The narrow range of his knowledge, however, transpired when I told him that eight days were required to go from London to America, and he immediately asked if the distance was 80 *farsakhs*, i.e. 320 miles, arguing from the maximum distance of a day's land march in Persia.[6]

Very characteristic too, and in strict accordance with the practice of his family (his father, Reza Kuli Khan, put the same questions to Fraser, and the Ilkhani himself had repeated them seventeen years before my visit to Baker), were his interrogations as to my object and motive in travelling. 'Why do you come to Kuchan? What do you want? Do the English Government pay you to travel? How much do they pay you? If not they, then who pays you?' The taste for travel and gratuitous thirst for knowledge are emotions quite incomprehensible to the Oriental mind.[7]

I had great difficulty also in explaining to him my own profession and the position of my family. Parliament he had never heard of; and when I told him that I was a member of the great *mejilis* (council), he replied, 'Are you a soldier?' The status or rank of an English nobleman conveyed nothing to him; but he put the pertinent questions, 'Has your father many soldiers?' and 'Who made him governor of his property?' He was positively amazed at a tenure of the same estates lasting over 800 years, but replied, in the spirit of Mr. Hardcastle in 'She Stoops to Conquer',[8] and with a Conservatism which I could not fail to admire, that Ferenghistan was a great country because of its antiquity; age, as he said, meaning authority.

Acting in unconscious imitation of Fraser, who, nearly seventy years before, had presented a silver hunting watch to the father of my host, I endeavoured to make some little recognition of the hospitality of which I was the recipient by offering the Ilkhani a watch, the hours and minutes upon the face of which were marked not by a revolving hand, but by numerals appearing on a disc. He was vastly interested in this novelty; but as he could not understand the figures, which did not correspond with the Roman numerals on watches which he had previously seen or possessed, I had to draw up a table with the ordinary numerals from 1 to 60 and their Roman equivalents, to which his secretary appended a Persian translation. Having accepted the watch, the Shuja somewhat staggered me by inquiring how much it had cost. I attributed this question, which in a European would have implied impertinent curiosity, to the Oriental desire to make a return of as nearly as possible equivalent value to the donor, the notorious character of the Ilkhani for stinginess rendering it certain that he would not give a farthing in excess. What the quality or worth of his return gift may have been I never discovered; because, although he brought a bundle with him on his valedictory visit the next day, which I afterwards heard contained an intended present of carpets or embroidery, he failed to offer it to me, and it was said to have been purloined by some of his servants.

Such were the main incidents of my intercourse with the old chief of Kuchan. I am glad to be able, if not to contradict the versions of his character and accomplishments that have been given by my predecessors, at least to depict another and more favourable side of his nature. I note that on Sir C. MacGregor in 1875 he left the same impression of dignified manners and considerable intelligence. In the evening I had an opportunity both of becoming acquainted with the Persian *cuisine* and of testing the quality of the Khan's own kitchen. A dinner that would have fed a regiment was brought ready cooked from his house to that which he was pleased to call mine, and deposited in dishes upon the floor of the room. There were soup, chickens cooked in no less than three different ways, leg of lamb, mutton *ragoût*, excellent *kabobs*, a

Persian omelette, three gigantic platters of rice, two of them containing the famous Persian *chilau* or plain boiled rice, the third a *pilau*, or rice mixed with meat and currants,[9] and other dishes for which I cannot find a name. The cooking of such as I tried was excellent, and the rice especially was prepared in a manner that no Parisian artist could emulate. For drink there was Kuchan wine, which I thought extremely nasty, sour milk, which is equally distasteful to the untrained palate, and native sherbet, which, though little else than iced sugar and water, is a most agreeable and refreshing beverage. Delicately carved and transparent pear-wood spoons from Abadeh floated in the sherbet-bowl. Lastly there were piles of grapes. I more than once afterwards partook of a Persian dinner, and thought the fare, though excessive in quantity, better than in any of the other Oriental countries whose native styles I have tested.

While at Kuchan I rode out to inspect the town and its environs. I was informed that it now contains 12,000 inhabitants, but cannot help regarding this as an exaggerated estimate. The walls, of which I made the tour and which, along with the ditch, were constructed by the father and grandfather of the present Ilkhani, have never been repaired since their bombardment by the siege train of Abbas Mirza, and have been still further reduced by frequent shocks of earthquake since, notably one in 1872. Indeed, MacGregor in 1875 said the town was such a mass of ruins that he felt absolved from giving any description of it. The old ramparts are now in many places no more than shapeless heaps of mud. Outside the town are a large number of brick-kilns,

Kuchan, I was informed, now contains 12,000 inhabitants, an exaggerated estimate.

and several ice-houses with lofty mud cones, built in beehive fashion over a pit in which the ice is stored. I was also taken to an extensive garden or orchard belonging to the Khan, the interior of which, ten or twelve acres in extent, was planted with vines, and avenues of apple, pear, apricot, pomegranate, mulberry, peach, plum, and quince. In the centre was a raised platform of beaten clay about a foot high, on which the Shah's pavilion was pitched when he stopped here on his second journey to Meshed in 1883, and where the Khan sometimes camps out when there is danger of earthquakes. Outside the town are also pointed out an elevated plateau known as Takht-i-Shah (i.e. Throne of the King), where Fath Ali Shah's tents were pitched in his expedition against Kuchan; and a hill called Nadir Tepe, at a distance of a mile and a half from the walls, where Nadir Shah met his fate in June 1747.

The only building in Kuchan, in addition to the palace, that lifts its head above the horizontal level of the dusty roofs or is of the least importance, is a mosque with a dome and two stunted minarets, one of these having a wooden gallery at the top from which is given the summons to prayer. As the Shiah Mahometans do not allow unbelievers to enter even the gateways of their mosques, combining a peculiar fanaticism in this respect with excess of laxity in others, neither here nor elsewhere was I able to do more than gaze through the Arabic archway into the inner court.

I am sorry that it was not till later that I read Fraser's account of his visit to Kuchan in 1822; because I should have liked to ascertain the whereabouts of the fragments, described by him, of a magnificent Koran which had been brought by some of the Kuchan soldiers of Nadir Shah from the grave of Timur at Samarkand. Seventy years ago about sixty of these pages, ten to twelve feet long by seven to eight feet broad, and covered with beautiful calligraphy, were seen by Fraser lying upon a shelf in an *imamzadeh*, or saint's tomb.

---

[1] Valentine Baker (1827–1887) who was dismissed from the Army for kissing (or worse) a lady in a train on the London–Camberley Line. Editor.

[2] A Persian grandee will frequently try to get the better of his guest in this manner, not so much with the intention of being rude as to magnify his own importance.

[3] It is a cardinal point of Persian etiquette when you go out visiting to take as many of your own establishment with you as possible, whether riding or walking on foot; the number of such retinue being accepted as an indication of the rank of the master.

[4] The *kolah*, as the national headdress of the Persians, was only introduced by the Kajar family a century ago. Up till that time the turban was universal. Even after the introduction of the *kolah*, a shawl was sometimes wrapped round it; but this was a distinction limited to the King, the Royal Family, and a few of the great officers of State. It is now only seen in the Court dress worn at the Shah's levées. On the other hand, the *kolah* itself has changed in shape; for whereas at the beginning of the century it was about a foot and a half in height, and sloped up to a peak at the top, it is now ordinarily from six to ten inches in height and is level round the top.

[5] This was an allusion to the coagulated milk, called *mast* or *ab-i-dugh*, which is a favourite drink with the Persians and Kurds; and the meaning was, 'We are not such a simple and agreeable draught as some suppose'.

[6] This answer, which is typical of the ignorance on all matters concerning geography that is universal in Persia, reminds me of the story told by Morier (*First Journey*, p. 215) of Fath Ali Shah, who was very curious about America, and asked Sir Harford Jones, 'What sort of a place is it? How do you get at it? Is it underground?' Similarly, a Persian envoy to London, half a century later, being told that the steamer which was carrying him had engines of 500 horse-power, exclaimed delightedly, 'Oh, show me the stables'.

[7] 'These people cannot conceive that any one should travel for pleasure or from curiosity. Who, argue they, would voluntarily undergo the fatigues and dangers, not to mention the heavy expense, of a long journey merely for the sake of collecting information? If, therefore, there be no ostensible motive for the journey, as that of business or of traffic, they at once assign the one in their opinion most likely.'—Fraser, *Journey into Khorasan*, p. 579.

[8] 'I love everything that's old: old friends, old times, old manners, old books, old wine.'

[9] The *chilau*, which is a triumph of cooking, comes up in the form of 'a white pyramid of steamed rice, every grain of which is dry outside, but inside is full of juice,' and is served with a large number of *entrées*. For its recipe, *vide* Thielmann (*Journey in the Caucasus*, vol. ii. p. 26), copied from Polak's *Persien*. As for the *pilau*, Chardin declared that there were above twenty sorts, for which he gave the recipes, made up with mutton, lamb, pullets, &c. The results of a long experience are condensed in these words: 'It has a wonderful, sobering, filling, and nourishing effect. One eats so much that one expects to expire; but at the end of half an hour you do not know what has become of it all; you no longer feel the stomach loaded' (edit. Lloyd, vol. ii. p. 226; edit. Langlès, vol. viii. p. 187).

From Kuchan to Kelat-i-Nadiri

And one a foreground black with stones and slags,
Beyond—a line of heights, and higher
All barred with long white cloud and scornful crags,
And highest snow and fire.

TENNYSON, *The Palace of Art*.

FROM Kuchan it was my intention, if possible, to visit the famous frontier stronghold of Kelat-i-Nadiri, the Fort of Nadir Shah, described by previous travellers as one of the most extraordinary natural phenomena in the world, and famous even in this land of mountain fastnesses and impregnable defiles for its inaccessibility and amazing natural strength. Ever since the rumour had been spread, and even circulated in Europe, that Russia coveted this particular possession [a question was asked in the House of Commons in the spring of 1889 as to whether it had not actually been ceded to the Czar], the Persians had looked with a jealous eye upon any intruder, and I accordingly judged it prudent to say nothing of my desire. I had ascertained that it was impossible for me to fortify myself before starting with a special permit from the Shah, the latter not having as yet returned to Teheran from Europe, and the British Minister not being at the capital, in order to approach the sovereign's representatives. Nor in any case should I have solicited such permission, knowing that if granted it would at once have been treated as a precedent by the Russians for demanding a similar concession, which might in the case of their emissary have meant something very different from the visit of so innocent a traveller as myself. I was still less willing to telegraph for leave to the Governor-General of Khorasan at Meshed, because I doubted his ability to grant it, and felt certain that my footsteps would at once be dogged by spies, if I was not actually turned back. The Persians are so extravagantly suspicious of foreigners, and particularly of such as sketch, or ask questions, or measure, or pull instruments out of their pockets, that no successful exploration would ever be undertaken if they were to be forewarned of the traveller's intention. I determined, therefore, to take no one into my counsels, but to announce that I was going to Meshed and might possibly diverge on the way to hunt in the mountains; my secret resolve being to strike across country by whatever route I could find, and ascertain for myself whether it was possible for a single individual, unexpected and unannounced, to penetrate into Kelat.

I had the greatest difficulty in eluding the vigilance of the Ilkhani, who was not only full of curiosity as to my movements, but also insisted upon my travelling in his brand-new Russian victoria as far as Meshed, threatening to return me the silver watch if I would not accept the loan of his vehicle. It was in vain that I said that I preferred to ride. 'You will have plenty of riding later on,' was the reply. Or that I wanted to stop at the villages *en route*. 'So can the carriage,' was the rejoinder. Finally I compromised by accepting the victoria, with the intention of sending it back at the end of the first stage; and concluded by a most ceremonious departure from Kuchan. The Khan walked with me through the streets, holding me by the hand, and deposited me in the vehicle, which was of Moscow build and of the newest and most elegant description (I fell to wondering from whom the present had come), and to which were harnessed four grey horses with postillions. With mounted *gholams* clearing a way in front and attendants walking by the side, the victoria, with myself inside it, rolled slowly out of the town.

The first part of my route lay along the highway to Meshed; as, in order to avoid suspicion, I had decided upon pursuing it as far as Radkan, on the outskirts of the Shuja's government, and forty miles from his city. The road runs across an almost dead level, although at about twenty miles from Kuchan it crosses the watershed between the Atrek and Keshef Rud drainage. It was unmetalled, in bad repair, and reflected no credit on the engineer who had constructed it. My postillions, as a rule, preferred to drive over the open plain, for the road was frequently intersected by irrigation trenches of a foot or more in depth, which caused excruciating scrunches to the springs of the light victoria. For the first ten miles the country, though at this season destitute of verdure, was richly cultivated, every square yard being turned by the plough. Wrapped up in a shroud of dust, I could scarcely see a yard in front. At intervals on either side of the plain occurred small mud villages, clinging to the shade of tiny clumps of trees, which owed their existence to some stray watercourse or to a happily unchoked *kanat*.[1] Of these villages we passed in succession Fathiabad, two miles from Kuchan; Sarkhan, seven miles; Jafirabad, a collection of low cubical domes, fifteen miles, and Dashtabad. Black goats'-hair tents scattered here and there showed that not all the Kurds had taken to sedentary life, but that some retained their nomad instincts; while an occasional deserted village marked the site of a destroyed *kanat* or exhausted spring. At Kelata, about twenty-two miles from Kuchan, I dismissed the victoria, with instructions to go

Every square yard of land was turned by the plough.

25

It is impossible to tire of the interest and humours of camp life.

home on the morrow; and mounting my horse, and leaving the high road to Meshed and the telegraph poles on the right, continued for another eight miles on the level to Chamgir, a small village some way short of Radkan. As we rode along the plain, now quite destitute of vegetation, a lovely lake of water, the creature of the Eastern mirage, trembled and glittered on the horizon, and ever receded while we advanced. Towards evening the north-east hills, on which the declining sun shone with full orb, acquired a startling glory with tints of rose and coral; the opposite range, plunged in the shadow, was suffused with an opaline vapour that temporarily endowed it with almost ethereal beauty. Presently they both relapsed, the one into a russet brown, the other into a cold and ashen grey. I camped in an orchard outside the village.

At one of the hamlets which we had passed during the day I saw a decidedly primitive manner of threshing barley straw. A threshing-floor was prepared of trodden earth outside the walls, and upon this the straw was spread out; while a long wooden cylinder or roller, armed with big wooden spikes, like the barrel of a colossal musical box, and drawn by bullocks, was driven slowly round and round over the heaps. The result was that the straw was chopped up into small pieces, which constitute the *kah*, or fodder, that is the common food of horses and mules in Persia. This mode of threshing and the implement employed are as old and unalterable as are most of the habits and utensils of the East. It is described at length by Chardin over two hundred years ago, and by even earlier travellers, and will doubtless be visible in remote hamlets two hundred years hence.

It is impossible to tire of the interest and humours of camp life. The traveller arrives first on his superior mount, and selects a favourable spot, beneath the protection of trees, and if possible near to running water. Stretching himself at full length upon an outspread carpet, he enjoys the luxury of relaxation and repose. The villagers crowd round and stare. Some firewood and forage are bought for a few coppers. A flame is soon crackling and blazing; the *samovar* puffs out its grateful steam; and an excellent cup of tea proves to be the best beverage in the world. By this time the remainder of the camp has arrived. The horses are unsaddled by their grooms, currycombed, wrapped in thick felts from ears to tail, picketed, and fed from nosebags containing grass and chopped straw. The tents and beds and cooking utensils and baggage are pulled with a crash from the backs of the mules, who, relieved of their burdens, immediately seek the nearest tree to scratch their hinder parts, and then incontinently lie down, and kicking their heels in the air, do their ineffectual best to turn a somersault in the dust. Meanwhile the cook is hard at work on one side scooping a hole in the ground, into which he transfers the already lighted fuel, and over which he props an iron grid. On the other side the tent-pegs are driven in; the tent soon rises, and, extended on his couch, the traveller recalls the incidents of the day, tries to summon up resolution to write his diary, and awaits the crowning consolation of dinner. By 8.30 or 9 P.M. all is still save the tinkle of the mule bells and an occasional sneeze from the horses; for at five next morning the forward movement must again begin.

And here, before I proceed further, let me introduce to my readers, for the purposes of this chapter only, the names and individuality of my attendants, who will appear several times within its pages. Their leader was Ramzan Ali Khan, an Afghan of Persian extraction (i.e. a descendant of a Persian ancestor who had accompanied either Nadir Shah or Ahmed Shah Durani into Afghanistan in the previous century, and had settled there), himself a *duffadar*, or sergeant, in the Indian Corps of Guides, who are recruited on the north-west border of India very largely from these sources, and whose members are commonly employed upon frontier expeditions or foreign service. Ramzan Ali had accompanied General Maclean, the British Consul-General at Meshed, from India, and was a fine specimen of the Asiatic. Courageous and resourceful, a good horseman, with the manners of a perfect gentleman, he entertained a profound conviction that there was no people in the world like the English. Colonel Stewart, then acting as substitute for General Maclean at Meshed, had kindly given me the loan of his personal servant, Gregory, an Armenian of Julfa, who, knowing English fairly well, and Persian thoroughly, proved himself a most efficient interpreter,[2] and also of his cook. He had, moreover, sent as a personal escort two of the Turkoman *sowars*, or horsemen, a small contingent of whom are kept by the Indian Government at Meshed, and are employed as a private mounted post between that city and Herat. They are chiefly Sarik Turkomans of Penjdeh, who threw in their lot with Great Britain before the Russian advance of 1885, and have preferred to maintain this allegiance rather than join the conquerors, whom they cordially dislike. I present upon the accompanying page a portrait of Nobad Geldi, the senior of these Turkomans, which I took with my 'Kodak' at Imam Kuli. He rode a white Turkoman horse, whose tail was dyed with henna, and which, though of unprepossessing appearance, could always go both faster and longer than any other animal in the caravan. Its favourite pace was the peculiar amble or run which the Turkomans teach their horses, and which it performed with its hind legs very wide-apart. The Persians look upon this idiosyncrasy as a good sign in a horse, proving that it is not knock-kneed, and call an animal thus gifted *asp shulwari gushad*—i.e. 'a horse with broad trowsers'. Riding behind him, I never failed to be tickled at the paces of Nobad Geldi's red-tailed charger, and used to amuse both myself and him by taking him off, as he was ambling along, with my photographic

A portrait of Nobad Geldi, the senior of these Turkomans, which I took with my 'Kodak' at Imam Kuli.

camera. Finally, the only other servant whom I need mention was the Persian groom, Shukurullah, who had met me at Ashkabad, and of whom it was impossible to say whether he was more willing or more stolid.

I will give my diary for the ensuing week according to each day's march, as the information may conceivably be useful to a later traveller following the same line.

October 15.—Starting at 7 A.M., we reached Radkan (seven miles), a largish village of 400 to 500 houses and superb orchards, inhabited by Kaiwanlu Kurds, at 8.30. Away to the right I could discern Saidan (or Saidabad), a village on the road to Meshed; and the curious tower, or Mil-i-Radkan, one of those lofty circular structures, evidently dating from the times that succeeded the Arab conquest of Persia, but whose exact purpose has never clearly been ascertained. Its exterior consists of fluted brick columns, round the summit of which, beneath the conical roof, ran a gigantic Kufic inscription in blue tiles. The interior originally contained three storeys, which have fallen in and disappeared. O'Donovan, who carefully examined the structure, says it could neither have been a dwelling nor a tomb. Why not the latter he does not state; and good authorities have regarded it as the mausoleum of one of the Tartar rulers of

Khorasan, although the theory that it was designed as a watch-tower is also worthy of consideration. Colonel Stewart conjectures that it was intended for a hunting-tower. It is a curious fact that a somewhat similar tower is to be seen near another village, also bearing the name of Radkan, on the road between Astrabad and Gez; from which we may infer that the name, which is neither modern Persian nor Turkish, contains some reference to the object of the building.

Halting outside the village, I sent Ramzan Ali to hire a guide to lead us to Kelat, having heard from an Afghan trader at Kuchan that there was a track from here across the mountains. A man was found who, for three *krans*, offered to conduct us to Pushtah, six *farsakhs*. Further he had never been, but another guide would be procurable there. As we were waiting outside the walls in some fields that formed part of the *rakf* or endowment of the shrine of Imam Reza at Meshed, the leading personage of Radkan—a green-turbaned *seyid* who administered the domain—came out with a posse of townsfolk behind him to inspect some tobacco with which the ground had been planted. He loudly expressed his dissatisfaction with the crop, and his intention to sow wheat another year. We started again at ten. It was a long wearisome ride to Pushtah, for the sun was piercingly hot, and a brisk wind sprang up and blew the desert into suffocating whirlwinds of dust. At about ten miles from Radkan the track passed into the first fold of the foot hills on the north side of the plain, and then struck boldly up a dried torrent bed to a higher plateau, the first of a series of similar terraces between the main range and the Meshed valley. There were no villages, water, or vegetation in this arid desert. At twenty miles from Radkan we came to a kind of circular crater with ragged walls, at the extreme end of which, under a rock once crowned by a fort, nestled the village of Shiri by the side of a genuine stream. Skirting this and continuing to the north, we now passed on to a second and higher terrace that stretched for several miles to the base of the Hazar Musjid,[3] or main range. Dotted at intervals along its length could be seen the villages of Girri, Pushan, and Ardokh. We camped at the village of Pushtah, on the southern side of this plateau, six good *farsakhs* from Radkan. On the plain outside was a very large encampment of Kurd nomads, with black many-peaked tents, and innumerable flocks.

October 16.—Started at 6.45 A.M. We marched straight across the plain to the village of Ardokh (or Ardràkh), two miles, at the foot of the mountain range. Here we entered the bed of a broad but empty torrent that clove a winding passage in the wall of rock. Coming, after a mile or more, to a plain where two gorges converged, we followed that to the right, and proceeded up a mountain valley to the village of Oghrah, picturesquely situated upon a rocky slope at its extremity. Here we procured a guide, following whom we plunged into a deep and narrow gorge that cut straight into the heart of the rock wall, as though some Titan's axe had slashed a savage gash in the solid stone. Its walls were absolutely perpendicular, and shaped in parts by the storms of centuries into windy buttresses and towers, while at the bottom brawled a stream, which had hollowed pools in the rock, and up and across the bed of which it was with difficulty that our horses could be persuaded to climb. The formation and the scenery of this magnificent gorge, whose walls were in receding terraces, are a precise reproduction on a miniature scale of the little known but unequalled cañon of the Colorado River, in Arizona. After two hours' marching in this splendid defile, we scaled the right or east side, and followed a line over the mountains in a north-easterly direction, crossing a second sweep of hills, and emerging upon another valley, richly watered both by springs and streams, and tilled by the villagers of Maresh. This was the most remarkable of the mountain villages that I saw. Clinging to the side of the steep rock, its houses were built entirely of stone, rudely quarried and loosely put together, the ruins of an old stone castle frowning from a peak above the whole. It was a sombre-looking place, even in the full blaze of the sunshine. Here we again turned northwards, and after climbing another ridge of hills descended upon yet another valley, commanded by the romantic village of Bolghor. There we halted for the night, having been on the march for nine hours; although, owing to the extraordinarily rugged ground, we had probably not covered more than twenty-four miles.

After we had encamped I heard that the peasant who had guided us in the afternoon had, while returning to his village, been overtaken and soundly thrashed by a Persian *sowar*. He had, apparently, told my muleteers that he expected this chastisement for showing us the way. But three *krans* were too tempting a bait to be resisted. One of my men overheard the howls of the poor wretch, and watched the soldier beating him; but we neither saw nor heard any more of the latter. He was probably the solitary representative of the Imperial Government in these parts, and did not care to assert its majesty in the face of a numerous caravan.

October 17.—Undeterred by the fate of his predecessor, another guide was forthcoming this morning. For an hour we were occupied in climbing and descending the ridge immediately to the north of Maresh; and then, facing due northwards, we struck the track from Meshed to Kelat, the passage of which along a deep gorge was marked by telegraph poles and a single wire, so loosely hung that we had frequently to dip our heads in order to avoid being struck in the face. At this point I joined the principal caravan route from Meshed to Kelat-i-Nadiri, which has been followed by most English visitors to the stronghold of Nadir. It runs here through a profound and narrow gorge, whose sides are so close that in places there is only room for a single horseman to pass between. The pass is called Dahaneh-i-Zaupirzan, or Old Woman's Gorge, any peculiarly horrible piece of country in Persia being described, as I shall have reason again to observe later on, by this quaint but in Persia most apposite simile. After an hour's laborious marching, we emerged upon a more open valley, where two roads diverged, to the east and to the west. I was informed that the latter also led to

He rode a white Turkoman horse, whose tail was dyed with henna, and which, though of unprepossessing appearance, could always go both faster and longer than any other animal in the caravan.

Kelat, but was very rough and almost impassable for horses, and that the other was the easier and more ordinary way. Accordingly we turned our faces towards the sun and struck eastwards along a rolling upland valley, having upon our left hand the main range of the Kara Dagh (Black Mountains), whose splintered limestone crags were dotted on their inferior slopes with mountain juniper. At one point of this valley, where an elevation is crossed, a most superb view unrolled itself to the east. In tier after tier the mountain ridges descended towards the basin of the Tejend River (formed by the junction of the Keshef Rud and Heri Rud) and the Turkoman plains; while like a yellow scarf against the sky hung the dim outline of the desert. After pursuing this valley for an hour and a half, we turned sharply to the left and scaled the ridge by a path known as the Dewah Boini, or Camel's Neck, so steep, and alternately so rough and so slippery, that, although on foot ourselves, it was with much difficulty that we could prevail upon our horses to ascend. At the crest we gazed down upon a second valley parallel with that which we had just left—i.e. running from north-west to south-east, in the bottom of which appeared a little hamlet with a ruined fort perched upon a knoll, and beyond this again the larger red-coloured village of Vardeh.

Leaving these villages on our left hand, we struck eastwards, following the telegraph poles in the direction of Kelat, the horizontal ramparts of which we thought we could now discern against the distant sky. At noon, having been in the saddle for over five hours, I stopped for lunch by a rivulet running at the valley bottom, which here deepens into a rocky ravine. At this juncture one of the Turkomans, whom I had left behind to point out our direction to the muleteers, arrived with the news that in scaling the Camel's Neck one of the mules had slipped and rolled down for fifty feet, maiming or breaking its leg. I was not in the least surprised at this intelligence, as there are certain places which even Persian mules cannot attack with impunity, and of which this horrible natural ladder was most assuredly one. We left the poor brute behind to be looked after till our return, and followed the gully down for two miles till at its eastern end we came to the small village and crumbling fort of Baghkhan.

Here the wire turned sharply to the north-east, and an hour was occupied in crossing a rolling hump of hills, at whose further edge a deep ravine disclosed itself below, and a second magnificent panorama burst upon our view. Now we could distinctly see the corrugated battlements of the southern outer wall of Kelat, dipping at the point where is the solitary rift in this portion of their circumference. Beyond to the north fold succeeded fold of lower undulations, until like a sea upon the horizon spread the blue band of the Kara Kum (Black Sand), which I had left little more than a week before at Ashkabad. A bee-line due north from where I was standing would have struck the Russian station of Kaahka, on the Transcaspian Railway, from which, or from the neighbouring station of Dushak, a year before my companions and I had lightly and without any preparations contemplated an expedition to Kelat and Meshed, litte recking of the appalling stretch of country that intervened. On that occasion we had been stopped by the Russian authorities;[4] and I had since travelled some thousands of miles in order to renew the experiment from the opposite quarter. We now commenced a very steep and prolonged descent, having to lead our horses most of the way, the ravine breaking at times into a sheer precipice upon our left hand. The opposite side of the gorge had sloping sides of coloured clay and marls, above which rose sandstone pinnacles and towers; and as we contemplated the strange and variegated spectacle, it was as though the mountain had been draped for festal purposes in a particoloured skirt with purple and crimson flounces. The defile was alive with partridges, in coveys of from four to eight. They started up with a whirr almost under our feet, but seldom flew more than a hundred yards. Indeed, they seemed to be greater adepts on foot than on the wing, for they scudded up the bare vertical cliffs just like squirrels. At the bottom of the descent we followed the dried-up bed of a torrent till through a rocky portal, it opened upon the last valley but one before that of Kelat. Here the telegraph poles and track diverged to the right, but as it was now late in the afternoon, and our animals were dead beat, we turned to the left, following the course of a plentiful stream that ran down the valley and made it green with *chenars* (the Oriental plane) and poplars. At the mouth of this valley is a gigantic *chenar* springing from the base of a rock which contains an *imamzadeh*, or saint's tomb. Its boughs were positively covered with rams' horns, a favourite offering of the pious Mussulman to the distinguished dead, and with other emblems of reverence. After a mile and a half I reached the secluded little village of Issurcha or Ab-i-garm (i.e. hot water), so called from some warm springs which rise near by.

Realising that my mules, which I had left far behind, would be unlikely to arrive for hours, if indeed they succeeded in coming at all before it was dark, I made up my mind for a night in a Persian hovel. The inhabitants of Issurcha, however, were by no means glad to see a stranger, and at first declared that they could provide me neither with forage nor with accommodation. After a little delay a villager was found who placed at my disposal an empty mud apartment, in which, with nothing but what I had on me, I made myself as comfortable as I could. Fortunately, about 10.30 P.M. the mules appeared, having found a guide who brought them safely down the mountain.

During the last two days I had, from such natives as we met and interrogated, heard the most conflicting reports of the possibility of entering Kelat. Some declared that any one could go in or come out as he pleased; others that a strict guard was kept at the entrance, and no strangers permitted to pass. The question accordingly presented itself how and in what guise I was to make the attempt. I did not want, after all this trouble, to be turned back. On the other hand, I was reluctant to do anything that, if discovered, might arouse suspicion, or bring discredit upon the English name. I imagine from what I saw later that it would have been possible to ride in at night, though I cannot be sure. I resolved, however, as I had no motive in concealing my intentions, and as they were of the most innocent description, to ride down to the gate, if gate there was, at daylight, and either enter uninterrupted or not at all. My presence, moreover, was likely so soon to become known in the neighbourhood, that disguise or concealment, even if temporarily successful, would be liable to detection in the end.

October 18.—I was called at 4.30 A.M., and started at five in the moonlight, having a rough ride of nearly ten miles before me. Descending the valley of Issurcha to the point where we had entered it on the previous day, we followed the course of the stream, which here turned northwards and plunged into a black and rocky gorge called Derbend-i-Jaur, where we threaded our way between sombre walls in and out of the river bed. The moon hung high overhead, and straight in front the Great Bear twinkled solemnly, standing upon his tail. At the exit of the gorge was a ruined and unoccupied fort. The track now broadened into a flat and open valley, across which were drawn the segments of a curious rocky ridge which had been burst through by some convulsion of nature, and whose strata were strangely contorted and inclined. Streams of water, impregnated with naphtha, gushed from the mountain side and joined the river channel, from which a flock of wild duck started with a prodigious clamour. The sun rose as we were about half down the valley, and disclosed the southern wall of Kelat on our right hand, a magnificent and lofty rampart of rock, springing from the valley bottom to a height of 700 or 800 feet, as level along the summit as though pared by a plane, but scarred and fluted down its absolutely vertical and impervious sides. Four times I passed to and fro beneath this stupendous barrier, and never failed to think it one of the most astonishing natural phenomena that I have ever seen. Its outer slopes or glacis consist of steep acclivities and shelving spurs, which swell up to it from the plain, and resemble colossal piles of *débris* that might have been shot from its summit. From the point where they terminate the rock rises sheer and abrupt to its aërial battlements. As this wall encloses Kelat on the south-east side, it does not catch the morning sun, but remains plunged in shadow. In the evening, however, towards sundown, the red sandstone under the descending rays glistens like columns of porphyry and jasper, and the entire rocky rampart seems to be on fire.

In descending the valley, where not a soul was to be seen, I had observed a place ahead of us where the level top of the rocky parapet ended abruptly in a jutting point, and its continuity was evidently broken by some sort of rift or cleft. As we drew nearer this spot, at a distance of about seven miles from the gorge by which we had entered the valley, the sides began to converge and close, until presently they left only the narrowest passage, the bottom of which was filled by the bed of the stream. Following this natural cutting through one or two zigzags, we came in sight of a rocky portal, some twenty yards in width, completely barred by a wall, the only aperture in which consisted of three arches that admitted the stream, and were also the sole gateway for any visitor to Kelat. The upper part of the wall above the arches was loopholed and had a parapet, but there was no one upon it and no sign of life or movement. This is the famous Derbend-i-Argawan Shah, or Gate of Argawan, or Arghun Shah, the passage having originally been fortified by that monarch, who was the grandson of Hulaku Khan, and is said to have retired to Kelat after being defeated on one occasion in battle by his uncle, Ahmed Khan.[5] A fine inscription on a smoothed surface of rock upon the right-hand wall of the defile beyond the gate records this act of the sovereign. The present barricade is only a modern substitute for that which was built by Nadir Shah, and which, I do not doubt, was a far more substantial structure.

Following this natural cutting through one or two zigzags, we came in sight of a rocky portal, some twenty yards in width, completely barred by a wall, the only aperture in which consisted of three arches that admitted the stream, and were also the sole gateway for any visitor to Kelat.

In the fond belief that all my previous fears had been groundless, I put my horse into the bed of the stream, and, accompanied by Ramzan Ali Khan, Gregory, and Shukurullah, also on horseback, rode through the central arch. No one appeared or challenged. I had time upon the other side to note the inscription of Argawan Shah, and to observe a round tower at the summit of an eminence commanding the entrance, and had already advanced about a hundred yards towards the houses of a village that appeared upon either side of the defile, when suddenly a terrific shouting was heard from the gate behind us, and a miserable soldier, still half asleep, and pulling his tattered cotton tunic about his shoulders, came running out, yelling at the top of his voice. Answering cries were heard; and presently there poured out of the wall, which was really a gate-tower and had casements on the inner side, a motley band of half-clad individuals, for the most part in rags, though an occasional button with the Lion and Sun upon it, and one pair of blue trousers with a red stripe, showed that I was in the presence of some of the *serbaz* or regular infantry of the King of Kings.

As I did not want to begin with a fracas, and as the soldiers were clearly doing their duty, although they had been within an ace of letting me slip through unobserved, I halted and we entered into conversation. At first they were very violent and tried to pull back our horses. But when I represented that I had no intention of going further without leave, they became calmer. I inquired for the officer in command. There did not appear to be such a person. I next asked where was the Khan of Kelat. The reply was given that he was at his village, two miles away. Accordingly I despatched Shukurullah (as a Persian and therefore free from suspicion), with a soldier mounted on the same horse behind him, to the Khan, to tell him who I was, and to request permission to pass through Kelat and out on the other side; or, if this could not be granted on his own responsibility, then to telegraph to Meshed.

While the Persian was away I remained in the rocky gateway conversing with the soldiers. It was bitterly cold, for the sun would not strike the chasm for some hours, so I bought some brushwood and lit a fire. When they heard that I was an Englishman they seemed disposed to be more friendly; for they said that if I had been a Russian they would have shot me down as I rode through the gate, though how they could have guessed my nationality when they never saw me, or have shot at all when they were fast asleep, I did not needlessly vex them by asking. They added that a Russian had come to Kelat last year and had beaten a Persian, and been beaten by them, and had then started to come with 300 Turkomans in revenge; but that they had marched out, and the Russian and the Turkomans had marched back again. They also asked me if it was true that the Zil-es-Sultan, the eldest son of the Shah, had put off the Persian costume, donned English dress, and sailed from Bushire for London. I interrogated them about their existence and service at Kelat. They said that the water was very unhealthy, being impregnated with naphtha, and that they suffered from it.[6] They also complained that, though they were to have been relieved in three months, they had already been there for five, and during that time had received no pay. I could not help feeling for the poor wretches, who were about as like what one ordinarily associates with the idea of a soldier as a costermonger's donkey is like the winner of the Derby.

After an hour and a half of tedious waiting, Shukurullah returned with the news that the Khan wished me to telegraph for leave to the Governor-General of Meshed, and that if the answer was favourable I might pass through. This was all that I desired; so I proceeded to write a telegram to Colonel Stewart, asking him to interview the Governor on my behalf and to wire me a reply. There was some difficulty, however, in finding any one to transcribe the message into Persian characters. Few of the lower

During the half-century since the Persian serbaz *(soldier) has ceased to be put through his exercises by British drill sergeants, and in the absence of any equivalent tuition, and the chronic stint of equipment, rations, and pay, he has sunk to a very low position in the scale of efficiency, courage, and fighting power. Military service is distasteful to him from the start. He is rarely, if ever, a volunteer. Ill-fed, ill-clad, and unpaid, in the intervals of service, and often while actually with the colours, he ekes out a scanty subsistence by plying the trade of a butcher, or porter, or money-changer, or common labourer in the bazaars; from which employment he emerges on parade days, struggles into a uniform supplied from the depot, and, his perfunctory duty fulfilled, returns to his civil avocation.*

orders know the Persian alphabet; if they want to write a letter they hire a scribe to do it for them. The solitary scribe of Kelat was reported to be asleep under the influence of opium; but I insisted upon his being severely awakened, and at length he appeared, and spent exactly half an hour in transliterating the despatch which it had taken half a minute to compose. I now proposed to return to my camp, leaving the Persian behind till an answer arrived from Meshed; but Gregory suggested, from a more profound knowledge of the national character, that I was not yet out of the wood, and that it would be advisable to wait. So I moved to the other side of the gateway and halted in the sunshine.

In an hour Shukurullah reappeared upon the scene with the news that the telegram had been refused on the plea that the line was broken between Kelat and Meshed. Presently arrived a mounted emissary from the Khan, who was voluble with explanations, and afforded me an interesting insight into Persian character. First he repeated that the wire was broken; but when I replied that if that were the case it was unlikely that the Khan would himself have invited me to use it, he shifted his position and said that the wire, though not broken, was trailing upon the ground. Upon my rejoining that communication was not thereby interrupted, he was ready with the counter plea that the Khan had meant me to telegraph not to Meshed but to Teheran. As there was no wire to Teheran from Kelat except by Meshed, this falsehood was easily exposed; but I confess I was scarcely prepared for the fourth, which immediately replaced it—viz. that the Khan had meant me to telegraph neither to Teheran nor to Meshed, but *from* Meshed on my return thither. As it was useless bandying words with so accomplished a liar, I resigned the verbal contest, but insisted upon receiving a direct answer or a direct refusal from the Khan to my request to telegraph; and it was agreed that Gregory, as a more befitting ambassador than Shukurullah, should ride back to the village and receive a definite answer to my ultimatum.

All this occurred within 100 yards of the gate of Argawan Shah on the outer side. As I was giving final instructions to Gregory, the Persian, who had remounted, suddenly clapped spurs to his horse, and disappeared like lightning through the archway, shouting to the guard not to let any one through. When Gregory arrived a few seconds later he was refused the passage. There was nothing more to be done; and thus ignobly ended my attempt to penetrate to the interior of Kelat-i-Nadiri! Shukurullah now told me that when he took the telegram to the office the clerk was about to accept it, when the Khan's son came in and said that his father absolutely forbade any message to be sent at all. I had heard a good deal of Persian artfulness before entering the country, but had scarcely expected so artistic a sample within the first fortnight; and I do not know whether I was more incensed at the treatment I had received or tickled at the illustration it afforded of Oriental tactics.

The most amusing episode, however, was yet to come; for on arriving at Meshed three days later I found the Governor-General in a great state of excitement, having been informed by the faithful Khan that the new British Vice-Consul had appeared at Kelat with an armed retinue, had tried to force a passage, and had drawn his sword upon the guard! The latter had gallantly performed their duty and had expelled the intruder.

October 19.—Before I left the neighbourhood I determined to make one more effort to see the interior of Kelat. I knew from MacGregor's book that, besides the two main entrances of Argawan Shah and Nafta, there were other pathways by which it could be entered; and at Ab-i-Garm a hunter was found who said that he knew one of these very well, but was afraid to conduct me himself. He had a nephew, however, who would act as his substitute, and would appear in the morning. I need hardly say that at the appointed hour the nephew was not forthcoming. That my presence in the vicinity of Kelat was beginning to be regarded with some suspicion, was evident both from this and from an incident which occurred that evening. As I was discussing plans in the mud hovel with Ramzan Ali and Gregory, I heard a scratching in the roof over-head, and, looking up, detected a man, who, it appeared, had come from Kelat, with his ear to a hole in the rafters, eaves-dropping. As no guide was procurable, I decided to go without one. I had noticed in riding down the valley to Kelat that there was one place where the otherwise unbroken parapet of the southern wall dipped, and formed a V-shaped indentation, which seemed to be accessible from below by one of the sloping natural buttresses that swell up against it from the plain. Any future visitor to Kelat who has read this description will not fail to recognise the spot, about halfway down the valley. I was called at 3.30 A.M., the mules were laden, and we all moved out of Issurcha at 4.30 on a black cold morning. Sending the camp on to Vardeh from the Derbend-i-Jaur, I rode down the valley for the last time, and leaving my horse at the foot of the hills began the climb. It did not take long to mount the stony skirts, though the slope was very steep; and I easily arrived below the craggy battlements. Here the rock, the natural conformation of which is in wavy horizontal bands, parallel with the summit, had been artificially scarped by some previous occupant, no doubt by Nadir Shah, so as to form a sort of rocky ledge or pathway running along the face, and defended at intervals by ruined circular towers. There were two such rocky ledges, one about thirty feet above the other. I scrambled on to the lower and pursued it as far as the V-shaped gap. There were only about thirty feet of rock above me; and it was to be climbed. But the face of the rock was very steep and smooth; I was alone, and though I could have scrambled up it was the kind of place that could have been very awkward to come down from again. Accordingly, I resigned the attempt. With the aid of a friend and a rope it could easily have been managed, but from what I know of the interior of Kelat I doubt whether the panorama afforded from the top of the wall would be as striking as might be expected from its external configuration.

On my way back, however, I climbed the highest mountain in the neighbourhood, the name of which I do not know, but whose elevation is far higher than the perimeter of Kelat; and from there my ambitions were so far and unexpectedly realised that, though I could not see the interior level of Kelat, the angle of vision being too obtuse, I could trace the entire circuit of its walls from east to west on both sides; the southern wall, which I had attempted to climb, appearing from the height on which I stood to be the lower of the two, and the summit of the north wall rising above it on the further side. From this point I could follow, without difficulty, the whole southern rampart, nearly twenty miles in a straight line, running as regularly as though it had been built by design, and scarped and scarred along its vertical sides down to the point where the buttress-slopes shelved away to the valley. If in their war with Olympian Zeus the Titans had ever had occasion to build for themselves an unassailable retreat, such might well have been the mountain fortress that they would have reared. I made a sketch from this point of the entire circumference, which is reproduced on the next page. The mountains in the foreground are the range that separate the valley of Issurcha from the valley that leads down to Argawan Shah's gate.

And now, having related with so much minuteness what I did see, I propose to describe from a variety of sources, some of which have not been accessible to the public, what I did not see, in order that my readers may be able to form an accurate idea of Kelat-i-Nadiri as it is at the present moment. They will already have gathered that, though literally translated and commonly called the Fort of Nadir Shah, it is not a fort at all in the accepted sense of the term; consisting as it does of a mountain plateau,

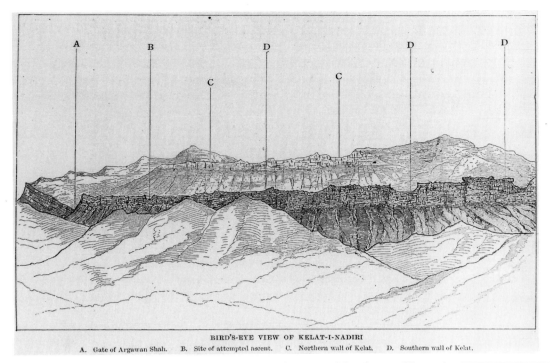

BIRD'S-EYE VIEW OF KELAT-I-NADIRI

A. Gate of Argawan Shah.   B. Site of attempted ascent.   C. Northern wall of Kelat.   D. Southern wall of Kelat.

with a mean elevation of 2,500 feet above the sea, intersected by deep gullies and ravines, some twenty miles in total length by from five to seven in breadth; and only so far resembling a fortress that this vast extent of ground, comprising a probable area of 150 square miles, is surrounded as with a ring fence by a mighty natural rampart enclosing it from end to end with a cliff-wall of naked and vertical rock, 700 to 1,000 feet in sheer height above the valley bottom. From early times the extraordinary character of the place, which must have resulted from some abnormal convulsion of nature, impressed itself upon the imagination of the neighbouring peoples; and Iranian legend localises here one of the mythical combats between the hero Rustam and the alien forces of Turan under Afrasiab, who, expelled from Kelat by the victorious hosts of Iran, fell back upon the Oxus, where they sustained a final and crushing defeat. Here too, according to the Shah Nameh of Firdusi, settled Ferud, the brother of Kai Khosru, and here he was attacked and slain by Tus. The inscription to which I have alluded proves that as a defensible and defended retreat it was known to the Mongol successors of Jenghiz Khan. Timur is said to have possessed himself of it by stratagem.

But it was not till the times of Nadir Shah that full use was made of its invaluable natural gifts. Returning from India, laden with the spoils of conquered kingdoms and with the rifled treasures of the Great Mogul, he saw in Kelat, with which he must have been familiar from childhood,[7] the ideal storehouse where this vast wealth could be deposited, and also an invulnerable place of arms. Accordingly, he constructed powerful fortifications at all the entrances, placed watch-towers on every peak and point of vantage, artificially scarped the rocky battlements both within and without, in order to render them still more impossible of access, built himself a residence on a plateau in the interior (which it is said he rarely occupied), and provided for a supply of good water. Entrance to the interior is gained by one of five gates, of which the two principal are Argawan Shah on the south and Nafta on the north. The three others are Kushtani on the south-east, Chubast on the west, and Dehcha on the north-west. All of these

I made a sketch from this point of the entire circumference of Kelat. The mountains in the foreground are the range that separate the valley of Issurcha from the valley that leads down to Argawan Shah's gate.

gates are said to be fortified and defended by troops; of the two main entrances it is undoubtedly true. There are also several footpaths (it is said nine) by which it can be entered; and I doubt not that in that large circumference shepherds must have discovered goat tracks by which approach, though difficult, is feasible. Nevertheless, the character, no less than the paucity of the acknowledged entrances, which are in each case through easily barred defiles, confirms the general opinion which I have expressed as to the phenomenal nature of this mountain stronghold.

The inhabitants are Turks chiefly of the Jallayer and Benjat tribes, with a few Arab and Kurdish families as well. Their total number does not exceed 1,000. They are to be found in two villages, situated in the valley by which the stream which I followed enters and traverses Kelat, and in six hamlets upon the uplands or higher elevations. Of the two main villages, I saw that of Argawan Shah, clustered upon either side of the gorge, at a short distance within the gate of the same name. The other, Giuk Gumbaz (i.e. 'Vault of Heaven' in Turkish) or Ja Gumbaz, locally contracted into Gugumaz. is a little over two miles down the valley from the same entrance, and is the spot to which I had twice despatched Shukurullah to interview the Khan and to send the telegram. Here is a curious circular tower of red sandstone, with fluted half-columns on the outer surface, rising from a big octagonal substructure. It is called Makber-i-Nadiri, having been built (for what purpose does not appear clear) by that king, and is now used as a residence by the Khan. From Gugumaz the river continues to run for six miles at the bottom of the same valley, which intersects Kelat from south to north, and deepens into a rocky gorge, until upon reaching the northern wall it passes out through a cleft not unlike that of Argawan Shah, similarly fortified, garrisoned, and closed by a wall pierced with arches across the bed of the stream. The latter, emerging from the defile, makes its way down through the lower ranges, and ultimately irrigates the cornfields of Dushak.

In addition to Nadir's tower at Gugumaz, there are other but quite inconsiderable relics of that king's occupation. To the north-west of the village, upon an elevated open plateau, are the ruins of what purports to be his palace, and is called Imaret-i-Nadiri, the largest remains being those of an enclosure, called the Diwan-Khaneh, twenty yards square. Beyond this, again, most travellers have been taken up the summit of the Kuh Khisht, which is 1,500 feet above the level of the plateau and 4,000 feet above the sea; but than which MacGregor was of opinion that finer views are afforded by other elevations. The water tanks and conduit constructed by Nadir have already been mentioned.

O'Donovan compared Kelat with the Happy Valley of Rasselas; but he would probably have shifted his simile had he been condemned to reside for a time within its walls. Of the total inside area, only a small portion is under cultivation, the water supply consisting merely of the stream so often mentioned and of five small springs. This scarcity renders the support either of a large population or of a powerful garrison impossible, except by supplies brought from the outside. Cultivation in the interior is limited to two areas, the river valley and the uplands. In the former, along the banks of the stream and in the flat spaces, rice, cotton, lucerne, vines, melons, and cucumbers flourish under the persuasive influence of water. On the higher ground, which rises to 1,000 and even 1,500 feet above the valley bottom, are grown barley and wheat. There are few trees or shrubs inside Kelat; and the grass cannot be remarkable either in quantity or quality, seeing that the inhabitants frequently send their flocks outside to graze. To represent the place, therefore, as an oasis is a misnomer.

From this point I may resume my return march to Meshed, the first stage of which was by the route already traversed and described between Kelat and Vardeh. The distance is said to be five *farsakhs*; I should call it a bare twenty miles. My camp was pitched outside the tiny hamlet on the knoll, and here I found the mule which had tumbled down the Camel's Neck, but whose leg was fortunately not broken, but only severely sprained. From standing out in the cold at night, the limb had grown so stiff that the poor brute could scarcely hobble.

October 20.—We marched to Kardeh, nominally seven *farsakhs*, but according to my reckoning not more than twenty-six miles. For the first part of the route I was repeating my journey of three days before, up the point where the lateral ravine comes in from Bolghor. From here we continued down the main gorge, following both the telegraph poles and the stream which flows along and often entirely fills its bottom. For miles we threaded this intricate and precipitous defile, clambering over the boulders in the river-bed, now confined in a narrow chasm, now emerging upon a neat little valley. MacGregor, who was a good judge of country from the soldier's point of view, paid no ordinary, though a well-deserved, tribute to this section of the Meshed-Ketal road when, in his graphic way, he said:

I certainly have never seen a stronger bit of country than the twenty-seven miles between Kardeh and Vardeh, it being one continual succession of impregnable defiles, any one of which would make the road celebrated....The country is more like what one would see in a nightmare than anything one has ever beheld awake.

On the way we pass a mighty lump of sheer rock, perched upon the top of a 1,000-feet slope, and known as the Kuh-i-Panjmana or Five-*man* (= about 32 lb) Mountain, from a story about a facetious monarch who invited one of his courtiers to weigh the airy trifle. A little further, on the left hand, is an Arabic and Persian inscription upon the smoothed surface of a big limestone block, some twenty feet above the path, which records a victory of Sheibani Mohammed Khan, the Uzbeg conqueror of Bokhara, over the Persian unbelievers in the year of the Hejira 916. We then came to a little village, the name of which was pronounced to me as Hark (or Whark), where I found an agreeable shade in an orchard sloping down to the stream. After another six miles through the same defile, the valley widened into an open plain, at the head of which, surrounded by trees, was situated the larger village of Kardeh. It is an insignificant place, but is the residence of the chief of a petty district.

October 21.—After skirting the eastern slope of the hills that enclose the valley of Kardeh, the track to Meshed plunges into a narrow gorge, called the Derbend-i-Kardeh, through which the stream, coursing in rapid zigzags between the walls, occupied the whole of the slender space between. Above the lower slopes the cliffs rose in craggy magnificence to a sheer height of 1,000 or 1,500 feet. This ravine equalled in savage splendour anything that I had seen even during the past week of astonishing scenery; and I could not help thinking that if those who rave about the Alpine passes, set though they be in the incomparable framework of snow and ice, could travel to this unvisited corner of Asia, even their senses would be bewildered by so amazing a succession of natural phenomena, each one of which would attract a stream of pilgrims in any better-known land.

At this point we finally left the mountains and debouched on to the eastern continuation of the same plain from which I had diverged a week before at Radkan. The moment, therefore, is an opportune one for casting an eye in swift retrospect over the country and surroundings in which I had been travelling since I entered Persia, and which embrace the least known and yet most typical characteristics of North-eastern Khorasan. I summed up my impressions, without, however, describing my journeys, in *The Times* in these words:

'After leaving Kuchan, I struck eastwards through the mountains, and spent eight days in wandering about amid the mountain valleys of this rugged and almost inaccessible corner of Khorasan. Being hampered by a camp and mules, I was limited to about twenty-five miles a day, but even so succeeded in traversing about 200 miles of this interesting and rarely visited country. The names of most of the villages are not upon any English map, and only a few larger or more notable localities, such as the famous stronghold of Kelat-i-Nadiri, are known to European ears. It is astonishing how difficult it is in these parts to procure reliable information about anything, most of all about that which should be best known—namely, the distance between adjoining places. A *farsakh*, nominally about four miles, is the sole unit of measurement, but, judging by my own experience, it may mean anything from two to five. The commonest thing is to be told that a place is half a *farsakh* distant—a term which, being used to imply any fraction less than the whole *farsakh*, may describe a distance of either one mile or three miles and a half. The scenery through which I travelled, and which may be said to extend over the whole of North-eastern Khorasan, is singularly uniform in its characteristics. A series of lofty mountain ridges, with an axis inclined from north-west to south-east, run parallel to each other at varying distances, the intervening hollows being in the more northern parts deep gorges admitting little more than a torrent bed at their bottom, while further south they widen into valleys watered by mountain streams and dotted with villages, and eventually into broad, rich plains, such as that of Kuchan to the north and Nishapur to the south of the Binalud Kuh mountains. Transverse ravines cut these ridges, often at right angles, and provide a way of communication from valley to valley. These gorges are frequently of almost inconceivable abruptness and grandeur. Each one presents a score of positions of absolute impregnability; and I do not suppose that more savage mountain scenery, in zones below the snow line, exists anywhere in the world. The base of these defiles seldom admits more than a torrent bed blocked with enormous boulders, and the walls are frequently vertical to a height of from 500 to 1,000 feet. The higher mountains rarely display even the scantiest vegetation, being sterile, stony, and forbidding to a degree, though the loftiest peaks are majestic with splintered outline, and occasionally some astonishing natural phenomenon is encountered, like the southern wall of Kelat. Cultivation is almost wholly confined to the valley bottoms, and is there dependent upon precarious streams and watercourses dug therefrom to the arable plots. Each village is like an oasis in a brown desert; and the squalid mud huts, with their fringe of green poplars and orchards, present an appearance almost as refreshing to the wayfarer as the snuggest of English homesteads.

'The ordinary beasts of burden in these mountain villages are very small grey donkeys, camels being only seen when belonging to a caravan, and a horse being beyond the means of the poorer people. The arid hill slopes provide a slender herbage that sustains large flocks of black sheep and goats, which are met with everywhere, guarded by big dogs. Mutton is consequently cheap and abundant. Rude wooden ploughs unshod with iron are drawn by yokes of black oxen; but cows and milk are not to be met with in every village. Fowls abound, and can be always bought for about 3*d*. apiece. The valley of Kuchan revels in every kind of fruit, but further north I was not able to procure any. Rice appeared to be the staple food of the peasantry. These struck me as a fine and masculine race, and as a very different type from the Persian of the towns. They spring for the most part from a different stock, being not of Iranian, but of Turkoman or Turkish origin, and are far more like the Uzbegs or Tartars in appearance than the Persians. They wore sheepskin bonnets on their heads, not unlike those of the Turkomans, but less lofty in the crown, canvas bound round their legs with thongs, and big loose shoes of untanned cowhide similarly attached. The women were everywhere visible, but, as a rule, carefully concealed their features, not with a veil, but with the upper cotton garment drawn over the lower part of the face. Such as I saw were prematurely old and ugly, the melancholy law of the East.'

In extension of what was here said, I may add two other observations upon the peculiar orography of the country. In the first place the dividing lines between the watersheds are seldom the highest ranges or crests; illustrations of which phenomenon I noticed in the case both of the dividing line between the Atek or Transcaspian and Kuchan drainage, and again of that between the Kuchan and Meshed drainage— i.e. the streams that run respectively to the Caspian and the Heri Rud. Secondly, the rivers, instead of pursuing a course parallel to the axis of the mountain ranges, or, in other words, running down the deep valleys between them, and then turning the corner where the saddle dips, prefer to pierce the ranges almost at right angles to their previous course; Nature having provided for that purpose transverse fissures and gashes through the very heart of the rock, which they could never have forced for themselves, and which do not betray the symptoms of aqueous detrition, but must rather have been caused by extreme tension at the moment of original elevation.

Once upon the plain, we passed in quick succession the villages of Anderokh and Rezan, which appeared to revel in an abundant water supply and in a wide area of cultivation. Far away on the southern side of the expanse the mountains behind Meshed could be seen, broken up into detached ridges, with sharp and serrated points. I strained my eyes to catch in the distance the glint of the golden cupola and minars of the holy Imam. Slowly the mist curled upward, as though a silken window-blind were being delicately raised by cords; and first a sparkle, and then a steady flash, revealed at a distance that must still have been from twelve to fifteen miles the whereabouts of the gilded dome. Though my emotions were not those of the devout pilgrims who have very likely travelled hundreds, perhaps thousands, of miles to see the hallowed spot, though I did not break into wild cries of 'Ya Ali, Ya Husein', and though I did not tear off fragments of my dress and suspend them upon the nearest bush, according to the

The ordinary beasts of burden in these mountain villages are very small grey donkeys, camels being only seen when belonging to a caravan, and a horse being beyond the means of the poorer people.

formula of the pious Shiah, I yet looked with the interest of one who has heard and read much from afar upon the famous city which I was approaching; and, putting spurs to my horse, I sped as quickly as I could over the intervening plain.

Nobad Geldi and I were galloping in front, and the old red-tailed charger was showing the best of his speed, when, ceasing to hear the clatter of the rest of the party behind me, I turned round to see what had befallen. At a distance of 200 yards Gregory's horse was lying on its back, furiously kicking its heels in the air. Its load lay scattered in every direction on the ground. The unhappy Armenian was slowly extracting himself from under the horse and ruefully rubbing his knee. Ramzan Ali Khan, also on foot, and covered with dust, was seen careering over the plain after his horse, which was disappearing in an opposite direction. It appeared that Gregory's animal, overtired, and unable, with its heavy load, to keep the pace at which we were going, had stumbled and fallen on top of Gregory; and that the Afghan, dismounting in order to extricate his colleague, had received a kick on the head which knocked him over. All was soon right again, and, leaving the slow movers to follow at their own pace, I pushed on. At five miles from the town we came to a massive high-backed bridge, of eleven arches, spanning the slender current of the Keshef Rud. The bridge, which is called Pul-i-Shah (King's Bridge), looked ridiculously out of proportion to the attenuated volume of the stream, which was only about twenty-five feet in width, and was barely moving. The ramps of the bridge had originally been paved with big cobbles, but, in common with all good work in Persia, these had for the most part disappeared, and the ruined causeway was better adapted to break legs than to save them.

In one of my Times *letters I wrote as follows: 'It is to be regretted that so far the British Government has not been able to house its representative in a similarly becoming fashion', but my latest information is that a new property is being built within the walls.*

Continuing for a mile, we reached the enclosure of the tomb of Khojah (or Khwajah) Rabi, a holy man who is variously reported as having been the personal friend and the tutor of Imam Reza, and whose body, in order to be near that of his sainted companion, was interred in this spot. The tomb is surrounded by a garden, in which there is abundance of trees, and which is entered by a lofty gateway containing rooms in arched recesses. From the surroundings it was evident that it is a favourite holiday resort of the people of Meshed, being indeed the only place of any attractiveness in the environs of the city. Thinking that the building also contained a mosque, and was, therefore, of an ecclesiastical character, I did not attempt to enter it, but merely took a photograph from the outside. I heard afterwards that, as with other tombs, any one can visit it who will. The present building is not the original mausoleum, but, as the inscription says, was raised by Shah Abas the Great on the remains of the earlier structure. A second restoration was now in course of execution; for the building was enveloped in a scaffolding, and workmen were replacing the blue tiles on the exterior of the dome, most of which had peeled off and disappeared. MacGregor spoke of the tile-work, in 1875, as better than any in Persia. But of this, too, a great deal had vanished; and what had once been a magnificent circular frieze below the spring of the dome now existed only in segments and patches. Hard by is buried the father of Agha Mohammed Shah (the founder of the reigning dynasty), Fath Ali Khan Kajar, who incurred the hostility of Nadir Shah, and was beheaded by his orders.

Soon the road passed between dusty earthen walls and over small ditches, the uniform suburbs of the cities of the East. The long line of the city wall now appeared, projecting towers connected by a curtain, and defended by a shallow ditch. Passing through the gateway, where a shabby guard sprang to his feet and presented arms with an ostentatious rattle of his musket, we rode for nearly half an hour through the blank and unlovely alleys that constitute four-fifths even of the proudest Oriental capital; and after crossing the Khiaban, or central avenue of Meshed—more about which will belong to my next chapter—pulled up at a low door, over which a large painted shield displayed the insignia of the British Government and indicated the residence of Her Majesty's Consul-General and Agent of the Viceroy of India. In a minute's time I was shaking hands with Colonel Charles Stewart.

---

[1] I shall have occasion so frequently to speak of *kanats*, and they constitute so striking and almost invariable a feature of the Persian landscape, that, for the benefit of those who have not seen them, I will describe what they are. A *kanat* (identical with the Beluch and Afghan *kariz*) is a subterranean gallery or aqueduct conducting the water from its parent springs in hill or mountain to the village where it is required either to promote cultivation or to sustain life.

[2] The poor fellow died a few weeks later on the march from Meshed to Teheran.

[3] 'Hazar Musjid' signifies 'A Thousand Mosques', the needle-like pinnacles and crags of the mountain range being compared by the facile imagination of the Mussulman pilgrim to the minarets of many mosques—*hazar* being frequently used in Persian as a round number. Others say that the Mohammedans believe in the existence of 1,000 prophets, with a mosque for each.

[4] Vide, *Russia in Central Asia*, p. 101. Reprinted in *Travels With a Superior Person* (Sidgwick & Jackson) 1985.

[5] This monarch, called by the Persians Argawan Shah, but more commonly spoken of as Arghun Khan (1284–1290 A.D.), was the remarkable man to whom Marco Polo was sent by Kubla Khan from China in charge of a Tartar bride, who opened diplomatic intercourse with the sovereigns of Europe, including King Edward I, and who, like his father, Abaka Khan, was almost a Christian, and degraded the Mussulmans from all public office.

[6] The unhealthiness of Kelat is notorious, whether it be due, as is generally supposed, to the water-supply or not. When Colonel Baker was there in 1873 he found the population decimated by typhus, and the proportion of sick among the garrison is invariably exorbitant.

[7] Nadir Shah was born in a tent near Mohammedabad, the capital of the neighbouring district of Deregez.

Meshed

Some reverence is surely due to the fame of heroes and the religion of nations.
GIBBON, *Decline and Fall of the Roman Empire.*

MESHED has in the course of the past half-century been visited and described at great or less length by several Europeans, among whom Englishmen have been in the ascendant, in merit as well as in numbers. I shall, as far as possible, avoid the repetition of what has been better said by them, believing implicitly in reference to the original source where that is feasible. But it will be within my power both to correct certain errors into which they have fallen, and to impart greater verisimilitude to the picture by bringing it up to date. The fixed residence of an official representative of the Queen in Meshed is alone sufficient to mark an epoch in its history.

I may dismiss with the briefest notice the rudiments of knowledge about the holy city. Its name (Mashhad = 'Place of Martyrdom or Witness') and fame are alike due to the fact that in the ninth century A.D. the remains of the pre-eminently holy Imam Reza, son of Imam Musa, and eighth of the twelve Imams or Prophets, were here interred. Rumour relates, but apparently without any very certain foundation, that, having incurred the jealousy of the Khalif Mamun (son of the renowned Harun-er-Rashid), whose capital was Merv, the saint, then residing at the city of Tus, fifteen miles from the modern Meshed, was removed at his orders by a dish of poisoned grapes; although another tradition represents the holy father as having comfortably died in his bed, or whatever was the ninth century equivalent thereto, at Tus. Whichever be the truth, the body of the departed prophet was interred in a tower in the neighbouring village of Sanabad, where also (a curious corollary to the story of the murder) lay the remains of the Khalif's father, the illustrious Harun. Sanabad gradually became an object of religious attraction and worship, and Ibn Batutah, who travelled hither about 1330 A.D., found the mosque of the Imam in existence, and highly revered. In 1404 the courtly Spanish Ambassador, Don Ruy Gonzalez di Clavijo, passing Meshed on his way to the Court of Timur at Samarkand, left a similar record.[1] Shah Rukh, the youngest son of Timur, subsequently embellished the mausoleum; while his wife, Gowher Shad, erected the magnificent mosque which still exists alongside. It was not, however, till the accession of the Sefavi dynasty, at the beginning of the sixteenth century, that Meshed, as it had now for long been designated, became a centre of world-wide renown. Having established the Shiah heresy as the national creed, it was in the highest degree necessary for the new occupants of the throne to institute some shrine which should divert the flow of pilgrimage and money from Mecca, and appeal to the enthusiasm of the entire Shiah community. Just as Jeroboam set up the golden calves at Dan and Bethel, in order to divert the Israelitish pilgrims from Jerusalem, so the Shahs Ismail, Tahmasp, and Abbas loaded the mosque of Imam Reza with wealth and endowments, visited and sometimes resided in the city,[2] and left it what it has ever since remained, the Mecca of the Persian world. It does not indeed rank first among Shiah shrines; for just as Ali (son-in-law of the Prophet and in succession to him, according to the Shiah canon, the true leader of the faith) and his son, the martyred Husein, are superior in holiness even to the Imam Reza, so their tombs at Nejef (or Meshed Ali) and Kerbela, near the Euphrates, possess a superior sanctity to the shrine of Meshed. But Nejef and Kerbela are both situated on Turkish—i.e. on alien—soil; and unpatriotic would be the soul that, while paying its devotions

to those sacred spots, did not also burn with the desire to behold and to offer its prayers at the religious centre of Iran, and to kiss the railings of the Imam's grave.[3] The situation of Meshed, however, so near the confines of Turan, rendered it liable to constant inroad and attack, and in common with all the border cities of Khorasan it has had a stormy and eventful history. In the reign of Shah Abbas (A.D. 1587) it was once taken and sacked by the Uzbegs. It suffered severely during the Afghan invasion of Mahmud. But it revived under the patronage of the conqueror Nadir Shah, who, although after his accession to the throne he eschewed and endeavoured forcibly to expunge the Shiah faith, yet often held his court at Meshed, restored and beautified the sacred shrine, and built in the city a tomb both for himself and for the son whom he had blinded in a fit of jealous passion. After his death, Meshed remained in the possession of his blind grandson, Shah Rukh, under whose infirm rule its population, harried by almost yearly invasions of the Uzbegs, sank from 60,000 to 20,000, until at the end of the century he was deposed and tortured to death by the brutal eunuch

Meshed was often the subject of attack and was itself several times in rebellion against the sovereign power.

Agha Mohammed Khan Kajar, the founder of the reigning family of Persia. During the present century Meshed has several times been in rebellion against the sovereign power, having inherited a detestation of the Kajars, recurrent outbreaks of which have necessitated more than one punitive expedition; but along with the rest of the kingdom it has now passed in peaceful subjection into the hands of Nasr-ed-Din.

Meshed is surrounded, as are all Oriental towns of any size, by a mud wall with small towers at regular distances, and projecting bartizans at the angles. The wall was originally nine feet thick at the bottom and four feet thick at the top, besides having a parapet one foot in thickness, but is now in a state of utter disrepair. There was formerly a small ditch or *fausse-braye* below the rampart, with a low parapet on the crest of the counterscarp, and a broader ditch beyond. But the process of decay has merged these structural features in a common ruin, and in most parts they are not to be distinguished from each other. The circumference of the walls has been variously calculated at four, four and a half, and six miles; but any calculation is difficult, owing to the irregularity of the plan. They are pierced by five gates: the Bala Khiaban, or Upper Avenue, and the Pain Khiaban, or Lower Avenue Gate, at the two ends of the main street; the Naugan, Idgah, and Sarab. The ark or citadel, my visit to which I shall presently relate, is situated on the south-west wall.

The main feature of Meshed (next to the holy shrines) which endears it to the Persian imagination and distinguishes it from other Oriental capitals, is the possession of a straight street, nearly one mile and three-quarters in length, which intersects the town from north-west to south-east, being interrupted only in the centre by the imposing quadrilateral of the sacred buildings.

This street is called the Khiaban (i.e. Avenue or Boulevard), and is regarded by the Oriental as the veritable Champs-Elysées of urban splendour. Down the centre runs a canal, or, as we should prefer to call it, a dirty ditch, between brick walls, about twelve feet across, spanned by frail foot bridges and planks. The kerbing and facing as well as the bridges are said to have been originally of stone. This canal appears to unite the uses of a drinking fountain, a place of bodily ablution and washing of clothes, a depository for dead animals, and a sewer. On either side of it is planted an irregular row of *chenars*, mulberries, elms, and willows, in which are many gaps, and the majority of which are very decrepit and forlorn. Then on either side again comes the footway, and then the ramshackle shops of the bazaar, the total width being about eighty feet. The Khiaban is filled in the busy parts of the day with so dense a crowd, that one can only proceed on horseback at a foot's pace, even with outriders to clear the way in front. Everyone seems to be shrieking and shouting at the same time. All classes and nationalities and orders of life are mingled: the stately white-turbaned *mullah*, the half-caste dervish; the portly merchant, the tattered and travel-stained pilgrim; the supercilious *seyid* in his turban of green, the cowering Sunni who has ventured into the stronghold of the enemy; black-browed Afghans and handsome Uzbegs, wealthy Arabs and wild Bedouins; Indian traders and Caucasian devotees, Turk, Tartar, Mongol, and Tajik—an epitome of the parti-coloured, polyglot, many-visaged populations of the East. Conolly, Ferrier, Vambéry, and O'Donovan have left such graphic descriptions of the living kaleidoscope in the Khiaban that I will not strive to emulate their achievements. Perhaps the most novel feature of the boulevard at the time of my visit was a row of lamp-posts, at distances of fifty yards apart, which had just been erected by the Governor.

As soon as we diverge from the Khiaban, we plunge into the familiar labyrinth of intricate alleys, wandering between mud walls, turning odd corners that seem to lead nowhere, occasionally stumbling upon a small piece of bazaar, now emerging upon

All classes and nationalities and orders of life are mingled in the Khiaban.

open spaces and heaps of rubbish. The houses of the wealthier citizens are concealed behind high walls; the poorer hovels are entered by low doorways often below the level of the street. Suddenly we come upon a vast open area, the surface of which is broken into irregular heaps, and littered with broken slabs of stone. This is one of the cemeteries, for a portion of whose hallowed soil a large price is paid by believers, and for a final resting-place in which corpses are frequently transported for thousands of miles. Hard by, masons in their sheds are busy chiselling the memorial stones, of a coarse granite quarried in the neighbourhood; engraving upon their surface a text from the Koran, or some symbol of the craft or status of the deceased. No more permanent or irremovable tombstone is tolerated; for it is essential to the requirements of the restricted area and to the revenues of the shrine that the ground should be constantly re-available for use, and as soon as the covering of an old grave has fallen in a newcomer is interred in its place. Over several of the graves were erected small white awnings or tents, in which *mullahs* are hired by the friends of the deceased to sit and moan prayers, and thus to expedite his path to heaven.

In spite of the number of these cemeteries and the outrageous violation of sanitary laws with which they are managed; in spite of the crowded numbers of human beings constantly packed in the city, and of its frequent and filthy cesspools, the average health of Meshed is superior to that of many Persian towns. Though situated in very nearly the same parallel of latitude as Teheran, and at a lower altitude (3,100 ft. as against 3,800 ft.), its average temperature is lower and its rate of mortality less high. Khanikoff attributes this immunity to its situation on the northern slope of a mountain range, by which it is shielded from the suffocating desert winds. The water of Meshed is abominable and quite unfit to drink, being strongly impregnated with sulphuretted hydrogen. I left my razor standing in a cup for one night, and the next morning it was as black as a steel gun-barrel.

Above the level of the rooftops rise several of the *badgirs*, or wind-towers, which are such a prominent feature in the maritime towns of the Persian Gulf. Their principle of construction is as follows. A tall square or four-sided tower is built from the roof, and is covered at the top, but contains in its sides long vertical slits or apertures, by which the air enters and passes down corresponding partitions in the interior into a room below, where the inmates live in the hot weather, and where there is consequently a perpetual current of air. In still hotter places in the South, these rooms are replaced by *serdabs*, or underground chambers. Another very prominent feature of Meshed is the number of *karaoul-khanehs*, or guard-houses, scattered throughout the city and occupied by small detachments of the regular infantry. They consist, as a rule, of a low verandah with a guard-room behind. The muskets, which are old muzzle-loading smooth-bores, are usually standing piled in front. But as a European rides by, a ragged soldier, in a blue serge tunic and a sheepskin shako, who is probably lounging behind, jumps up, and with a prodigious rattle seizes one of these weapons and presents arms. It is then put down again and the guard resumes his seat.

MacGregor in 1875 truly remarked that 'there is very little in this city to induce any one to visit it, or stay long if fortune has cast him into it. There is just one building, the Imam Reza's tomb, worth seeing; and that one there is no chance of any European being permitted to see, except at a risk quite incommensurate with the reward'. It is indeed most irritating, as one rides down the Khiaban, suddenly to find the passage barred by an archway in a wall surrounding the mysterious parallelogram that contains the holy places, and shutting it off as inexorably from the Christian's gaze as Aaron's cord between the living and the dead. From the descriptions, however, that have been left by such Europeans as have entered it, and from the accounts that have been given by Mohammedans themselves, we can form a correct idea of what is to be seen within.

Immediately beyond the barrier, above the archway of which is a European clock, the street continues to run for 100 yards or more through a crowded bazaar up to the main entrance of the mosques. Here the greatest throng was always congregated, and the busiest barter seemed to be going on. Pilgrims who reside within the enclosure can purchase there all the necessaries of life; while mementoes of their visit are pressed upon them, in the shape of the local manufactures of the city, of amulets and trinkets, and of turquoises engraven with sentences from the Koran. The most remarkable feature about this section of the parallelogram is that, belonging to the Imam, it is holy ground, and consequently affords an inviolable sanctuary, or *bast*, to any male-factor who succeeds in entering its precincts. Some writers declare that even Christians, Jews, and Guebres (the Persian name for the Parsis) are permitted to use it for the same purpose; but this I elsewhere heard denied. To a Mohammedan, however, it is a safe refuge from his pursuers, with whom, from the security of his retreat, he can then make terms, and settle the ransom with which to purchase his immunity if he comes out. The idea of sanctuary is of course familiar to the Oriental mind, and is embodied in the Cities of Refuge of the Pentateuch. Nor should it excite the indignant surprise of the English reader, seeing that in our own country and capital at no very distant date a similar refuge to debtors existed in the famous Alsatia between Blackfriars Bridge and Temple Bar, which also had an ecclesiastical foundation, having originally been the precincts of the Dominicans or Black Friars. The Bast at Meshed is so emphatically the property of the Imam, that any animal entering its limits is at once confiscated by the authorities of the shrine.

At the end of the bazaar of the Bast, a lofty archway, rising high above the adjoining wall, leads into the Sahn, or principal court of the Holy Buildings. This is a noble quadrangle, 150 yards long by 75 yards wide, flagged with grave-stones of the wealthy departed, whose means have enabled them to purchase this supreme distinction, and surrounded by a double storey of recessed alcoves. In the centre of this court stands a small octagonal structure or kiosque, with gilded roof, covering a fountain which is supplied by the main canal, and surrounded by a stone channel constructed by Shah Abbas. The water of this fountain is used for purposes of ablution by the pilgrim as he enters. Upon the four sides the walls between and above the recesses are faced with enamelled tiles; and in the centre of each rises one of those gigantic portals, or *aiwans* (archways set in a lofty rectangular frame), which are characteristic of the Arabian architecture of Central Asia. These arches are embellished with colossal tiles, bearing in Kufic letters verses from the Koran. An inscription on the southern *aiwan* says that it was built by Shah Abbas II. in A.H. 1059. The lower bands of Kufic characters on all the *aiwans* were, we learn from a similar source, added in A.H. 1262. Upon the summit of the western *aiwan* rises a cage, very rashly assumed by Eastwick to be made of ivory, from which the *muezzin* gives the call to prayer.[4] The eastern *aiwan* is that which leads to the Holy of Holies, the tomb-chamber of the Imam; and its special character is indicated by the gilding with which its upper half is overlaid. An inscription upon it says that it was finished by Shah Sultan Husein in A.H. 1085; and some later verses record that it was gilded by Nadir Shah in A.H. 1145 with the gold that had been plundered from India and the Great Mogul. The Sahn contains two minarets, which, according to descriptions, and from what I myself saw from the roof of a bazaar within the Bast, do not appear to be placed in analogous positions on either side of the main entrance. The older minaret, built by Shah Ismail or Shah Tahmasp, springs from the mausoleum itself. When Fraser was here on his second visit in 1834, it had been 'so shaken or damaged, that for fear of its falling they had taken it down'. It was afterwards rebuilt. The second or larger minaret was erected by Nadir Shah, and rises from behind the opposite gateway. The upper part of these minarets is in each case overlaid with gilded copper plates, and is crowned with the cage-like gallery that is common to the Persian style. The sun flashes from their radiant surface, and in the distance they glitter like pillars of fire.

And now we approach the chief glory of the whole enclosure, the mosque and sepulchre of the immortal Imam. I say immortal advisedly, for the theory upon which the shrine and the vast system dependent upon it subsist is that the sainted Reza still lives, and responds miraculously to the petitions of his worshippers. The Hazret, as he is called—i.e. His Highness—is the host of his guests. He supplies their bodily wants while they remain within his domain; and equally he answers their prayers, and furthers their spiritual needs. It is open to any pilgrim to consult him, and Delphic responses are easily forthcoming in return for a suitable fee to one of the attendant priests. From time to time also the rumour goes abroad that some astonishing miracle has been effected at the shrine of His Highness. The cripple has walked, or the blind man has seen, or some similar manifestation has occurred of god-like effluence.[5]

The tomb itself is preceded by a spacious chamber, whose marble floor is overlaid with rich carpets. Above it, to a height of seventy-seven feet, swells the main cupola, whose gilded exterior marks the sacred spot to the advancing pilgrim, and gladdens his weary eyes from afar. The walls of this chamber are adorned with a wainscoting of *kashi*—i.e. enamelled tiles, above which are broad bands of Arabic writing in the same material. There is a hum of voices in the building; for servants of the shrine are heard reading aloud from the Koran, *seyids* are mumbling their daily prayers, greedy *mullahs* are proffering their services to the new arrivals; and many are the exclamations of pious wonder and delight that burst from the bewildered pilgrim, as, after months of toil and privation in the most cheerless surroundings, there flash upon his gaze the marbles and the tile work, the gold and the silver, the jewels and the priceless offerings of the famous shrine. 'Encrusted within and without with gold, it is,' says Vambéry, who himself saw it, 'unquestionably the richest tomb in the whole Islamite world. Although since the date of its first erection it has been several times plundered,[6] the cupolas, towers, and massive fretted work of the interior still contain an incalculable amount of treasure. The walls are adorned with the rarest trinkets and jewels: here an *aigrette* of diamonds, there a sword and shield studded with rubies and emeralds, rich old bracelets, large massive candelabra, necklaces of immense value'. Well may the worshipper, as he enters, bow his head till it touches the ground, before he approaches the main object of his devotion, the sepulchre itself.

At different times the tomb has been surrounded with railings of gold and silver and steel. The first of these was originally set up by Shah Tahmasp, but was in part dismantled and plundered by the grandson of Nadir Shah. The last was the gift of Nadir himself. Three doors lead to the shrine, one of which is of silver, another of gold plates studded with precious stones, the gift of Fath Ali Shah; the third being covered with a carpet sewed with pearls. Upon the railings round the tomb are hung silver and wooden tablets with appropriate forms of prayer and inscriptions. 'Before each of them a little group of the devout is posted, either to pray themselves or to repeat the petitions after the leader of their common devotions. This they do with cries and sobs, as though thus to open to themselves the gates of eternal bliss. It is indeed a singular and sublime spectacle to see how these rude sons of Asia kiss with unfeigned tenderness the fretwork of the grating, the pavement, and especially the great padlock which hangs from the door. Only the priests and the *seyids* are uninfluenced by these feelings of devotion. their only concern is with the pence which they may collect. They force their way

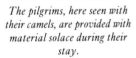

The pilgrims, here seen with their camels, are provided with material solace during their stay.

everywhere among the devout, nor do they retire till by felicitations or other good offices they have obtained the desired mite. When the pilgrim, filled with awe, walking backwards, has at last left the building, he has earned for himself the honorary title of Meshedi, a title which he has inscribed on his signet and his tombstone, and which he ever after prefixes to his name as an *agnomen*.

In the absorption consequent upon visiting the mausoleum of the Imam, the pilgrim probably recks little of the dust of the famous Harun-er-Rashid, which reposes beneath a sarcophagus hard by. Nor, perhaps, will he think much of the tomb of Abbas Mirza, the son of Fath Ali Shah, and grandfather of the present monarch, which also stands beneath the sacred roof. Other tombs and chambers, moreover, there are opening out of the principal shrine, but of minor importance, and these may be dismissed without further notice.

Perhaps the most extraordinary feature of Meshed life, before I leave the subject of the shrine and the pilgrims, is the provision that is made for the material solace of the latter during their stay in the city. In recognition of the long journeys which they have made, of the hardships which they have sustained, and of the distances by which they are severed from family and home, they are permitted, with the connivance of the ecclesiastical law and its officers, to contract temporary marriages during their sojourn in the city. There is a large permanent population of wives suitable for the purpose.[7] A *mullah* is found, under whose sanction a contract is drawn up and formally sealed by both parties, a fee is paid, and the union is legally accomplished. After the lapse of a fortnight or a month, or whatever be the specified period, the contract terminates; the temporary husband returns to his own *lares et penates* in some distant clime, and the lady, after an enforced celibacy of fourteen days' duration, resumes her career of persevering matrimony. In other words, a gigantic system of prostitution, under the sanction of the Church, prevails in Meshed. There is probably not a more immoral city in Asia; and I should be sorry to say how many of the unmurmuring pilgrims who traverse seas and lands to kiss the grating of the Imam's tomb are not also encouraged and consoled upon their march by the prospect of an agreeable holiday and what might be described in the English vernacular as 'a good spree'.

Here, in the city which he patronised and adorned, was originally laid the body of the great conqueror, Nadir Shah. In his own lifetime he caused the buildings to be raised both for himself and for his son, Reza Kuli Mirza. They were situated about halfway between the mosque of the Imam and the Bala Khiaban gate. Not a trace now remains of their existence. The brutal eunuch Agha Mohammed Khan Kajar, mindful of the source to which he owed his calamity, as soon as he became Shah, gratified the instincts of a long-nurtured revenge by razing the structures to the ground; while the bones of Nadir were removed at his orders to Teheran and deposited (along with those of his other rival, Kerim Khan Zend) beneath the threshold of the palace, so that whenever he went abroad he might trample upon the dust of the great persecutor of himself and his family. In Fraser's day the desecrated buildings at Meshed were heaps of rubbish. Ten years later Burnes found a crop of turnips springing from the soil which had sheltered the body of the conqueror of Hindustan.

There still exist a considerable number of Jewish families in Meshed, although the practice of their own worship is strictly forbidden, and is only pursued in secret. The story of their enforced conversion to Mohammedanism in the year 1838 is well known, and has been repeated by more than one traveller. Dr. Wolff, who was twice at Meshed, both before and after the incident, described it in these terms:—

The occasion was as follows: A poor woman had a sore hand. A Mussulman

*I was greatly disappointed
with such articles as I saw.
A more unfavourable
hunting-ground can hardly
be imagined.*

physician advised her to kill a dog and put her hand in the blood of it. She did so; when suddenly the whole population rose and said that they had done it in derision of their prophet. Thirty-five Jews were killed in a few minutes; the rest, struck with terror, became Mohammedans. They are now more zealous Jews in secret than ever, but call themselves *Anusim*, the Compelled ones.

Wolff does not add—what is necessary to explain the sudden outburst—that the incident of the Jewess and the slaughtered dog unfortunately occurred on the very day when the Mohammedans were celebrating the Feast of Sacrifice. Superstition and malice very easily aggravated an innocent act into a deliberate insult to the national faith; and hence the outbreak that ensued. There is much less fanaticism now than in those days; but it still behoves a Yehudi, or Jew, to conduct himself circumspectly and to walk with a modest air in Meshed.

Khanihoff is responsible for the statement that there are fourteen *madressehs* and sixteen caravanserais in the city; as also for an enumeration of their names and the dates of their foundation. Any reader who requires information upon these points may be referred to his pages.

I had heard or read a good deal about the native manufactures of Meshed, but was greatly disappointed with such articles as I saw. A more unfavourable hunting-ground for the would-be purchaser can hardly be imagined. The manufacture of damascened sword-blades has long been a trade here, having originally, it is said, been introduced by a colony transported for the purpose by Timur from Damascus. Now, however, that rifles and revolvers have taken the place of swords and daggers, there is not the same demand for new blades. Silk and cotton and velvet stuffs are made here, but of a quality greatly inferior to those of Bokhara. There are in the town 650 silk looms and 320 shawl looms. On the other hand, good carpets are procurable, particularly those of genuinely Oriental pattern, close texture, and imperishable vegetable dyes, that hail from Kain and Rajand. The Kurdish carpets are also original, but less artistic. In Meshed itself are forty carpet-looms. Turkoman carpets, jewellery, and weapons were formerly a common object in the bazaars, but are now almost entirely bought up by the Russians in Transcaspia or exported to Europe. Astrabad, near the camps of the Goklan Turkomans, is probably, next to Teheran (whither everything converges), the best place in Persia for procuring Turkoman articles. Old Tartar and even Bactrian coins are frequently to be met with at Meshed. I naturally anticipated that, being in such close proximity to the famous turquoise mines of Nishapur, the bazaars would be well stocked with specimens of that stone. I saw little but rubbish. All the best stones are bought at the mouth of the mines and are exported to foreign countries. Meshed seems to receive the residue, of a price and quality likely to attract the itinerant pilgrim. Nor was I any better pleased with the carved objects, cups, bowls, basins, ewers, which are hollowed with the aid of a very primitive lathe and tools out of a soft slate or steatite that is found in the neighbourhood. There are two varieties of this stone, a dull reddish brown, and a blue-grey. But though previous travellers have spoken in terms of great admiration of these works of art, I failed to appreciate either the material, the shape, or the workmanship.

---

[1] 'Imam Reza lies buried in a great mosque in a large tomb, which is covered with silver gilt. On account of this tomb the city is crowded with pilgrims, who come here in great numbers every year. When the pilgrims arrive, they dismount and kiss the ground, saying that they have reached a holy place' (Hakluyt Society edition).

[2] Abbas the Great is said, upon one occasion, as a proof of his piety, to have walked with his court the entire distance from Isfahan to Meshed, while the Astronomer Royal measured the distance with a string, and returned the total as 199 *farsakhs* and a fraction.

[3] I asked a Shiah *seyid* of Kerbela the order in which the Holy Places of the Moslem faith are esteemed by his persuasion, and his answer was as follows:—(1) Mecca, (2) Medina, (3) Nejef, (4) Kerbela, (5) Kasimein, near Baghdad, (6) Meshed, (7) Samara, on the Tigris, (8) Kum. But a Persian Shiah would rank Meshed after Kerbela. The pilgrimage to Mecca confers the title *Haji*, that to Kerbela *Kerbelai*, and to Meshed *Meshedi*.

[4] Chardin says that the reason why these cages were constructed for the *muezzins* in Persia was the fear lest from the summit of the minarets they should see too much of female life in the courts of the neighbouring houses.

[5] This is no new thing, for, 200 years ago, the French missionary, Father Sanson, narrates and mercilessly analyses the same phenomena. 'Shah Abbas has made this tomb famous by a great many false miracles he caused to be practised there; for, placing people there on purpose who should counterfeit themselves blind, they suddenly received their sight at this sepulchre, and immediately cry'd out, "A miracle", he procur'd so great a veneration for this tomb of Imam Reza that most of the greatest lords in Persia have desir'd to be bury'd in this mosque; and to which they give great legacies.'

[6] By none more than those who should have been responsible for its safety. The two sons of the blind Shah Rukh and grandsons of Nadir Shah in particular could not keep their avaricious hands from the shrine which their grandfather had honoured and embellished. Nasrullah Mirza pulled down part of the gold railing round the saint's tomb, and Nadir Mirza took down the great golden ball, weighing 420 lbs, from the top of the dome; while both brothers freely plundered the lamps, carpets &c., inside.

[7] A *sigheh* or temporary wife may be married for any period from one day to 99 years. Women often prefer being *sighehs* for the full period to being *akdis* or real wives. The *akdi* can be divorced at any time, the *sigheh* not before the end of her contract, except for misconduct. Short-period *sighehs* in the big cities are quasi-prostitutes.

From Meshed to Teheran

There is nothing which has yet been contrived by man by which so much happiness is produced as by a good tavern or inn.

DR. JOHNSON, *Boswell's Life*.

Persicos odi, puer, apparatus.

HORACE, *Carm.*, Lib. I.XXXVIII.

[Persian gewgaws, boy, I loathe]

HAVING spent eight days at Meshed, I started upon the long *chapar* ride to Teheran. The distance is given by the Persians, and is therefore paid for by the traveller, as 154 *farsakhs*. At the full complement of four miles to a *farsakh*, this would amount to 616 miles; but, though the Khorasan *farsakh* is famed beyond all others for its odious and seemingly inexhaustible length,[1] a compliment in reality to the funereal monotony of the road—the distance (comparing my own estimate with that of previous voyagers) is under rather than over 560 English miles. It is surprising how soon, if a man be riding alone and have nought to distract him but the paces of his steed and the thought of his destination, he can arrive at an approximately correct calculation of the distance he is covering from stage to stage. The route between Meshed and Teheran is divided into twenty-four stages, the post-houses being established at distances varying from fifteen to thirty miles, but averaging twenty-three miles apart. This distance I accomplished in the comfortable time of nine days, doing an average of sixty miles a day, but in reality combining days of seventy miles with shorter spans. This is slow rather than speedy travelling for Persia;[2] and I afterwards became easily habituated to journeys of seventy-five to eighty miles in the day. Telegraph officials and residents in the country seldom do less, and frequently more. The post which goes through from Meshed to Teheran without stopping, but with first claim upon the horses at each station, covers the distance in from five to six days. Dr. Wills reports having ridden from Isfahan to Teheran, about 280 miles, in thirty-nine and a half hours; whilst officers travelling by day alone and resting at night have accomplished 120 miles between dawn and leaving the saddle.

Quick riding is indeed an accomplishment for which the Persians have always been famous, and notable records in which have been achieved even by their kings. Abbas the Great, 300 years ago, rode from Shiraz to Yezd in twenty-eight and a half hours, the Astronomer Royal being commanded to take the time. Malcolm gives the distance as eighty-nine *farsakhs*, or 303 miles; but, though modern measurements have reduced it to 220 miles, it was still no mean peformance. Agha Mohammed Khan, the founder of the reigning dynasty, fleeing from Mazanderan on the death of Kerim Khan Zend, rode from Shiraz to Isfahan—a distance, by whatever route, of not much under 300 miles—in less than three days. Fath Ali Shah, his nephew, upon succeeding to the throne, rode from Shiraz to Teheran, a distance of at least 550 miles, in six days. Fraser mentions the case of a Persian, Agha Bahram, who kept the best horses in the country, and who once on the same Arab horse rode from Shiraz to Teheran in six days, rested three days, rode back in five days, rested nine days, and performed the journey a third time in seven days. But the most remarkable, because the most sustained performance of which I have ever read was that of the dragoman who, in 1804, rode from Constantinople to Demavend (near Teheran), a total distance of 1,700 miles,

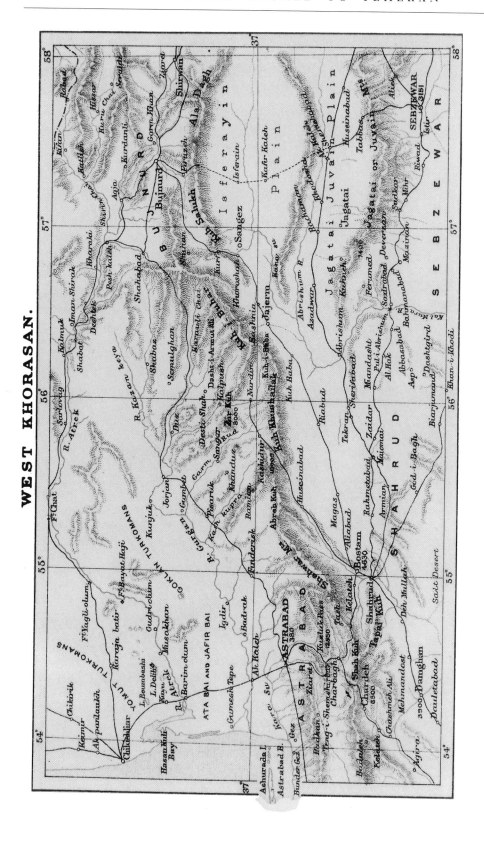

WEST KHORASAN.

in seventeen days, with the news of Napoleon's escape from Elba. On the other hand, when there is no purpose in haste, no rider can be so slow as a Persian. If he is not proceeding at a headlong gallop, he affects a dignified crawl; and in the whole of my *chapar* rides I never once met a native who was moving at more than a foot-pace on horseback.

The postal system in Persia, about the inauguration of which I shall have something to say later on, is under the superintendence of a Minister of Posts; but as the present tenant of that office holds two other portfolios in addition, besides being President of the Council, it may be inferred that it is not regarded as one of commanding import-ance. The Government allows him a certain annual sum for the repair and equipment of every posthouse upon the Government roads, as well as an annual allowance of barley and straw as fodder for the horses. The Minister does not, however, work the system himself. That would be a shocking violation of all Persian usage. Each road is farmed to a publican, probably some merchant or wealthy person, who pays a certain sum per annum to the Minister for the privilege. He then provides the servants and animals at each station, and makes as much money out of the business as he can; the only check upon his parsimony being the fear of losing his contract in favour of a higher bidder at the end of the year. It is not surprising, therefore, that the posthouses are mostly in a state of extreme and disgraceful dilapidation, or that the horses are among the sorriest specimens of the equine race that were ever foaled. The system is a vicious one, and it is hard to say whether the traveller or the poor brutes whom he is compelled to flog along are the more to be pitied.

Let me, however, endeavour to balance the pains and the pleasures, if any there be, of *chapar* riding, so as to arrive at a fair verdict. The system has been variously de-scribed by travellers according to their tastes, endurance, and fortune, as an exhilaration, a tedium, or a torture; and there is perhaps something to be said for each opinion. Much depends upon the extent to which the road adopted is travelled upon, and, in consequence, supplied; something upon the season of the year or the weather encoun-tered; a good deal upon the luck of the voyager. The route between Meshed and Teheran is but little traversed (except by pilgrims, who move in *kafilahs*, or caravans), and there are accordingly not above five or six horses, sometimes less, at each station. These I found to be for the most part underfed, broken-down, and emaciated brutes, with ill-regulated paces, and open sores on their backs that sometimes made it almost unbearable to bestride them. The best that were supplied to me would anywhere else be classified at a low level of equine mediocrity. To ride the worst was a penalty to which any future Dante might appropriately condemn his most inveterate foe in the lower circles of hell. Subsequently, however, upon the Teheran-Shiraz line, which is more travelled upon and better provided, I found a larger number and a superior quality of animals. They were generally tolerable and sometimes positively good; and when I succeeded in covering by their means an average of between eight and nine miles in the hour throughout the day, when they invariably cantered and sometimes galloped, it can be imagined that a day's ride of from seventy to eighty miles may become quite endurable, and, under favourable conditions of climate, at times almost pleasant. In the last resort, however, more depends upon the fortune of the traveller than upon any other consideration. If he can avoid clashing or competing with the Government post, which has universal priority of claim; if he is lightly equipped himself and does not require many animals; above all, if he can get ahead and keep ahead of any other party of travellers on the same road, he will fare passably well. If he is unlucky in any or all of these respects, he will leave Persia muttering deep and un-repeatable curses against a land of rascals and jades. That this is the more common experience may perhaps be inferred from the fact that the main solace of a European's life in Persia appears to be the desire to cover a specified distance in quicker time than it has ever been done before. A furious competition prevails. Where there is a telegraphic line along the route the wire conveys to anxious ears the news of the rider's progress; and a man is seldom so happy, or leaves so enduring a reputation, as when he succeeds in cutting the record.

At this stage let me describe the *chapar-khaneh*, and its meagre, but peculiar properties. Sometimes in the heart, sometimes on the outskirts of a town or village, sometimes planted in absolute solitude upon the staring waste, but usually in the neighbourhood of water, is to be seen a small rectangular structure, consisting of four blank mud walls surrounding an interior enclosure, with a stunted square tower rising above the gateway, and a projecting semicircular tower or bartizan at each corner. The whole presents the appearance of a miniature mud fort. And such indeed it is intended to be; for in a land till lately desolated by Turkoman forays, and where promiscuous thieving is indubitably popular, every possession, from a palace down to an orchard, has to be safeguarded from attack, as though the country were in a state of open war. Entrance to the *chapar-khaneh* is gained by a big wooden door in the gateway; and when this is closed it is unassailable except by ladders. Riding into the gateway, one observes a low seat or platform against the wall on either side, and two doorways leading into dark and dirty rooms on the ground floor. The gateway conducts into the interior court, which is an open space about twenty to twenty-five yards in length and twelve to fifteen yards in width. In the middle is a *chabutra*, or mud platform, usually occupied by fowls and filth, but designed for *al fresco* slumbers of the traveller in the summer season. The walls of the court, on two and sometimes on three sides, are pierced with holes or mangers, into which the chopped barley, or *kah*, is placed for the horses, and to which they are tethered in the warm weather. In the interior of the two side walls, however, are long dark stables for winter use, unlighted save by the low

The chapar-khaneh, *or Persian post house. Entrance to the* chapar khaneh *is gained by a big wooden door in the gateway; and when this is closed it is unassailable except by ladders. Riding into the gateway, one observes a low seat or platform against the wall on either side, and two doorways leading into dark and dirty rooms on the ground floor.*

door, unventilated, and reeking with accumulated refuse. In one of these, along with the horses, the postboys and attendants usually sleep, stretched around a low fire. The interior walls of the court have at one time or another been faced with plaster; but this has uniformly peeled off, and the entire fabric looks what it is—mud. As the weary traveller rides in, the *chaparchi*, or post-house keeper, who sometimes wears the semblance of an official dress, comes out to meet him. Eager inquiries are exchanged as to the supply of fresh horses in the stables; and while these are being gratified or disappointed, the baggage is pulled off the exhausted beasts and piled upon the *chabutra*, and the English rider stretches himself at full length or boils a cup of broth or tea. His Persian attendant takes a pull at the *kalian*, which is always ready, and the wearied animals, stripped except for their tattered horsecloths, are slowly walked up and down for ten minutes by the postboy, and finally marched off to water. In a quarter of an hour, if lucky, sometimes not for one hour or even two, a fresh batch of horses having been brought out, and the traveller having selected the best for himself, he will remount, and will once again pursue the uneven tenor of his way. If, however, no fresh animals are forthcoming, or if he has been anticipated by some other voyager, then ensues the most heartrending experience of all. For, after a tedious wait of perhaps two hours, the same miserable brutes that have borne the burden of his last twenty-five miles' stage are brought out again to be urged and flagellated through twenty-five more. I confess that my sympathies were always with the beast rather than with his rider; and considering the pitiless daily, nay, almost hourly, task that is imposed upon these wretched crocks, it was sometimes a surprise to me that persuasion, however extreme, could extract from them anything more than a hobble.

But supposing the traveller to have reached the end of his day's journey and to have arrived at the post-house where he proposes the pass the night, what then? The answer to the question is contained in the projecting square tower above the entrance gateway. Access thereto is gained by stairways of almost Alpine steepness, fashioned in the mud at the angles of the court inside. Clambering up these with difficulty, we reach the flat roof that runs right round the building, and find that the tower consists of a single chamber, which invariably has two, sometimes three, doors (that are never known to shut), and usually a couple of open window spaces in the walls, so that it may literally be said to stand

Four-square to all the winds that blow.

This is the *bala-khaneh*, or upper chamber, specially reserved for the comfort of foreign guests, and within this forlorn and wintry abode, which is not much less draughty than the rigging of a ship, the wayfarer must spend the night. The interior has at one time been plastered and whitewashed. Its only decorative features are a number of shallow niches in the walls, in which Persian visitors have sometimes scrawled the most fearful illustrations, and occasionally, but not always, a fireplace. Of furniture, it is absolutely destitute. To have the floor swept clean of vermin, to spread a felt or carpet in the corner and one's sack of straw upon it, to buy firewood and light a fire, to stuff up the open windows and nail curtains over the ramshackle doors—all these are necessary and preliminary operations, without which the dingy tenement would be simply uninhabitable, but which it is sometimes hard work to undertake in a state of extreme stiffness and exhaustion after a long day's ride upon a freezing winter's night. Even so, this aërial roost is sometimes too chill for endurance, and one is compelled to descend and seek refuge in the dank and cellar-like apartments below. In half an hour's time, however, when the work has been done, as the genial warmth begins to relax stiff joints and weary limbs, and as the *samovar* puffs out its cheery steam, a feeling of wonderful contentment ensues, and the outstretched travel-

As the weary traveller rides in, the chaparchi, *or post-house keeper, who sometimes wears the semblance of an official dress, comes out to meet him.*

ler would probably not exchange his quarters for a sheeted bed in Windsor Castle. But it is upon the following morning, when, aroused at four or five A.M. in the pitchy darkness and amid biting cold, he must get up to the light of a flickering candle, dress and pack up all his effects, cook his breakfast, and finally see the whole of his baggage safely mounted in the dark upon the steeds in the yard below, that he is sometimes tempted to think momentarily of proverbs about games and candles, and to reflect that there are consolations in life at home.

A word more about the Persian post-horse, for a man does not ride from sixty to seventy of these beasts in the space of a few weeks without being driven to generalise somewhat upon the species. The traveller of course selects the best out of a bad lot for himself, but an eye must be kept on the *chapar-shagird*, or post-boy, who knows the 'form' of each animal to a nicety, and who, if left alone, is apt to consult his own rather than his employer's comfort. As you emerge from the post-house, and, after a short walk, try the paces of your new mount, there is a moment of acute suspense. Within 300 yards you know whether your next three or four hours are to be a toleration or an anguish. The pace which, after a little experience, a European usually adopts is a sharp canter alternating with a walk. The Persians, when not cantering or galloping, seem to prefer a rough jog-trot shamble, which on an English saddle is excruciating. In the whole of my *chapar* rides I only twice encountered a horse that could trot in English fashion. The post-boy carries, and each rider must carry, a long whip made of twisted leather with a leathern thong, and appalling are the whacks that are administered by the former, often without exciting the faintest response from his habituated steed. In this place it may be well to remark that, though called a boy, the *shagird* is much more commonly a man. He does not ride upon a saddle, but usually sits perched upon the top of a vast pile of baggage with his legs sticking out on either side; nor does he use reins, but only a single rope or halter attached to one side of the bit. He is supposed to lead the way and to set the pace, but I soon found that seventy miles in the day could never be accomplished in that fashion, and that it was better even in a strange country to lead the cavalcade oneself. As a rule it is difficult, if there is light, to mistake the track; for though there is no road and the route is simply a mule track which crosses plains, climbs mountains, and descends gorges, sometimes, so to speak, a single rut, and sometimes a wide belt of parallel paths, yet the passage of countless animals has left such impressions upon the soil that the direction to be followed can often be traced in advance for miles. At night a stranger would be lost at once but for the guidance of the post-boy, whose sight and memory are unerring.

The best known characteristic of the Persian post-horse is his incurable predisposition to tumble. Most of them have bare knees in consequence, and the first law in mounting is to select an animal with some hair still adorning that portion. I could not make out that either a tight rein or a slack rein had very much to do with the occurrence of this phenomenon, and I ended by concluding that the Persian post-horse has a certain regulation number of falls in the year, which may be distributed either by accident or as he pleases, but the full tale of which some hidden law of necessity compels him to complete. The fact that I rode through the country from the east to the centre and from the centre to the south without a single fall, tended to confirm rather than to invalidate my theory, for there was no conceivable reason why I should be so favoured, except that others would have or had had to pay the price. It became quite a trite occurrence to hear the groan with which my Persian servant riding behind me sank or was hurled on to mother earth; while the *chapar-shagird* would be seriously disappointed at an entire day without a fall. There is this to be said for the instability of the Persian post-horse, that it appears very seldom to be vindicated at the lasting expense of his rider. The number of accidents or injuries that take place in proportion to the number of falls is ludicrously small. Two other tricks I noticed which were widespread and popular. Some of the meanest of the animals would very much resent being mounted, a curious proof that their memories had profited by experience; and the only approach to an accident that I had was when a horse from which I had dismounted ran away as I was putting my foot into the stirrup, and as nearly as possible pitched both himself and me down the shaft of an open *kanat*. The lifting of the right arm, whether with or without a whip, had, further, such a provocative effect upon the memory of these beasts that they would frequently swerve and spin right round to the left. The Persians, if peculiarly disgusted with a post-horse, sometimes revenge themselves by docking his tail, which incapacitates him from further use in a country where a tail is considered *de rigueur*; but this is a spiteful, if not a cruel act, from which strangers can afford to abstain. Perhaps I shall not inaptly conclude this digression upon the Persian post-horse and postal system if I quote the sententious observation with which Tavernier prefaced his Persian travels more than three centuries ago: 'A man cannot travel in Asia as they do in Europe; nor at the same hours, nor with the same ease.'

The road from Meshed to Teheran is one whose intrinsic attraction is so small that no one would ever be found to traverse it but for the necessity of getting from one place to the other. For the entire distance of 560 miles there is scarcely a single object of beauty, and but few of interest. The scenery, at any rate in the late autumn, is colourless and desolate. The road, or rather track, winds over long, stony plains, across unlovely mountains, and through deserted villages and towns. There is frequent and abundant evidence that the country traversed was once far more densely or less sparsely populated, and for that reason more carefully tended, than it is at present. The traveller passes towns which have been entirely abandoned, and display only a melancholy confusion of tottering walls and fallen towers. He observes citadels and fortified posts which have crumbled into irretrievable decay, and are now little more than shapeless heaps of mud. He sees long lines of choked and disused *kanats*, the shafts of the underground wells by which water was once brought to the lands from the mountains. The walls of the cities are in ruins and exhibit yawning gaps; the few public buildings of any note are falling to pieces; rows of former dwellings have been abandoned to dust-heaps and dogs. The dirty, desecrated cemeteries that stretch for hundreds of yards outside every town of any size, in which the tombstones are defaced and the graves falling in, are not more lugubrious in appearance than is the interior, where the living seem to be in almost as forlorn a plight as the dead. The utmost that the traveller can expect in the way of incident—an expectation in which I have already said that I was disappointed—is that his *chapar* horse should tumble down, to break, if not its own knees, at any rate the paralysing monotony of the journey.

But though the route be thus devoid of external attraction, it has a twofold interest, historical and practical. The traveller is not merely pursuing the track that has been worn by countless thousands of pilgrims for at least 500 years, but he is following the stormy wake of armies, and treading in the footsteps of great conquerors and kings. And if, in the desolation that gapes around him, he sees no hint or reminder of what these countries once were, at least he is able to form some judgment of what the combined horrors of war, pestilence, and chronic misgovernment—which is worse than either—have done for them, and in this blighted zone of crumbling cities and forsaken homes to read the tale of Persia's long decline.

Before proceeding further it may be well to state that there is an alternative route for the first three stages between Meshed and Nishapur. The postal service and stations being upon the other southern route, this, which is a more northerly line, cannot be taken by *chapar* riders. It is, however, frequently adopted by caravans (other than camels), particularly in the summer; as though the road is much worse, and in parts excessively steep, it runs over higher ground (10,720 feet), and through scenery of quite exceptional verdure and beauty. It is a positive surprise to the traveller, within a few miles of the naked rocks and dusty plains of Meshed, to alight upon running water and a wealth of trees.

Colonel Stewart and other friends accompanied me on horseback—after the prevailing Persian fashion, which for polite good-fellowship might be commended elsewhere—for some distance outside the city gate. In deference to another excellent Persian habit, he lent me a horse from his own stables for the first stage; while, in obedience to a third, I proposed only to do one stage on the first afternoon, so as to allow servants and baggage to 'shake down', and to inure myself for harder work on the morrow. After I had been riding across the level plain for an hour, one of those violent winds arose, which the traveller in the East knows by sad experience, and drove like a hurricane across the land, whirling heaven and earth into one savage thundercloud of dust. Eyes, mouth, and ears were filled and choked with the gritty storm, which was blowing straight in my teeth, and yet was perfectly warm. About seven miles after leaving Meshed we arrived at the base of the mountains, in reality the south-east extremity of the Binalud Kuh, which separates the plain of Meshed from that of Nishapur. The Jagherk-Dehrud road boldly crosses this range; but the postal route avoids so steep a climb by a divergence in a south-easterly direction, and mounts only the lower spurs and slopes.

At the crest of each ridge, where the road, now rapidly ascending, topped the rise, grateful pilgrims wending to the holy city had, as they caught sight of the gilded cupola of the prophet, piled little heaps of stone in pious thanksgiving. The symbolism of these erections is said to be that the pilgrim is building in anticipation a home for the next world, either for the dear departed, or for those who may survive him, or for himself. Every knoll was thickly covered with these emblems of devotion. The topmost of all, where the new-comer first discerns the sacred pile, is known as Salaam Tepe, or Kuh-i-Salaam (the Hill of Salutation); and there is an analogous site upon the Dehrud road.

Here, as he first comes in sight of his destination, the excited Shiah Mussulman kneels, and strikes his forehead upon the ground, and sobs aloud at the recollection of the indignities that were heaped upon the martyrs of his faith; here he tears off little fragments of his dress, and ties them to a bramble or a bush, in order that the holy Imam may recognise them and plead for him in Paradise; here he unfurls his coloured banner; and here with loud cries of 'Ya Ali', 'Ya Husein', and 'Ya Imam Reza', he presses forward to the long-sought goal. Many times I turned back myself to look, but the entire valley was wrapped in a tornado of dust, the white clouds of which rolled upwards like the smoke of a prairie fire.

At the top of one of these hills is an upright slab of stone, which has been erected to commemorate the piety of a former Governor-General of Khorasan, who was exiled to this post after being both Sadr Azem, or Grand Vizier, and Sipah Salar, or Commander-in-Chief, at Teheran, and who earned a great reputation, particularly with pilgrims, for improving the Meshed road and adorning it with substantial caravanserais. His name still lives, both on the slab of slate and on the lips of many a grateful Meshedi.

Following the telegraph poles, and winding over a succession of bleak but undulating ridges, we passed the caravanserai of Turukh, situated by a stream. The road was thronged with pedestrians, with camels, and donkeys; and I even saw a wheeled vehicle which had stuck fast on one of the hills. At length in a hollow we came upon the domed caravanserai of Sherifabad, erected by the famous Ishak Khan of Turbat-i-Haideri, of whom I have spoken in the chapter on Khorasan, at the beginning of this century. Here it was that in 1831 the eccentric Dr. Wolff, travelling for the first time to Meshed, so narrowly escaped being taken a prisoner by a band of wild Hazaras. There is a small village round the caravanserai, and the *chapar-khaneh* stands hard by.

There was no sun in the early morning, and a cold white mist ran shivering along the mountains. Two hours after starting we passed the village and caravanserai of Sultanabad, where my baggage horse, seeing his opportunity, bolted down the intricate alleys of the village, and we had quite a game of hide and seek before we could drive him out again. There were many hundreds of travellers upon the road, chiefly going Meshed-way, and all or nearly all on horseback, a sign of greater affluence than the employment of a donkey. I was on the look-out for coffins of defunct Shiahs on their way to the great necropolis of Meshed; and from the descriptions of previous travellers recognised the ghastly burden as soon as I saw it. Some that I passed were wrapped in black felt, and slung on either side of donkeys. One man, however, was carrying a very long coffin in front of him on his saddle-bow, and must have had moments of strange emotion. Sometimes a regular corpse-caravan is met, which has been chartered to convey so many score of departed Shiahs to their final resting-place. But as frequently an amateur carrier is encountered, who, to pay the expenses of his own journey and leave a little for amusement at the end, contracts to carry the corpse of some wealthier fellow-citizen or friend. It was a long and stony and fatiguing ride to the next post-house at Kadamgah.

At Kadamgah the Dehrud route from Meshed descends from the mountains on to the plain and joins that upon which I travelled. The name means 'the place of the step', the tradition being that the Imam Reza halted here on his way to Tus, and, in order to convince the local fire-worshippers of his superiority, left the imprint of his foot upon a black stone, which became a *ziarat gah*, or place of pilgrimage, ever afterwards. Over the sacred spot a mosque was raised, not, as Eastwick says, by Shah Abbas, but by Shah Suleiman, and the sanctity of the site has led to its being peopled by a colony of *seyids*, who are as eminent rascals as are most of their brethren. The mosque stands on a raised platform at the upper end of a large garden, which had once been beautifully laid out in terraces, with flower beds, and tanks, and channels of running water, and which, though in a state of hopeless decay, is still overshadowed by considerable trees. Inside the mosque is a single chamber, entered by a coffered archway, and covered by a large dome. The sacred stone is inside; nor is it surprising to find that the Prophet's footmarks are of more than ordinary size. All these great men had huge feet. I have seen Mohammed's footprint in the Mosque of Omar at Jerusalem, and Buddha's footprint on the summit of Adam's Peak in Ceylon; and in view of their prodigious magnitude I was surprised at the modesty of the Imam Reza in having been content with, comparatively speaking, so temperate a measurement. The exterior of the dome had once been covered with tiles; but all these have been stripped or have fallen off, though bands of a still perfect inscription encircle the drum and adorn the façade. From the garden of the mosque the stream flows down the middle of the roadway past a remarkably stately row of pines,[3] between the *chapar-khaneh* and a large caravanserai. Above the shrine, on a hill some 500 feet above the plain, stand the village and fort of Kadamgah, whilst upon a corresponding hill on the opposite side of the valley which here opens into the mountains, is perched an old fortress.

An hour after leaving Kadamgah we entered upon the famous plain of Nishapur, whose praises have been sung by so many chroniclers of the past. Its wonders were expressed in multiples of the number twelve. It was said to have twelve mines of turquoise, copper, lead, antimony, iron, salt, marble, and soapstone; twelve everrunning streams from the hills; 1,200 villages, and 12,000 *kanats* flowing from 12,000 springs. Gone, irretrievably gone, is all this figurative wealth; but fertile, though far less fertile than legend has depicted, is still the plain of Nishapur. Not that fertility in these parts, at any rate in the late autumn, bears the smallest resemblance to its English counterpart. There is no visible green except in the square patches, topped with trees, that mark the villages. But these occur at intervals of almost every quarter of a mile, and the numerous ditches and banks show that the whole country is under irrigation. Its return of the grain sown is said to be tenfold; but the chief local products are now rice, opium, and tobacco. Ferrier, who passed this way forty-five years ago at a more favourable season of the year, spoke quite enthusiastically of its charms. 'Never had I before seen in Persia such rich and luxuriant vegetation; and, as the eye revelled in contemplating it, I could understand without any difficulty the predilection which ancient sovereigns had for Nishapur.'

The shattered walls and towers of Nishapur—'the Nisaya or Nisoa blessed by Ormuzd, the birthplace of the Dionysus of Greek legend, and one of the "paradises" of Iran'—with the roof and minar of a lofty mosque looming above them, were visible long before we reached the city. Passing through an extensive cemetery, whose untidy graves were typical of the squalor that environs death as well as life in Persia, and skirting the town wall on the southern side, we came to the *chapar-khaneh*, immediately outside the western gate. The walls of the city, which had at one time been lofty, were in a more tumbledown condition even than those of Kuchan. Great gaps occurred every fifty yards, and whole sections had entirely disappeared. In one place, however, men were at work rebuilding a bastion, lumps of clay being dug out of a trench at the bottom and tossed from hand to hand until they reached the top, where they were loosely piled one upon the other; though what purpose this belated renovation can have been intended to serve, I am utterly at a loss to imagine. An enemy could march into Nishapur as easily as he could march down Brompton Road, and would find about as much to reward him as if he occupied in force Brompton Cemetery.

The name Nishapur is popularly derived from *nei* (reed) or *ni* = *no* (new) and Shapur, the tradition being that Shapur built the town anew, or built it in what had been a reed-bed. The city was older, however, than Shapur, its legendary foundation being attributed to Tahmuras, one of the Pishdadian kings, fourth in descent from Noah; and its true derivation is from *niw* (the modern Persian *nik*) = good, and Shapur. This town is said to have been destroyed by Alexander the Great, and subsequently rebuilt either by Shapur I. or by Shapur Zulaktaf (the two are constantly confused in Persian tradition), who is further said to have erected here a huge statue of himself, which remained standing till the Mussulman invasion. Shapur's city, however, was not upon the site of the modern Nishapur, but considerably more to the south-east, where its ruins are still traceable round a blue-domed tomb to the left of the road. Nishapur, which has certainly been destroyed and rebuilt more than any city in the world, rose again under the Arabs, and became successively the capital of the Taheride dynasty, of Mahmud of Ghuzni, when Governor of Khorasan, and of the powerful Seljuk family, whose first Sultan, Togrul Beg, resided here, and brought it to the zenith of its splendour. A long line of eminent travellers testified to its magnificence and renown. In the tenth century, the Arab pilgrim El Istakhri found the city a square, stretching one *farsakh* in every direction, with four gates and two extensive suburbs. In the

The tradition is that the town of Nishapur was built in what had been a reed-bed.

eleventh century, Nasiri Khosru declared that it was the sole rival to Cairo. An Arab wit said of its *kanats* and its people, 'What a fine city it would be if only its watercourses were above ground and its population underground!' Another writer, Abu Ali el Alewi, recorded that it was larger than Fostat (old Cairo), more populous than Baghdad, more perfect than Busrah, and more magnificent than Kairwhan. It had forty-four quarters, fifty main streets, a splendid mosque, and a world-famed library. It was one of the four Royal cities of the Empire of Khorasan.

But now the cycle of misfortune had come round; and from the twelfth century downwards it may be said that if Nishapur was only destroyed in order that it might be rebuilt, it was no sooner rebuilt than it was again destroyed. No city ever showed such unconquerable vitality. No city was ever the sport of such remorseless ruin. Nature herself assisted man in the savage tenacity of his vengeance, for what a conqueror had spared an earthquake laid low. Three great earthquakes are recorded in the twelfth, the thirteenth, and the fifteenth centuries. The long career of human devastation was inaugurated by the Turkomans, who in 1153 A.D., in the reign of the great Sultan Sanjar, ravaged it so completely that the inhabitants on returning could not discover the sites of their homes. But if the Turkomans had chastised with whips, the Mongol hordes of Jenghiz Khan might be trusted to chastise with scorpions. They fell upon the city with flame and sword in 1220 A.D., under the command of Tului Khan, son of the conqueror; and the appalling measure of their cruelty is said by a credible historian not to have been filled until they had slain 1,740,000 persons, and razed the city so completely to the ground that a horse could ride over the site without stumbling. Fifty years later, Nishapur was rebuilt, but it would be tedious to relate the vicissitudes of misery through which it has since passed. Mongols, Tartars, Turkomans, and Afghans in turn made it their prey, and gradually reduced it to what in the eighteenth century was reported to be one vast ruin. Upon the death of Nadir Shah in 1747 it held out against Ahmed Abdali the Afghan; but after a six months' siege was taken by him under circumstances which recalled, if they did not equal, the atrocities of Jenghiz Khan. The conqueror, however, was as prudent as he was successful. He restored as ruler to the city the Turkish chieftain, Abbas Kuli Khan, who had resisted him, but whom he learnt to respect, and whose sister he married. The vassal repaid the compliment by life-long loyalty, and by an energetic restoration and adornment of the town. In the time of his successor, in 1796, Nishapur passed tranquilly into the hands of the Kajar usurper, Agha Mohammed Khan, and has ever since remained an appanage of the Persian crown. Fraser in 1821 computed its population as under 5,000, Conolly in 1830 said 8,000, Sir F. Goldsmid in 1872 gave the same figure; the latest estimate is 10,000, which, with the growth that might be expected in a long period of peace, ought not to be excessive.

To a great many English readers Nishapur will perhaps be known only as the last resting-place of the Persian astronomer-poet Omar el Khayam (i.e. the tent-maker), whose name and works have been rendered familiar to the present generation by the masterly paraphrase of Fitzgerald, and by the translations or adaptations of many inferior bards. I remember reading in the preface of one of these latter the plaintive request that someone would take the volume and cast it as an offering at Nishapur before the poet's tomb. Had I possessed it, I should certainly have gratified the writer's petition, at the same time that I disencumbered myself of useless baggage by making the offering, although I fear that the condition of Omar's grave would have greatly shocked his English admirers. It stands in a neglected garden, which once contained flower-beds and rivulets of water, but is now a waste of weeds. There is no inscription to mark the poet's name or fame; and it is to be feared that the modern

Persians are as little solicitous of the dust of Omar el Khayam as a nineteenth-century citizen of London might be of that of Matthew Paris or William of Malmesbury.

Nishapur possesses a Telegraph station of the Meshed-Teheran line worked by a Persian staff. It is also the meeting-point of several important roads in addition to the two from Meshed. On the south a road comes in from Turshiz, and on the north a track runs *via* Madan (where are the turquoise mines) to Kuchan; while in a more westerly direction stretches the old long-forgotten trade route to the Caspian, which is believed to have been a link in the great chain of overland connection in the middle ages between China and India and the European continent. It ran from Nishapur to the Arab city of Isferayin in the plain of the same name, then struck westwards, and passing through the mountains by the defile known as the Dahaneh-i-Gurgan, through which the river Gurgan forces its way, descended the slope to the Caspian. The stages on this route are recorded in the itineraries of Isidore of Charax, and of El Istakhri, and the caravanserais built by Shah Abbas the Great are still standing, though in ruins.

About thirty-six miles in a north-westerly direction from Nishapur, on the first of the roads above mentioned, are situated the famous turquoise mines of Madan (i.e. mines), which from their proximity to the better known city have always been called the mines of Nishapur. Though turquoises are or have been found elsewhere in Persia, and, it is sometimes said, in other countries, these may for all practical purposes be regarded as the only mines in the world that are worked or that repay working on a large scale, and as the source of 999 out of every 1,000 turquoises that come into the market. The mines, of which there are an immense number, actually worked, fallen in, or disused, are situated in a district some forty square miles in extent, which is rich in mineral deposits, there being a productive salt mine, a neglected lead mine, and sandstone quarries within the same area. The turquoises are found in a range of hills, consisting of porphyries, greenstones, and metamorphic limestones and sandstones, at an elevation above the sea which has never exceeded 5,800 feet or fallen below 4,800 feet. They are obtained in one of two ways, either by digging and blasting in the mines proper, which consist of shafts and galleries driven into the rock, or by search among the *débris* of old mines, and amid the alluvial detritus that has been washed down the hill-sides on to the plain. The finest stones are now commonly found in the last-named quarter. The mining, cutting, &c., give occupation to some 1,500 persons, who inhabit the two principal villages of Upper and Lower Madan and several small hamlets in the neighbourhood.

It is believed that in former times and under the Sefavi dynasty, when Persia touched the climax of her wealth and renown, these mines were worked directly by the State. In the anarchy and turbulence of the eighteenth century they were either neglected or left to the villagers, who extracted from them what they could. As order was re-established, control was resumed by the Government, which throughout this century has farmed them to the highest bidder. Abundant relics, however, exist of the reign of 'every man for himself' that preceded. There was no system or science in the working, and the clumsy and sporadic efforts of individuals have resulted in the roofs and sides of most of the old mines falling in and thus completely choking the most lucrative sources of produce. Moreover, the march of science has itself tended to make the work more unscientific, for gunpowder is now used at random where the pick once cautiously felt its way; and many of the stones are smashed to atoms in the process that brings them to the light.

Conolly relates that when Hasan Ali Mirza was Governor of Khorasan the turquoise mines were rented for 1,000 *tomans*, and the rock-salt mine for 300 *tomans* per annum. In Fraser's time (1821), 2,000 Khorasan *tomans*, or 2,700*l*. were asked for the whole mines, and 1,300 *tomans* for the principal mine. In 1862, Eastwick says the rent was only 1,000 *tomans*, or 400l. Ten years later the Seistan Boundary Commissioners found the total rent of all the mines to be 8,000 *tomans*, or 3,200l., though in 1874 Captain Napier reported the figures to be 6,000 *tomans*, or 2,400l. The rent remained at 8,000 *tomans* up till 1882, when the Shah very wisely thought that he could make a better bargain. In that year he leased the mines for a term of fifteen years to the Mukhber-ed-Dowleh, Minister of Education, Telegraphs, and Mines, the rent to be 9,000 *tomans* in the first year, and 18,000 *tomans* in each succeeding year. The Minister took a few rich men into partnership, and the versatile and accomplished General Schindler, whose services are enlisted for whatever work of regeneration is contemplated (I wish I could say executed) in Persia, held the post of managing director for one year. This syndicate appears to have found the system of working the mines itself unremunerative; for at the time of my visit I found that they had been sublet to the Malek-et-Tajar, or head of the Merchants' Guild at Meshed—the enterprising speculator who had also undertaken the Kuchan road—and who was paying a rent of 10,000 *tomans*, or 2,850l., per annum as sublessee, himself subletting again to the villagers after the immemorial fashion to which every tenant in turn seems compelled to come back. He had just had a smart dispute with some of his own sublessees, who had discovered some larger and finer stones than he had bargained for, and whose tenancy he had accordingly terminated by the abrupt method of confiscation. In the past year (1890) the output of stones was estimated at not less than 80,000 *tomans*, or 22,850l.

It would be quite a mistake to suppose that by going either to Meshed or to Nishapur, or even to the pit mouth, the traveller can pick up valuable stones at a moderate price. Fraser tried seventy years ago, and was obliged to desist from the attempt by the ruthless efforts made to cheat him. Every succeeding traveller has tried and has reported his failure. All the best stones are bought up at once by commission agents on the spot and are despatched to Europe or sold to Persian grandees. I did not see a single good specimen either in Meshed or Teheran, though I made constant inquiries. I might indeed, to record my own experience, adopt the very words of Tavernier over two centuries ago:—

Formerly the Meshed jewellers brought some turquoises of the old rock out of Persia; but for these fifteen years last past there have been none found. The last time I was there I could only meet with three which were but reasonable. As for those of the new rock, they are of no value, because they do not keep their colour, but turn green in a little time.

Against the proverbial craftiness of the Oriental the would-be purchaser of turquoises must indeed be pre-eminently upon his guard. There is a plan by which the deep azure that should characterise the true turquoise can be artfully retained up till the very moment of sale. The stones are kept in moist earthenware pots or otherwise damp, until they are parted with. The purchaser hugs his *trouvaille*, only to see its colour fade from day to day, until it is turned to a sickly green. The commoner stones are much used in Persia and the East generally for the decoration of bridles, horse-trappings, dagger-hilts and sheaths; though even of the flat slabs so employed I could obtain no decent specimens; while the commonest of all are converted into charms and amulets, Arabic characters being engraved and gilded upon them so as to hide the flaws. A roaring trade in these trinkets is driven with the pilgrims at Meshed.

From this digression let me now return to my forward journey. The plain of Nishapur is separated from that of Sebzewar (which is 1,000 feet lower) by an undulating range of ugly hills over which the road passes. Fifteen miles from Nishapur, the big caravanserai of Zaminabad is passed, the hills are entered by a low pass, and after a while the post-station and hamlet of Shurab (salt water) are discerned in a hollow. It was during the next stage that my worst *chapar* experience in Persia befell me. The pitiful brute that I was riding smelt so abominably that I could barely sit upon his back, while he himself groaned (for I can call it by no other name) in a manner that testified to his own misery. Removal of the saddle soon showed the seat of mischief in a great open sore; but I only exchanged horses with the *gholam* to discover that his Rosinante was similarly afflicted. It was cruelty to man and beast alike to be compelled to ride these suffering skeletons for eighteen miles. A stretch of several miles across the level brought us to the station of Zafarani. There was once a magnificent caravanserai here, reported to be the largest in Persia. The Persians, eager for a fantastic interpretation wherever it can be suggested, explain the title (yellow or saffron) by a legend of a certain rich merchant who, when building the structure, mixed with the bricks some saffron which he had bought out of charity from a poor man, and which was forthwith converted by a miracle into gold dust, that is supposed to have glittered in the bricks ever afterwards. The building, which is said once to have contained 1,700 rooms, besides baths, shops, and gardens (all of which have disappeared), has been attributed by some travellers to Shah Abbas. But Khanikoff very appositely pointed out that the style and the inscriptions in the Kufic character alike referred it to the Arab period, and he conjecturally placed its foundation in the reign of the Seljuk Malek Shah. Upon its ruins a fine modern caravanserai was built by the public-spirited Sadr Azem before mentioned. From Zafarani the road leads across the Sebzewar plain at no great distance from the mountains on the north, until the city of that name is reached. The entire town, whose central street is a very long covered bazaar (newly constructed when Conolly passed through in 1830), must be traversed before we arrive at the *chapar-khaneh*, close to the western gate.

Sebzewar (i.e. green-having) is the capital of a district of some fertility, which suffered terribly in the famine of 1871, and is only now beginning to raise its head again. Before that year the population of the city was estimated at 30,000. It sank at once to less than 10,000, but is now said to have mounted to 18,000. The town is surrounded by the usual wall of mud bricks, and on the north is commanded by a ruined ark or citadel on a mound. The legendary foundation of Sebzewar, it is needless to say, goes far back into the past, but its historical birth is more justly attributed to the Seljuk dynasty, the style of whose architecture can be detected in certain of its remains. Like most of its neighbours, it has been several times destroyed; Timur completing in 1380 A.D. the operation which Mohammed Shah of Kharizm had left imperfectly done. Whatever of prosperity it subsequently regained was obliterated in true Afghan fashion by the Afghan invaders in the eighteenth century. The modern city is not a century old, having been rebuilt and fortified by Ali Yar Khan, of Mazinan, one of the rebellious governors in Khorasan in the reign of Fath Ali Shah. A good deal of trade has latterly sprung up in Sebzewar, for it is a considerable centre of cotton cultivation, as well as the local entrepôt for the export of wool: and there is an Armenian commercial establishment in the town whose occupants trade with Russia *via* Astrabad and Gez, exporting cotton and wool and importing sugar and chintzes. A coarse cotton cloth is manufactured in the bazaars, and rude copper pots are also fashioned from the produce of three mines in the neighbourhood, which are reputed to be the richest in North Persia and the proper exploitation of which is not unlikely to be undertaken by the Persian Mining Rights Corporation. Sebzewar is also said to be one of the strongholds of the Babis in North Persia.

Almost the only object of interest in Sebzewar to a stranger lies, if a bull may be

permitted, outside it. This is an isolated minaret called by the Persians (in their legendary vein) Khosrugird,[4] which stands about four miles beyond the walls of the present town on the west, but was no doubt within the limits of the ancient city destroyed by Mohammed Shah of Kharizm. That anyone should ever have been mystified by this tower, which has every feature of Arabic architecture about it, simply because it has lost the mosque which it once adorned, is difficult to believe. Riding out to inspect it in the early dawn, I found the mountain crests both to the north and the south of the town white with freshly fallen snow, the first of the winter. Glorious they looked as the rising sun shone on their glistening caps, and flushed the purples and reds of their lower skirts. O'Donovan, rather irreverently, but with some justice, compared the minaret at a distance to a factory chimney; but this illusion is dispelled as we approach. Then we see it to be a single lofty tower, 100 feet high, of brickwork arranged so as to form an exterior pattern on the surface, converging towards the summit, and adorned with two bands of Kufic inscriptions also in brickwork. The capital at the top is broken, and the shaft has, therefore, an unfinished appearance. It springs from a square plinth of mixed concrete and gravel, the whole of which to a depth of about six feet is exposed, and which stands upon a further terrace about eight feet high, in the corners of which are doors, and which is surrounded by low pillars and a low mud wall encircling the whole enclosure. Fraser ascended the tower in 1822 by an interior flight of spiral steps, and O'Donovan followed his example in 1880. The stairway is now in ruins.

No traveller who could read the Kufic character need ever have been in doubt as to the history of this interesting relic; for the inscription states that it was raised in the year 505 of the Hejira—i.e. in 1110 A.D.—when Sultan Sanjar ruled in Khorasan, in the reign of Sultan Mohammed, the son of Malek Shah the Seljuk. It suffered severe injury in the Afghan invasion in 1722, but was subsequently restored by Nadir Shah, and now stands the sole surviving reminder of a city and a splendour that have utterly perished.

Near Sebzewar the country was richly cultivated, especially with cotton. In less than an hour, however, the arable ceased, and in front and around stretched a desolate gravelly plain, in the middle of which in the distance a mountain with double cone stood up and expanded, as we drew near, into a small isolated ridge. Leaving this on the left, we turned towards the base of the snowy range on the north, and after a five-hours' ride reached the village of Mihr, the first inhabited place that we had seen for over thirty miles. The post-house is in the very centre of the village, down whose main street runs a rapid and brick-coloured stream. Between Mihr and Mazinan I caught my first glimpse of a *kavir*, or salt desert, one of those strange and weird expanses, sometimes hard plain, sometimes treacherous swamp, which cover so large a portion of the centre of Persia, and about which I shall require to particularise later on. The white patches of sand glittered under a thin saline efflorescence, and at a little distance might have been mistaken for shallow pools. Mazinan was once a place of considerable size, and was itself the centre of a cluster of fortified villages and towns, but was destroyed by Abbas Mirza in 1831, in punishment of a rebel chief. It is now a most miserable spot, full of tumble-down or abandoned houses. A relic of bygone days exists in the shape of a big caravanserai on the outskirts of the village, built by Shah Abbas. A once far finer structure, the work of Mamun, the son of Harun-er-Rashid and murderer of the Imam Reza, is now in partial ruin. All around are the remains of other towns or villages not less dismal or deserted. As I rode out of Mazinan at 5.30 A.M. on an icy morning, the caravans of pilgrims in the two big caravanserais were already astir; and some loud-lunged *seyid* or *haji* would be heard to chant the note of invocation to Allah, which the whole body would forthwith take up in a responsive volume of sound that rang far through the crisp chill air. From the other side of the village came a

The ice-house at Mazinan was once a place of considerable size, and was itself the centre of a cluster of fortified villages and towns, but was destroyed by Abbas Mirza in 1831, in punishment of a rebel chief.

chorus of similar cries; and with plentiful shouting and discord, another day for the holy wanderers began.

The mention of the pilgrims, or *zawars*, of whom I saw so much on each day's journey, and who all but monopolise the Meshed road, tempts me to vary the dull recital of my progress by a slight description of the human surroundings in which it was framed. The stream of progress appeared in the main to be in the opposite direction to that which I was pursuing. Sometimes for miles in the distance could be seen the *kafilah*, or caravan, slowly crawling at a foot-pace across the vast expanse. Then, as it came nearer, would be heard the melancholy monotone of some devout or musical member of the band, droning out in quavering tones a verse from the Koran; sometimes, in less solemn companies, a more jovial wayfarer trolling some distich from the Persian classics. As the long cavalcade approached, it would be seen to consist of every kind of animal and of every species of man. Horses would carry the more affluent, who would be smoking their *kalians* as they paced along; some would affect camels; mules were very common, and would frequently support *kajavehs*,[5] a sort of wooden pannier, with an arched framework for a hood, in which men as often as women were curled up beneath mountains of quilts. The donkey, however, was the favourite beast of burden. Tiny animals would bear the most stupendous loads, with pots and pans, guns, and water-bottles hanging on either side, and with the entire furniture of a household on their backs; the poultry of the owner perched with ludicrous gravity upon the top of all. It is a common thing for the poorer pilgrims to take shares in a donkey and to vary riding with walking. In the early morning the equestrians would often be seen fast asleep upon their asses, lying forward upon their necks, and occasionally falling with a thump on to the ground. Each *kafilah* would have a *caravan-bashi*, or leader, who not infrequently bore a red pennon fluttering from a lance. It was often difficult to discern the men's faces as they rode by shrouded in huge woollen blanket-coats, pulled up over their heads, while the stiff, empty arm-holes stood out on either side like monstrous ears. But, if it was not easy to discern the males, still less could be distinguished of the shapeless bundles of blue cotton that were huddled upon the donkeys' backs, and which chivalry almost forbade me to accept for the fairer sex. I confess to having once or twice, with intentional malice, spurred my horse to a gallop, as I was overtaking some party of wayfarers thus accompanied: for, to see the sober asses kick up their heels and bolt from the track as they heard the clatter of horse-hoofs behind, to observe the amorphous bundles upon their backs shake and totter in their seats, till shrieks were raised, veils fell, and there was imminent danger of a total collapse, was to crack one's sides with sorely-needed and well-earned laughter. There would usually be an assortment of beggars in every band, who would beg of me in one breath and curse me for an infidel in the next, or of tattered dervishes, who in Mussulman countries are beggars in their most offensive guise.

Not that every company we met or passed were pilgrims on pious mission bent. Far from it. Sometimes we would encounter merchants, absorbed and sedate; sometimes *mullahs* on sleek asses or mules; sometimes officials and soldiers; and sometimes whole families migrating. All classes and all ages were on the road: horsemen and footmen; rich men and poor men; *seyids* and scoundrels—a microcosm of the stately, commonplace, repulsive, fascinating Oriental world.

At night these varied and polyglot elements (for there will be pilgrims from many lands) seek shelter and sleep in the caravanserais erected at intervals of ten or fifteen miles along the entire route. I have so often spoken of these structures that I may here, in passing, describe what they are. The caravanserai is the Eastern inn. But with the name the parallelism ends: for no proud signboard, no cheerful parlour or burnished bar, no obsequious ostler or rubicund landlord welcomes your approach. The caravanserai, perhaps, contains a single custodian, and that is all. The wayfarer must do everything for himself. He stables his own beasts, piles together and watches his own baggage, lights his own fire, and cooks his own repast. As a rule, the building is a vast square or rectangular structure of brick or stone, built in the form of a parallelogram round an open court. The two exterior sides and the back walls are plain, and give the building from a distance the appearance of an immense fort—an idea which is frequently, and with full intention, sustained in the shape of projecting towers at the angles and a parapet above. In the front outer wall, or façade, is a series of large recessed arches, with a seat, or platform, about two feet from the ground. These are frequently used as sleeping-places in the warm weather. A huge gateway opens in the centre, with sometimes a tower and *bala-khaneh* overhead, and leads into the inner quadrangle, which is perhaps fifty yards square, and whose sides are divided into recessed compartments, open to the air, similar to those on the outside wall. In the superior caravanserais a doorway at the back of each of these arches leads into an inner cell, which is occupied on cold nights. Behind these, and reaching to the exterior wall, are long rows of hot, unlit stables, where the animals are lodged, and access to which is gained from the four corners. Such is the ordinary Persian caravanserai. In a few of improved style or recent construction, such as that at Borasjun, near the Persian Gulf—by far the finest that I saw in the whole country—there is a series of upstairs apartments for visitors of higher rank or means; but, as a rule, democracy is the prevailing law in the economy of the serai of Persia.

Perhaps the weirdest and most impressive of the many unwonted memories that the traveller carries away with him from such-like travel in the East is the recollection of the camel caravans which he has encountered at night. Out of the black darkness is heard the distant boom of a heavy bell. Mournfully, and with perfect regularity of

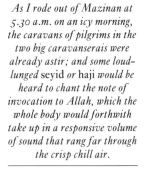

As I rode out of Mazinan at 5.30 a.m. on an icy morning, the caravans of pilgrims in the two big caravanserais were already astir; and some loud-lunged seyid *or* haji *would be heard to chant the note of invocation to Allah, which the whole body would forthwith take up in a responsive volume of sound that rang far through the crisp chill air.*

iteration, it sounds, gradually swelling nearer and louder, and perhaps mingling with the tones of smaller bells, signalling the rearguard of the same caravan. The big bell is the insignia and alarum of the leading camel alone. But nearer and louder as the sound becomes, not another sound, and not a visible object, appear to accompany it. Suddenly, and without the slightest warning, there looms out of the darkness, like the apparition of a phantom ship, the form of the captain of the caravan. His spongy tread sounds softly on the smooth sand, and, like a great string of linked ghouls, the silent procession stalks by and is swallowed up in the night.

And how wonderful and ever-present is the contrast in Eastern travel to all life and movement at home! No heavy carts and lumbering wagons jolt to and fro between the farmyard and the fields. No light vehicles and swift equipages dash past upon macadamised roads. Alas! there are no roads; and, if no roads, how much less any vehicles or wagons! Thatched roofs and tiled cottages, lanes and hedgerows and trim fields, rivers coursing between full banks, beyond all the roar and sudden, smoky rush of the train—these might not exist in the world at all, and do not exist in the world of the Persian, straitened and stunted, but inexpressibly tranquil in his existence. Here, all is movement and bustle, flux and speed; there, everything is imperturbable, immemorial, immutable, slow.

Between Mazinan and Shahrud, a distance of approximately one hundred miles, intervene four stages, which were formerly known as the 'Stages of Terror'. Here the western extremities of the Khorasan mountains, pushed out in long spurs of diminishing height from the knotted mountain cluster that surrounds the head-waters of the Atrek, descend on to the plain, and the road pursues a winding course through their lower folds and undulations. This entire mountain region was once desolated by Turkoman bandits, and through these valleys and ravines they dashed down in headlong foray upon the helpless bands of travellers making their way to or from Meshed. Sweeping up whatever they could get, driving off the animals, and chaining a few score of captives to their saddle-bows, they galloped off into their mountain-fastnesses with as much precipitation as that with which they had come. Already, along the route which I have described from Meshed to Mazinan, I had seen frequent proofs of their dreaded presence, in the shape of those small circular towers, dotted all over the plain like chessmen on a chessboard, which, from Ashkabad to Meshed, from Sarakhs to Farrah, and from Shahrud almost to Kum, marked the chosen hunting-grounds of these terrible moss-troopers of the border. In parts almost every field had one of these structures, into which, as soon as a rolling cloud of dust revealed the apparition of the enemy, the husbandman crept by a small hole at the bottom, and, rolling two big stones against the aperture, waited till the scourge had swept past. Similar evidence of the terror they inspired, and of the state of siege which self-preservation imposed upon their possible victims, is forthcoming along the entire belt of country above named, in the rude forts erected in every village as a refuge for the inhabitants. Once behind a mud wall the miserable peasants were safe; but woe betide them if caught in the open country—death or the slave-markets of Khiva and Bokhara were then the certain issue.

What the luckless peasant faced every day the timid pilgrim looked to encounter on this fateful stretch of road which I am about to describe. The most elaborate precautions were taken against the danger. An escort used to leave Shahrud and Mazinan twice a month, consisting of a number of so-called foot-soldiers armed with matchlocks, and a mounted detachment accompanying an old gun. At Miandasht the two escorts met and relieved each other. The support of the Mazinan detachment, consisting of 150 matchlock men and twelve artillery-men with their horses, was imposed, in lieu

A fateful stretch of road where pious pilgrims met perils and panicked.

of the ordinary taxes, upon the villagers of that place; and even so late as 1872, when the Seistan Boundary Commissioners passed this way on their return to Teheran, they had to travel with an escort of eighty matchlocks, a $4\frac{1}{2}$-pounder dragged by six horses, and 150 to 200 mounted *sowars*, between Mazinan and Shahrud.

Conolly, Fraser, Eastwick, O'Donovan, and other writers who journeyed with the pilgrim caravans have left inimitable accounts of the perils and panics of their pious companions. A Persian is a coward at the best of times: but a Persian pilgrim is a degree worse than his fellows; and a Persian pilgrim in the vicinity of a Turkoman almost ceases to be a human being. There would be long delays and anxious rumours at the beginning; several false starts would be made and abandoned in consequence of some vague report; finally the caravan would venture forth, moving frequently at night, when the darkness added to, rather than diminished, the terror. First would come the matchlock men blowing their matches, and either marching on foot or mounted on donkeys; then the genuine cavalry, with flintlocks and hayfork-rests; next the great body of the pilgrims, huddling as close as possible round the artillerymen and the gun, which was looked upon as a veritable palladium, but of which it is not on record that it was ever fired. Soldiers again brought up the rear, and, wrapped up in dust, confusion, and panic, the procession rolled on. The noise they made, shouting, singing, cursing, praying, and quarrelling, signalled their approach for miles, and, if they escaped, it was the positive worthlessness of the spoil (for a Mussulman pilgrim leaves all his valuables behind him), rather than the hazard of capture or the awe inspired by the bodyguard, that was responsible for their safety. To their fearful imaginations every bush was a vedette of the enemy, every puff of wind that raised the dust betrayed a charge, every hillock concealed a squadron. Loud were the shouts and clamorous the invocations to Allah, and Ali, and Husein, and all the watchful saints of the calendar, when the end of the march was reached and God had protected his own.

It is only just to add that, if the panic of a multitude was despicable, the terrors of individuals were not unfairly aroused. Many are the tales that are still told of the capture of isolated travellers or of small bands; and there was scarcely a single peasant in the villages in this strip of country that had not, at some time or other, been pounced down upon in the fields or at the water-springs, and who, if happily he were ransomed after years of slavery, did not bear upon his person the lifelong imprint of cruelty and fetters. Colonel Euan Smith is in error in stating that it was upon this piece of road that M. de Blocqueville, the French amateur photographer who had accompanied the disastrous expedition against Merv in 1860, in order to take photographs and paint a battle-scene for the Shah, was seized and carried off, and not redeemed until he had been a captive for fifteen months and a ransom of 11,000 *tomans* (then equivalent to 5,000*l.*) was paid by his royal patron.[6] He was captured in the successful attack made by the Turkomans upon the Persian column while at Merv. It was here, however, that a Persian general in command of 6,000 men, halting behind his column for two or three moments to take a final pull at his *kalian*, was snatched up and swept away in full sight of his troops, and within a few weeks' time was sold for a few pounds in the bazaar of Khiva.

Whatever may be said of the designs of Russia on this province of Khorasan, not Persia only, but every traveller between Teheran and Meshed, owes her a lasting sense of gratitude for the service she has wrought in putting an end to this unmitigated curse. It was certainly not for unselfish reasons, nor in the interests of Persia, still less out of pure philanthropy, that Russia undertook her successful campaigns against the Tekke Turkomans of Transcaspia. But here we may afford to ignore motives, and may be content with congratulating both ourselves and her upon the fact. Since the victorious campaign of Skobeleff in 1881, and the subsequent annexation of Akhal Tekke, the Meshed–Teheran road has been absolutely secure. No guard is maintained or needed, the pilgrims have no special ground of appeal to Allah, and the traveller is startled by nothing more serious than the whirr of wings as a covey of red-legged partridges—which abound in these mountains—rises almost from between his horse's legs.

Leaving Mazinan, our road struck northwards towards the hills. In the grey morning light I discerned a numerous herd of wild deer, as large as red deer, at a distance of 300 yards from the track; but the bullets of my revolver had no other effect than to accelerate their disappearance. After fourteen miles we came to the deserted caravan-serai and fort of Sadrabad. As the name implies, these edifices were raised by the great Minister, or Sadr Azem, before mentioned; but the fort and its garrison were practically useless: for the latter were only just strong enough to guard themselves, without turning a thought to the protection of others. A mile and a half beyond Sadrabad brought us to the Pul-i-Abrishum (or Bridge of Silk)—originally built by Nadir Shah, and recently restored—over the Abrishum River (a stream strongly impregnated with salt from salt-springs near its source), which flows down here from the north, and, under the name of the Kal Mura, subsequently disappears into a *kavir* to the south. The Kal Mura is generally regarded as the eastern boundary of Khorasan, and it marked the extreme north-west limit of the Afghan empire of Ahmed Shah Durani in the last century. At the time that I passed, the river-bed, which was about twenty yards in width, was absolutely dry. The rising sun just enabled me to take a photograph, which reveals a very typical Persian bridge, and I then hurried on.

A few miles beyond we came to a spot known as the Chashmeh-i-Gez (or Spring of Tamarisks), where a scanty rivulet supplies a number of little pools and fertilises some patches of grass. This was a notorious and dreaded spot in the old days, for hither came the Turkoman robbers to water their horses after the long mountain ride, and

The rising sun just enabled me to take this photograph, which reveals a very typical Persian bridge, called the Bridge of Silk.

here the luckless voyager was frequently swooped down upon and caught. It was close to this spot that Ferrier had a brush with them in 1845. The end of this stage is the remarkable-looking village-fort for Abbasabad, which rises in tiers upon an eminence, the lofty front being pierced with numerous windows and crowned with ruined battlements. Its inhabitants are the converted descendants of a Georgian colony of a hundred families, who were transported to this spot by Abbas the Great three centuries ago, as a link in his chain of military colonies along the northern frontier. He assigned them an annual allowance in coin (100 *tomans*) and wheat (100 *kharvars*), which after a while was not paid. In the third generation, being forbidden to use the Georgian tongue, they are said to have become Mussulmans; but traces of their mother language have been detected by some travellers in their dialect. During the Turkoman reign of terror there was said not to be a single adult man in Abbasabad who had not more than once been carried away captive.

A hilly ride over low, barren ridges, and up the gravelly bed of a valley known as the Dahaneh Al Hak, brings us to the squalid village of that name, where a corps of fifty militiamen were once stationed to guard the road. Through similar scenery and over undulating ground we mount 1,000 feet since leaving Abbasabad, and come at length to the magnificent caravanserai of Miandasht (lit. mid-plain), whose lofty embattled walls and projecting towers resemble a vast fortress, and can be seen for miles. This was the central point of the 'Stages of Terror', and here, one half of the peril over, the pilgrims foregathered to exchange felicitations or foment alarms. There is an old caravanserai built by Shah Abbas, whose name appears above the gateway; but the huge castellated structure is a new erection of burnt brick, with a parapet and walls twenty feet high. A courtyard, in which the *chapar-khaneh* is located, connects the two, and water is provided from three large *abambars*, or subterranean reservoirs, to which access is gained by steep flights of steps.

Beyond Miandasht occurs what was formerly the most perilous part of the journey. The road winds in and out of low passes between rounded knolls, where every turn discloses a hidden hollow, and where every elevation might hide an ambuscade. The hills are bare and stony, or clad only with a diminutive scrub. They are alive with partridges, in pairs or in small coveys of five or six, which were so tame that they ran along the road and crouched till one was within a dozen yards.[7] Here is the peculiarly noted Dahaneh-i-Zaidar, the gully by which the Turkomans usually descended to make their attack, and at its mouth was the small, now dismantled, fort of Zaidar, where was a garrison of fifty regulars. On emerging from the hills we see before us the twin-peaked mountains above Maiomai, and, skirting its northern base, reach the village of that name, where is a fine caravanserai, built by Shah Abbas II, and some superb old *chenars*. It was in the *bala-khaneh* of the posthouse at Maiomai, which I occupied, that O'Donovan was besieged by an infuriated band of Arab *hajis*, and had rather a narrow escape; and it was in the caravanserai that Dr John Cormick, for many years chief physician to Abbas Mirza, died of typhus in 1833.

The next march, from Maiomai to Shahrud, forty-one miles, used to be the longest in Persia, and has been bewailed by many victims. But, for postal purposes, it has now been divided by the station and *chapar-khaneh* of Armian. The first part of the road, along the base of the same mountain-range, is very stony. Two small villages are passed, each dependent upon a single small rill, whose passage from the mountains can be traced by a thin line of poplars. Armian is picturesquely situated on a hill-side, with an abundant stream flowing down the road just outside the posthouse door, and subsequently fertilising a series of well-kept terrace-plots below the village. The first half of the ride to Shahrud is spent in winding in and out of the lower ranges that gradually dip into the plain of Shahrud, 1,000 feet below Armian. The snowy crown of the Shah Kuh (King Mountain), the highest point of the Elburz between Shahrud and Astrabad, had been before my eyes the whole day, and at its feet, I knew, lay Shahrud. About eleven miles before reaching the latter, the first view is caught of the level plain, some ten miles in width, on which were visible three detached green clumps. The two nearer were unimportant villages, the farthest and largest, nestling at the very foot of the Elburz, was Shahrud. So buried in trees is the town, that, after riding for some time between garden-walls and orchards, I found myself in the main street, almost unawares.

The town is a great meeting-point of roads, from Herat to Meshed, from Tabbas and Turshiz, from Yezd, from Astrabad and Mazanderan, and from the capital. It is situated in a plain, of whose fertility I could form no just estimate in the month of November, but whose productiveness and abundant water-supply are unquestioned. The Rud-i-Shah (or King's River) flows down the street outside the *chapar-khaneh*, but at this season of the year was little more than a rivulet, and reflected no honour upon its name. The defensive properties of the place struck me as contemptible, and appeared to be limited to a ruined citadel, and to two small mud towers, perched upon a conical hill above the town. Shahrud is celebrated for its local manufacture of boots and shoes, which are said to be patronised by the Shah and the Royal Family; for the redoubtable *shabgez*, or *gherib-gez*, which attacked O'Donovan here but spared me; and as an entrepôt both of the local products of Mazanderan and of Russian imports *via* Gez and Astrabad, through the agency of Russian and Russo–Armenian traders. The Russian Caucasus and Mercury Company also keep an agent in the town. Its population is said to be 5,000. There is a Persian Telegraph-station here, and a wire to Astrabad, whence there is further telegraphic connection by Chikishliar with Kizil Arvat and Transcaspia—a line which is much used by the Russian Legation in Teheran in communicating with Ashkabad.

Having arrived at Shahrud early in the afternoon, I spent some time in inspecting the town. It contains a large covered bazaar, not thatched, but properly roofed, and with spacious and well-appointed shops. My observations and inquiries tallied exactly with what I had heard at Meshed. All the sugar was Russian, all the tea was Indian, brought from Bunder Abbas *via* Yezd. The greater part of the coloured cottons and chintzes were Russian, but the white sheeting bore the name of a Bombay firm, and I saw, not merely a large pile of Manchester glazed calicoes with a Bombay label, but also a number of unbleached cottons direct from Manchester itself. This was a gratifying fact, considering that Shahrud lies within four marches of what is practically a Russian port on the Caspian. I bought some delicious white grapes for a few pence. A wine is made from them in Shahrud.

Though Shahrud is the capital of the district of Bostam-Shahrud, it is not the residence of the Governor or the seat of government. The latter is at the town of Bostam, three and a half miles in a north-easterly direction from Shahrud (from which it is concealed by a rocky hill), and higher up the course of the same river. Bostam, a Mazanderani proper name, is a place of superior fertility and luxury to Shahrud. It is, further, a site of great sanctity among Mohammedan pilgrims, for here was buried the famous Sheikh, or Sultan, Bayazid, the leader of a dervish sect, who died, and was interred in the court of a beautiful mosque, now much ruined, in the year A.D. 874. Attached to the same mosque, whose cupola was erected by a Mongol prince in A.D. 1313, is a shaking minaret, similar to those which I shall afterwards describe at Isfahan, and which can be made to vibrate by rocking it at the summit. Colonel Lovett has attributed this phenomenon to the elasticity of the bricks and cement employed, the latter becoming more elastic with age, and has compared it with the kindred phenomenon of slabs of elastic sandstone. There is, further, at Bostam a curious brick tower, whose outer circumference is, so to speak, dog-toothed by a number of salient angles, similar to the tower of which I shall speak later at Rhey.

Already, upon arriving at the posthouse of Shahrud—which is unique in the possession of a threefold *bala-khaneh*—I had observed unfamiliar symptoms of refinement, in the shape of a druggeted floor and curtained doorways. On my return from the bazaars I was proceeding to make my toilet, and was already in a state of semi-*déshabille*, when, without the slightest warning, I became aware of a further act of official attention. Two Armenians first entered unannounced, both of whom could speak a little French. One was the agent of Messrs. Ziegler in Shahrud, the other of a firm named Tumanianz. I presumed that they had come out of curiosity, as they offered no explanation. But in the East such amenities cannot be resented, requiring rather to be interpreted as tokens of civility. Wherefore I continued my toilet while discussing the trade and commerce of Shahrud. Presently, however, the doorway of the *bala-khaneh* was again darkened, and a trio of Persian officials marched in, while a posse of attendants stood outside. They were succeeded by some menials carrying a tray, on which were two packets of tea and four sugar-loaves wrapped up in blue paper; following whom appeared two other individuals holding by the legs a kicking sheep, while a third balanced a couple of cane-bottomed chairs behind. I really think that I am justified in presenting this to my readers as a spectacle of no mean dramatic effect.

Scene.—A mud room in a Persian posthouse.
Dramatis Personæ.—Englishman in flannel shirt, breeches, and stockings only; Armenian traders; Persian chamberlains; struggling sheep.
Dramatic Accessories.—Sugar-loaves and cane-bottomed chairs.

I now realised that I was the recipient of a formal deputation from the Prince-Governor of Shahrud, who had sent to welcome and to invite me to become his guest at Bostam, and that the Armenians had been despatched as a sort of advanced guard to reconnoitre and interpret. By their aid I was enabled to acknowledge the hospitality of the Governor and to accept his gifts—a process which naturally involved the return of an equivalent present to the deputies. Having pocketed a few *tomans* with much satisfaction, these worthies forthwith realised that no more business was to be done. Accordingly, they announced that the hour for repose had arrived, and bowed themselves out. For my part, I slew the sheep and had a capital leg of mutton for dinner.

Shahrud is rather more than the halfway stage between Meshed and Teheran, but it serves to divide the journey into two portions, of which it is difficult to determine which is the less attractive. There is a curious identity between their respective features: for, just as the Meshed–Shahrud section presents two cities of ancient fame, Nishapur and Sebzewar, so the Shahrud–Teheran section displays Damghan and Semnan; and, just as the only structures worthy of observation in the first section are the minarets and towers of Sebzewar and Bostam, so, in the second, we must be content with the analogous monuments of Damghan and Semnan. Finally, to complete the parallelism, just as the first section terminates after threading the famous Turkoman passes, so does the second conduct us, on the penultimate day's journey, through the even more famous Caspian Gates that lead into the Plain of Veramin. Stones, sand, *kavir*, and execrable horses are the common prerogatives of both.

It was on one of the worst of these brutes that, over a track scarcely less atrocious, I pursued my way to Deh Mullah ('the Village of the Priest'). The *chapar-khaneh* is on the outskirts of the village, which lies a little farther in the plain, and is remarkable only for a huge mound of clay, once crowned by a citadel, whose riven and crumbling walls stand up in melancholy ruin. The ride from Deh Mullah to Damghan is over rather better ground, but is unutterably tedious. On my right hand was the scarped red rampart of the Elburz, rising sheer from the plain, and, like a wall of brass, shutting off the defiles and gorges of that mighty range; and behind them, again, the steamy lowlands of Mazanderan, sloping to the Caspian. On the left, or south, whereas on most maps I see marked a salt desert, or *kavir*, my own notes record that, throughout the entire day's journey, the horizon was bounded on that side, at an average distance of about ten miles, by a range of hills of quite sufficient elevation to appear upon most maps, although I cannot find any trace of them upon the majority of those that I have studied. The road to Damghan passed several villages, one of which, Mehmandost, was evidently a favourite halting-place for travellers, as there were crowds of wayfarers and horsemen in the single street. About three miles from Damghan we rode through the ruins of a deserted city, Bostajan. A more sorrowful spectacle than an abandoned town of mud cannot be conceived. The buildings, and roofs, and walls gradually waste away into indistinguishable heaps of clay; but, so compact and solid do these become in the process, that they last for scores, and sometimes for hundreds, of years. Nor is it fair to assume that, along with each deserted city or site, its inhabitants, as an item in the population, have been wiped off the face of the earth. Were such the case, one might be led to infer that Persia, which is now as sparsely peopled as Palestine, was once as densely crowded as China. I believe that this would be a false inference. Just as each great Persian monarch or founder of a dynasty, from Cyrus downwards, has shifted the capital and seat of government, so as to associate a fresh glory with his name, so has each petty governor or chieftain striven to emulate his sovereign by a new urban plantation; and, in a yet lower grade, each father of a family has thought to better himself and to transcend his forerunners by erecting a new abode. It is to this universal instinct, permeating every rank of life, not less than to the ravages of famine, disease, and war, that must be attributed the countless wasting skeletons of tenements and cities that litter the soil of Persia.

From a distance of some miles the two minarets of Damghan, the counterparts of that of Sebzewar, rise in view. They stand some way apart, in different quarters of the town. The better preserved of the two, which is mountable and has a small turret of later date at the top, with a door for the *muezzin*, is situated just off the main street of the town, and is in close proximity to a mosque—not, indeed, that to which it was originally attached, but a comparatively modern structure. Like the minar at Sebzewar, it is faced with bricks, so laid as to form geometrical patterns on the circumference, and has, further, a band of Kufic letters in high relief. The two minarets belong to the *imamzadehs*, or tombs of two saints, named respectively Jafir and Kasim; and, for an account of their shrines, as well of a third tomb raised over a saint named Mohammed, the son of Ibrahim, and called Pir-i-Alamdar, I cannot do better than refer my readers to the erudite pages of Khanikoff. Damghan, though a considerable place, even in the present century, is now in a pitiable state of decay. The deserted ruins of a huge square citadel—a room in which used to be preserved and shown as the apartment wherein Fath Ali Shah first saw the light—rise above the cubical domes of the bazaar, but are fast crumbling to pieces. I rode through the bazaar, which consists of a long covered street, far less cleanly and decorous than that of Shahrud. Through the town runs a stream, flowing down from a spring in the mountains called Chashmeh-i-Ali, where is both a summer residence of the Shah, and also a place of pilgrimage, as one of the spots where Ali's charger appears to have stamped so fiercely with his hoof as to leave a permanent indentation in the rock. On a hill-top near this miraculous site a further miracle exists in the shape of a spring, called Chashmeh-i-Bad (or Fountain of the Wind), which, if stirred at certain times, is said to produce a hurricane that blows everything to destruction.

Damghan has a twofold historical interest—legendary and modern. It is always supposed to mark the site of the ancient Hekatompylos (or City of a Hundred Gates), the name given by the Greeks to the capital of the Arsacid dynasty of Parthian kings, although, with the exception of a number of mounds and of several underground conduits, built of large slabs of stone, there does not exist, and is not on record as having existed, at Damghan a single remain that could be identified with so illustrious a past. Ferrier, I think erroneously, endeavours to combat this theory by the argument that the City of a Hundred Gates must mean a city in which many roads met, whereas at Damghan there are only two. He, therefore, prefers the Shahrud–Bostam site for that of Hekatompylos. Apart, however, from the fact that more roads meet at Damghan than two, it is by no means certain that the Greeks, when they used this descriptive epithet, referred to city gates at all. The title was equally applied by them to Egyptian Thebes, where it has been conjectured to refer to the *pylons*, or gateways, of the many splendid temples by which the capital of the Rameses was adorned; and it may have had some similar application in the case of the Parthian city. Dismissing, however, the identity of Damghan with Hekatompylos as a question of purely speculative interest, we may find enough of romance in the history of the town under its modern name. It is needless to say that Jenghiz Khan destroyed it once, or to add that Timur destroyed it again. That was a compliment invariably paid by those rival scourges of humanity to urban magnificence. Don Ruy di Clavijo, passing through Northern Persia on his embassy from the Castilian King to the Court of the Great Tartar in 1404, found still standing at Damghan two towers of human heads set in mud, which, but a few years before, the latter had erected as a trophy. Shah Abbas rebuilt the town and constructed its citadel. Here, in October 1729, Nadir Shah gained his great victory over the Afghan Ashraf, which heralded the final expulsion of the aliens in the following year. Here, in 1763, Zeki Khan, the savage half-brother of Kerim Khan Zend, being despatched to quell a revolt of the Kajar tribe, planted a garden with his prisoners, head downwards, at even distances; and here, in 1796, perished the miserable grandson of Nadir, Shah Rukh, from the effects of the inhuman torture inflicted upon him at Meshed by Agha Mohammed Shah. In the present century Damghan is said to have been finally ruined by a friend, instead of a foe, having never recovered from the encampment here, for three months, in 1832, of the army of Abbas Mirza on its way to Herat. No flight of locusts could have inflicted a more wholesale devastation. The population is reported now to be 13,000. I cannot credit it.

After leaving Damghan the road strikes due west, and traverses first a gravelly, and afterwards a richly-cultivated, plain to Ghushah, a place consisting only of two buildings—a caravanserai and a posthouse, which the exigencies of travel have conjured up in an otherwise untenanted expanse. The only interesting spot passed on the way is the deserted fort of Dowletabad, with a triple wall of enclosure, surrounded by a deep fosse. Sixty years ago Sergeant Gibbons, an Englishman serving in the army of Abbas Mirza, said it was 'one of the best little forts he had seen in Persia'. Its chief, who had held out for some time against the exactions of the provincial Governor, offered Abbas Mirza a bribe of 30,000 *tomans* if he would continue him in the government. The Prince pocketed the money and carried off the chief to Meshed, the local Governor taking advantage of his absence to capture the fort. Like most other places in the neighbourhood, it is now abandoned and is rapidly falling to pieces.

Throughout this day, and, indeed, in all parts of my journey, I passed several of those great tumuli, or barrows, which have so puzzled the traveller in North Persia. They consist of immense circular or oval mounds, from fifty to a hundred feet in height, supporting, as a rule, no traces of buildings, but composed of solid masses of clay, worn smooth by the long passage of time. Local tradition, of course, assigns them to Jamshid—which is tantamount to a confession of utter ignorance as to their origin. By some they have been regarded as the sites of fire-temples, raised in the old days of Zoroastrian worship. I entertain very little doubt that they were mostly, if not all, raised as citadels or forts of defence for villages, long since perished, below. They are invariably to be found upon the plains where Nature has provided no ready means of defence, and where artifice was consequently required to create them. Many still exhibit upon their summits the crumbling, shapeless walls of the mud citadels by which they were once crowned. Good illustrations of this stage of existence are visible at Bidesht, near Shahrud, and at Jajarm, between Bujnurd and Shahrud. Where the tumuli (or *kurgans*, as they are called) are smooth and bare, the superstructure has entirely perished. A long line of these mounds is still traceable along the valley of the Gurgan, starting from Gumesh Tepe (or Silver Hill)—an obviously artificial erection— on the shores of the Caspian, and forming part of a triple line of earth ramparts, attributed to Alexander the Great, which extends as far as Bujnurd. The regularity of their occurrence in some places, as, for instance, between Kazvin and Teheran, has led to the plausible conjecture that they may also have been used as signal-stations, or beacons, from one camp to another. But, in either case, their purpose was military. There seems to be no ground for regarding any of them as sepulchral barrows.

The road from Ghushah lay over a desolate and uncultivated plain, and then gradually mounted, until, having traversed an easy pass in the hills, it suddenly dropped down upon a gloomy hollow, where stood the caravanserai and posthouse of Ahuan. The existing brick serai was built by Shah Suleiman Sefavi; an older one of stone, attributed to the Sassanid Nushirwan, is in ruins. The name Ahuan, which has apparently much perplexed previous travellers, signifies antelope or gazelle,[8] tradition ascribing to this spot one of the astounding miracles by which the Imam Reza signalised the various stages of his eastward journey to Tus. Here he found a captive female antelope, which, detecting his sacred personality, found speech, and invoked the assistance of the saint on behalf of her motherless young. The Imam bade the hunter release the animal, and himself went bail for her reappearance. The antelope, however, found the joys of home too much for her plighted word, and failed to keep the tryst; whereupon the prophet, being appealed to, 'willed' her back again to her captor, with whom she remained a prisoner, or a pet, ever afterwards. Here the mountain range is entered that separates the plains of Damghan and Semnan. From the highest point of the dividing crest the latter city was visible, twelve miles away, lying like a green splash upon a floor of stones. The descent on the far side, though easy, is very stony, and cantering down was no pleasure. Meeting a closed carriage drawn by four horses, with two postillions, outriders, and a guard, I had a horrible momentary dread that I was in for an *istikbal*, or official entry; but was reassured by finding that the occupant was the *hakim* or Governor, who presumably was making a tour through his not very extensive dominions.

Semnan is held remarkable in Persia for its extensive and well-irrigated gardens, for its ancient trees, for an old minaret which enables it to compete with Damghan, for a smart and well-preserved modern mosque, for its local manufactures of teacakes and blue cotton pyjamas, for the beauty of its women, and for the unintelligibility of its speech. Perhaps in none of these respects does it quite answer to expectation. There is a great deal of water flowing in rivulets down the smaller streets, which usually serve as watercourses in Persia as well as roadways; but the environs of the town did not appear to profit thereby to the full extent, although a good deal of tobacco is cultivated. Outside the bazaar is an open space in which there are some venerable *chenars*, and one magnificent veteran is enclosed in the bazaar itself, and protrudes his stupendous bole through the roof. The old minaret is also encountered in the middle of the bazaar, attached to the Musjid-i-Jama, which is in ruins. The tower is one hundred feet high and contains a hundred steps leading to the summit, which is fitted with a prayer-gallery. Earthquakes and age have caused it to slant. Fath Ali Shah's mosque, a little distance away, contains a spacious quadrangle, fifty yards square, and two fine *aiwans*, or recessed arches, set in tile-enamelled frames. Attached to it is a *madresseh*, or religious college. As for the teacakes, when Vambéry asked in vain for them, having heard of their fame as far away as in Herat, he received the truly Persian reply that, so great was the demand for these articles, and so enormous the export, that none were left for local consumption. I did not see the beautiful women any more than Vambéry found the teacakes. Upon the speech I am not qualified to pronounce; but so learned a philologist as Khanikoff, having made fruitless efforts to ascertain something by queries, came to no more definite conclusion than that it was a Mazanderan dialect, enriched by more vowels; whilst a legend relates that a *savant* who was once employed by a Persian monarch to report upon the languages spoken by his subjects illustrated that of Semnan by shaking some stones in an empty gourd before his royal patron. Semnan is reported to contain 4,000 houses and 16,000 inhabitants—a probably altogether extravagant estimate. Jews are prohibited from residing here; but there are some twenty-five Hindu Buniahs engaged in trade, Semnan being the point where a route from Bunder Abbas, *viâ* Yezd and Tabbas, comes in from the south and supplies the northern provinces. A mud wall of the usual character, with flanking towers and gateways, and in the usual state of dilapidation, surrounds the town; and the Governor lives in a fortified *ark* (or citadel) projecting from the city wall on the north-west.

A long stony ascent leads us to one of the few interesting spots on the road between Meshed and Teheran. This is the remarkable man-roost—for I can call it by no more appropriate name—of Lasgird. Here there has once been a citadel, built upon a lofty circular mound to a total height of perhaps eighty feet from the plain. The citadel has fallen into ruin, and the buildings in its interior are a litter of rubbish and bricks. But the villagers have established themselves in the deserted *enceinte*, and, on the very top of the outer walls, have built a double storey of mud houses, which are only accessible by flights of crazy steps from the interior, and the most remarkable feature of which is a ledge or balcony built out from each storey with rude logs of wood plastered over with mud. Upon this rickety platform, which has nothing in the shape of a railing to prevent anyone from falling off, and which is full of holes, the inhabitants appear to live their outdoor life. The place, from a little distance, looks as if a gigantic colony of birds had settled there and built out their nests from the walls, the outer shape of the entire mound resembling a huge cask. It is entered by a steep stairway from the ground, mounting to a small postern, the door of which is a single block of stone swung on a pivot. I entered, and scrambled up the rude flights of steps in the interior, and poked my nose into some of the nests—I cannot call them cottages—in the upper storeys. The women were unveiled and steeped in squalor. The general condition of the tenements was very much like what the domestic economy of a rookery might be expected to be. Here the same dialect is spoken as at Semnan. The citadel is surrounded by a deep broad fosse, converted into garden-plots, the revenues of which go to swell the endowment of the Imam Reza at Meshed.

After leaving Lasgird the route conducts through a hilly region which has been furrowed by winter torrents into deep gullies and ravines crossed by bridges. Upon descending again into the plain, the village of Deh Nemek (Salt Village) can be seen, at least twelve miles away, in the middle of an unutterably barren and repulsive desert. Few things are more treacherous in Persian travel than the false expectation induced by the sight of one's destination at the apparent distance of a few miles only, or more wearying than the disappointment that follows as the miles lengthen out into *farsakhs*, and the end never seems to come. What, in the distance, had appeared a settlement of two buildings only, turned out to be a village with a good many houses, hidden in a little semi-fertile depression of 'the level waste, the rounding grey'. In the succeeding strip of country—which is not less desolate—we pass, at the villages of Padeh and Aradan, further specimens of abandoned, though not, as at Lasgird, re-inhabited, citadels on the top of great artificial clay mounds. When originally raised, and crowned with battlements and towers, these *kalehs* must have been imposing structures. They are now in a sort of intermediate stage between the recognisable fort and the indurated bare mound which I have discussed and explained in a preceding paragraph. Beyond Aradan an abundant stream descends from the mountains and separates into many channels, of which I must have crossed twenty in the space of half a mile. Cultivation improves in the same ratio, and at Kishlak (lit. winter quarters), which is *khalisah*, or Crown property, is responsible for the grain and fodder with which the royal stables are supplied at Teheran. This is the district of Khar, so often mentioned in earlier history and travel, and renowned as one of the granaries of North Persia. Here the route turns towards the north-west, and, at a distance of eight miles from Kishlak, enters a range of hills by a path which is commonly identified with, and which therefore raises the question of, the famous Pylæ Caspiæ (or Caspian Gates).

I do not here propose, and I have not the space at my command, to discuss that question at full length. Its essential points may be said to have been argued, if not determined, by the labours of previous writers. The Pylæ Caspiæ were the pass through which Darius fled towards Bactria after the defeat of Arbela, and through which he was pursued by the army of Alexander.

It was soon after emerging upon the plateau beyond the pass that an isosceles cone of perfect shape and dazzling whiteness rose in view above the browns and greys of the nearer ranges, and disclosed to my enchanted vision the mighty Demavend. From that day, for over a month, I never, except in the mist of early morning, lost sight of the lordly spectacle, which always overhangs Teheran, and which attended me on my southward ride to a distance of 160 miles. What Fujiyama is to the Japanese, Demavend is to the Persian landscape. Both are ever-present, aerial, and superb. Both have left an enduring mark upon the legends of their country;[9] and if the peerless Fuji has played a far greater part in the art of Nippon than has Demavend in that of Iran, it is because the Japanese, while not inferior in ingenuity, are a vastly more imaginative people.

Traversing a level, uncultivated plain, we reached the village and posthouse of Aiwan-i-Kaif, fording a rapid but muddy stream which flows over a broad bed outside. The name indicates Portal, or Hall, of Delight, although other derivations have been suggested—viz. Aiwan-i-Kai (i.e. Hall of the Kaianians—tradition interpreting a ruin in the neighbourhood as a palace of Cambyses), and Aiwan-i-Key (or Royal Drinking-hall). Whichever it be, the place appeared to me to have no attractions for the modern votaries of Epicurus. A great many of the houses had no occupants, and seemed to have been abandoned; and ill-advised would the monarch be who sought refuge in so squalid a retreat. Between Aiwan-i-Kaif and Kabud Gumbaz (Blue Dome) the River Jajrud descends from the mountains, and was divided at this season of the year into at least twenty-five different channels, straggling over a pebbly bed—in all, quite a quarter of a mile in width. I forded all these, and at Kabud Gumbaz encountered the first returning symptoms of proximity to that civilisation to which I had now been a stranger for nine days, in the shape of a vast pile of letters (the first I had received since leaving England) and a good hack sent out for my use by a friend in Teheran. Right gladly did I speed over the Plain of Veramin, whose ruins, presenting in the distance the appearance of four solitary columns, rose from a mound far away in the hollow of the plain. From a distance of quite ten miles the flash, as of a beacon fire, on the horizon showed where the sun's rays splintered on the golden dome of Shah Abdul Azim. Formerly the caravan route lay past this sanctuary and round the base of the range which separates the plains of Veramin and Teheran. Still is that line followed by the pilgrims, upon whom, whether starting for or returning from Meshed, it is incumbent to call and do reverence at the prophet's shrine; but pack animals and the postal road now both cut off an angle by striking in a due northerly direction over the ridge itself. Mounting to the summit of the pass, the new road winds up and down through dusty folds, until, the northern crest being reached, far down upon the plain that expands below is seen spread out the belt of verdure, topped only by a few edifices, that marks the capital of Persia. Beyond, again, at a distance of about seven miles from the city, rises the abrupt ferruginous face of the Elburz range, like a prodigious rampart of rusty corrugated iron.

The first appearance of Teheran is agreeable after a long journey, but in no sense imposing. As I descended the slope and drew nearer, it was difficult to believe that that green band could shroud a great city with a population of nearly 200,000 souls. The only buildings that rose to any height above the level of the tree-tops appeared to be a large mosque, with four tile-covered minarets, that looked from a distance like painted organ-pipes, and, upon nearer approach, like sham Corinthian columns; one or two detached towers, and a domed structure whose roof consisted only of skeleton ribs of iron, like the framework in which a schoolroom globe is hung. The latter turned out subsequently to be the Takieh, or Theatre of the Passion Plays, within the precincts of the palace. Outside the walls on the southern side are a large number of brick-kilns, a monopoly of which industry is possessed by the Grand Vizier. Here, too, are the slaughter-houses, the lease of which brings in an income of 2,230*l*. per annum. Entering the fortifications by a gaudily decorated gate at some distance from the populated quarter, I rode quite two miles through the streets before reaching the British Legation, which is situated on the northern outskirts of the city.

---

[1]'What a long *farsakh* is that of Khorasan!' says a traveller who has toiled from sunrise nearly to sunset, and who can no longer cling to his jaded horse but by the prong in front of his saddle. 'By the beard of the Prophet,' said one of the party as we neared our halting-ground, 'the road is longer than the entrails of Omar, for my back and my knees have lost their feeling.' There is also a local proverb, worthy of being quoted (Burnes' *Travels into Bokhara*, vol. iii. p. 89), which says that the Khorasani *farsakh* is as endless as the chatter of women, and that he who measured them must have done so with a broken chain.

[2] And yet I find a French officer (*Notes de Voyage d'un Hussard*, par le Comte de Sabran, p. 225) who, having accomplished the journey in the same leisurely time in 1888, writes a book to say that General Maclean expressed himself as stupefied with his astonishing performance, and told him that an English officer, who had done the journey in ten days, had fallen seriously ill in consequence! Sir H. Rawlinson once rode it in six.

[3] The seeds or cones from which these pines sprang are said to have been brought by a pilgrim from the Himalayas nearly four hundred years ago.

[4] It is astonishing that so intelligent an observer as Colonel Val. Baker should have been seduced thereby to speak of this 'curious old minaret of burnt brick *of the time of Khosro*' (*Clouds in the East*, p. 166). He might just as reasonably have attributed it to Edward the Confessor or to Confucius. O'Donovan, too, regards this tall shaft as an unusual feature in Persian architecture, where the call to prayer is commonly given from a balcony; quite ignoring the fact that it was raised in Sunni, and not in Shiah, times. Khosrugird was the chief place of the district of Beihak, identical with the modern Sebzewar.

[5] The *kajaveh*, which is very small and rocks disagreeably, is a most uncomfortable and almost impossible vehicle for Europeans, whose nether limbs are not inured to the telescopic contractions common in the East. Adam Olearius, the Secretary of the Embassy from the Duke of Holstein in 1637, graphically described his woes as follows: 'The Physician and myself were set in *ketzaweha* upon the same camel, whereby we were put to great inconveniences— one proceeding from the violent motion caused by the going of that great Beast, which at every step gave us a furious jolt; and the other from the insupportable stink of the camels, the infectious smell of whom came full into our noses.'

[6] It was said that the Turkomans had at first priced the luckless photographer at 3*l* 10*s*. But as soon as they found out that he was a European, and of some value, their demands rose in a steady crescendo. Meanwhile the Khan of Khiva, hearing that the captive had instruments, and thinking he must be a military engineer, was very anxious to get hold of him to fortify his capital. Colonel Val. Baker gratuitously doubles the ultimate ransom. M. de Blocqueville wrote the history of his adventures in the *Tour du Monde*, April 1866.

[7] This is the *kabk*, or ordinary red-legged partridge. There are also in Persia the *kabk-i-darah* (variously explained as 'royal partridge', or 'partridge of the defiles'); the *durraj*, the black partridge of India, commonly called the francolin; the *tihu*, or sand partridge, which, as Fraser said, 'runs like the very devil'; the *jirufti*, or bush partridge; the *kabk-i-chil*, or grey partridge; and the *bakhri-kara*, or *bakir-ghirreh*, the sand-grouse.

[8] *Ahu* = an antelope or gazelle. Hence *ahubara* (little antelope) is the name for the elegant Persian bustard.

[9] 'According to the local legends, Demavend, or Divband, i.e. "Dwelling of the Divs or Genii", has been the scene of all the events veiled under the form of myths. Here, say the Persian Mohammedans, Noah's Ark was stranded; here dwelt Jemshid and Rustem, heroes of the national epics; here was kindled the bonfire of Feridun, vanquisher of the giant Zohak; here the monster himself is entombed, and the smoke of the mountain is the breath of his nostrils; here, also, is chained down the Persian Prometheus, Yasid ben Jigad, whose liver is eternally devoured by a gigantic bird. The caverns of the volcanoes are full of treasures guarded by snakes.'—Elisée Reclus, *Universal Geography* (English edition), vol. ix, p. 84.

Teheran

Over the utmost hill at length I sped,
A snowy steep—the moon was hanging low
Over the Asian mountain—and outspread
The plain, the city, and the camp below.

SHELLEY, *The Revolt of Islam*, Canto V.

TEHERAN,[1] the modern capital of Persia, has frequently been spoken of by travellers, with some suspicion of contempt, as a new city. In the sense in which they use the word—i.e. in the historical sense—it is by no means a new, but, on the contrary, an ancient city. In another sense—viz. structurally—it was made a new city by Agha Mohammed Shah, a century ago, and still more by his nephew and successor, Fath Ali Shah; and has become a yet newer city—so new that the visitors in the first half of this century would barely recognise it—during the last twenty years. Before I trace the incidents of this twofold renaissance, I propose to say something of the antique, forgotten, but withal not uninteresting Teheran of the past. Research can never be quite wasted upon the origin and youth of a great capital.

It has been conjectured that the name Teheran is identical with the Tazora that appears in the Theodosian tables as near to Rhages (Rhey). In the tables, however, it is not the Median Rhages, but a place of the same name near Yezd, that is spoken of; and the identity cannot therefore be sustained. Whatever its origin, Teheran must have been for long a small and insignificant place, for neither of those indefatigable geographers, El Istakhri and Masudi, whose travels illumine the tenth century, allude thereto, although they have much to say of the adjacent Rhey. The earliest irrefragable mention is in the pages of Abu Abdullah Yakut in A.D. 1179–80. His account, which is borne out by several native historians, represents the primitive Teheranis as troglodytes, living underground in a semi-savage state, at war with their neighbours, and in revolt against the sovereign. However this may be, the locality soon became quite famous for its rivulets and gardens, and a more normal and respectable city sprang into existence. Hamdallah, in the fourteenth century, described it as a town of some magnitude and importance, and as preferable, both for climate and water-supply, to Rhey. Don Ruy di Clavijo, the Spanish ambassador to Timur, halting here on July 6, 1404, delivered himself of a somewhat balancing opinion:—

> The city of Teheran was very large, but it had no walls; and it was a very delightful place, well supplied with everything; but it was an unhealthy place, according to the natives, and fevers were very prevalent.

Shah Tahmasp, the second of the Sefavi dynasty, seems to have been the first to favour it with a royal patronage; but Shah Abbas the Great, having fallen ill there from a surfeit of fruit, vowed he would never enter the place again. By him the province and city were placed under the government of a Khan.

At this time Teheran was visited by more than one European; and the descriptions of the Italian, Pietro della Valle (1618), and of the Englishman, Sir Thomas Herbert (1627), are so curious as to be worthy of reproduction. I quote from a translation of the former that appears in 'Pinkerton's Travels':—

> Teheran is a large city, more spacious than Cashan, but not well peopled, nor con-

Teheran was suddenly bidden to burst its bonds and enlarge its quarters. The old walls and towers were for the most part pulled down, the ditch was filled up, a large slice of surrounding plain was taken in, and, at the distance of a full mile from the old enclosure, a new rampart was constructed upon Vauban's system.

Panorama of Teheran.

taining many houses, the gardens being extremely large, and producing abundance of fruit of various descriptions, of such excellent quality that it is sought for by all the circumjacent country. The Khan ordinarily resides here. All the streets are watered by a number of considerable streamlets, which, serpentining in the gardens, contribute not a little to their fertility. The streets, moreover, are shaded by beautiful, lofty plane-trees, called in Persia *chinar*; some of them are so extremely thick that it would take from two to three men to clasp them round. Excepting these, Teheran possesses nothing, not even a single building, worthy of notice.

More humorously the English traveller, whose tender susceptibilities appear to have been inflamed by the Teheran ladies, writes:—

Seated is Tyroan in the midst of a large level or plain. The Houses are of white bricks hardened by the Sun. The City has about 3,000 Houses, of which the Duke's and the Buzzar are the fairest; yet neither to be admired. The Market is divided into two; some part thereof is open and other part arched. A Rivolet in two branches streams through the Town, serving withal both Grove and Gardens, who for such a favour, return a thankful tribute to the Gardiner. The inhabitants are pretty stately, the Women lovely, and both curious in novelties; but the jealousies of the men confine the temper of the weaker sex; yet by that little they adventured at, one might see *vetitis rebus gliscit voluntas.*

Under the later Sefavi kings Teheran sometimes became the temporary residence of the Court; a palace was built here by Shah Suleiman; and here Shah Sultan Husein received the Turkish Ambassador. Tavernier incidentally notices, but did not apparently see, the town; Chardin calls it a *petite ville du pays.* It was taken and pillaged in the Afghan invasion, but is mentioned by Hanway (as Tœhiran) in the catalogue of Von Mierop's stages to Meshed in 1744. It was here that Nadir, on his return from India, convoked a meeting of all the priests of religion, with a view to promulgating a new national faith. Here he blinded his son, Reza Kuli Khan, and here that helpless individual was afterwards murdered. Kerim Khan Zend added to and altered the existing Ark or citadel, but did not often occupy it. Ali Murad Khan stayed there while marching against Mazanderan. With the rise of the Kajar dynasty, at the close of the same century, the first epoch of the city's political ascendency began.

The seat and cradle of the Kajar family was at Astrabad; but this was too remote and too far situated to the East to suit the expanding ambitions of the eunuch candidate for the throne. For some time, while his fortunes were yet insecure, and while his sovereignty was practically limited to Mazanderan, Agha Mohammed fixed his residence at Sari; but, as he turned his eyes and aspirations southwards, and the dream of a Pan-Iranian kingdom became capable of realisation, a more accessible capital was required. Accordingly, he selected Teheran, and its elevation to metropolitan rank is commonly dated from 1788. It was not till seven years later that his rivals were all removed, and that he found himself firmly seated upon the throne; but what had been perhaps in the first place a choice of necessity remained the selection of prudence. Rebellion had been effectively stamped out of life in the south. The Afghans had ceased for a while to be hostile or formidable. On the other hand, at Teheran, the successful usurper was within easy reach of his own patrimony and tribesmen; and he was in a better position to watch the only enemy of whom he had real apprehension—Russia. The same considerations, aggravated rather than diminished by the events of the present century, have compelled his successors to endorse his judgment; and, whatever may be said against the site, there is very small likelihood, as long as Persia escapes dismemberment, of Teheran being dethroned from its position.

Agha Mohammed, though he elevated Teheran to the rank of his capital, either had not the taste or did not reign long enough to confer upon it any of the external distinction with which his predecessors on the throne had always striven to adorn their seats of government. Olivier, who was there in 1797, the year of the king's death, reported the city as being little more than two miles in circuit, and as containing a population of only 15,000, 3,000 of whom belonged to the court or army of the Shah. Fath Ali Shah, however, had more regal ideas. Under his rule the city increased in size, importance, and display. In 1807 General Gardanne, the French Envoy, found it containing a population of over 50,000 in winter, though all but deserted in summer, when the Court was away, and the inhabitants had retired to their *yeilaks*, or summer quarters, on the mountains. A very nearly identical estimate was made by the English travellers Morier and Ouseley, who were at Teheran within the next few years. The former said it contained 12,000 houses, the latter a population of from 40,000 to 60,000, figures which practically coincide. As such, or, at any rate, not very much larger, it remained during the first seventy years of this century, before it experienced the entire renovation at the hands of Nasr-ed-Din Shah, which I shall presently describe.

What, however, was the appearance of the city in this first epoch of modified rejuvenescence? The narratives and the illustrations of a long series of minute and accomplished writers enable us to ascertain with absolute certainty. Planted in the hollow of the plain, and surrounded only by the stark desert, with few or no suburbs, and with clearly-defined outline, stood the city—a fortified polygon, between four and five miles in exterior circuit, surrounded by an embattled mud wall twenty feet high, flanked with circular towers, and defended by a moat forty feet in width and from twenty to thirty feet in depth. The wall was mean and in parts ruinous, the ditch was clumsy and broken down—in both respects, that is to say, profoundly Persian. Six gates of somewhat gaudy construction, adorned with glazed tiles, admitted to the interior, where 'the streets were narrow and filthy, with uncovered drains in the middle', and where the only building of any pretentiousness was the citadel, or ark, in the northern part of the town. This contained the Diwan-khaneh-i-Shah, or Dar-i-khaneh (i.e. the Royal Palace). Beyond the city walls the country palace of Kasr-i-Kajar, built by Fath Ali Shah, upon an eminence to the north, was the sole object that relieved the brown monotony of the surrounding plain. Demavend soared loftily over all—that one noble feature in the landscape. Such was the Teheran that met the eyes of Malcolm and Harford Jones and Ouseley, and the long train of soldiers, diplomatists, and writers, who, escorted by brilliant cavalcades and equipped with costly presents, marched up hither from the Gulf in the first decade of the present century, to court the superb graces of Fath Ali Shah.

Up till the year 1870 this, with few alterations, remained the Teheran with which a wealth of writers has made us familiar. In this circumscribed city the British Legation, or Mission, as it was called, was situated in the southern part. The grounds originally belonged to one Mohammed Khan, the Zamburakchi Bashi, or Commander of the Camel Battery, which was one of the favourite military toys of Fath Ali. Upon this individual his sovereign bestowed that especial mark of confidence for which Persian monarchs have always been famous, by inviting him, *sponte suá*, to part with his property, which was forthwith transferred to the English Elchi. Sir Gore Ouseley built upon it a commodious house, whose Italian portico and pillars were a perpetual record of Europe in the heart of Asia. The Russians originally occupied a Legation in another part of the town, but, after the assassination of their Minister, Grebayadoff, in 1828, they moved for greater security into the precincts of the Ark. Until its disappearance, or rather expansion, in the years 1870–2, this transitional Teheran was in every respect an Oriental city—contracted, filthy, shabby, and what the French so well denominate as *morne*.

Nasr-ed-Din Shah, among other titles to distinction, may claim to have made his city a capital in something more than the name. After being twenty years upon the throne, it appears to have occurred to him that the 'Point of Adoration (*Kibleh*) of the Universe' was framed in a somewhat inadequate setting. Accordingly, Teheran was suddenly bidden to burst its bonds and enlarge its quarters. The old walls and towers were for the most part pulled down, the ditch was filled up, a large slice of surrounding plain was taken in, and, at the distance of a full mile from the old enclosure, a new rampart was constructed upon Vauban's system, copied from the fortifications of Paris before the German war. A good deal of the money sent out from England by the Persian Famine Relief Fund in 1871 was spent in the hire of labour for the excavation of the new ditch, which has a very steep outer profile, and for the erection of the lofty sloping rampart beyond. There is no masonry work upon these new fortifications; they are not defended by a single gun; they describe an octagonal figure about eleven miles in circuit; and, I imagine, from the point of view of the military engineer, are wholly useless for defence. Their main practical service consists in facilitating the collection of the town *octroi*. Nevertheless, Teheran can now boast that it is eleven miles round, that it has European fortifications, and twelve gates; while its interior features have developed in a corresponding ratio.

That the city has yet much to do before it realises the full aspirations of its royal Haussmann is evident as soon as we enter the gates. These consist of lofty archways, adorned with pinnacles and towers, and presenting from a distance a showy appearance,

Dowlet Gate in snow. After entering the gates, where a guard is stationed, we are again in the open country, for on most sides the city has not yet grown up to its new borders, which embrace a large extent of bare, unoccupied desert. This passed, a ride through squalid suburbs brings us to the more central and pretentious quarters of the town.

Dowlet Gate. Teheran. (in winter) Persia vol I 308

which has caused to some incoming travellers paroxysms of delight. A closer inspection shows that they are faced with modern glazed tiles, in glittering and frequently vulgar patterns, depicting the phenomenal combats of Rustam, or the less heroic features and uniform of the modern Persian soldier. After entering the gates, where a guard is stationed, we are again in the open country, for on most sides the city has not yet grown up to its new borders, which embrace a large extent of bare, unoccupied desert. This passed, a ride through squalid suburbs brings us to the more central and pretentious quarters of the town. At every turn we meet in juxtaposition, sometimes in audacious harmony, at others in comical contrast, the influence and features of the East and West. A sign-board with *Usine à Gaz* inscribed upon it will suddenly obtrude itself in a row of mud hovels, ostentatiously Asiatic. Tram-lines are observed running down some of the principal thoroughfares. Mingled with the turbans and *kolahs* of the Oriental crowd are the wide-awakes and helmets of Europeans. Through the jostling throng of cavaliers and pedestrians, camels, donkeys, and mules, comes rolling the two-horsed brougham of some Minister or grandee. Shops are seen with glass windows and European titles. Street lamp-posts built for gas, but accommodating dubious oil-lamps, reflect an air of questioning civilisation. Avenues, bordered with footpaths and planted with trees, recall faint memories of Europe. A metalled and watered roadway comes almost as a shock after weeks of mule track and rutty lane. Strange to say, it does not appear to be mistaken by the inhabitants for the town sewer. We ride along broad, straight streets that conduct into immense squares and are fringed by the porticoes of considerable mansions. In a word, we are in a city which was born and nurtured in the East, but is beginning to clothe itself at a West-End tailor's. European Teheran has certainly become, or is becoming; but yet, if the distinction can be made intelligible, it is being Europeanised upon Asiatic lines. No one could possibly mistake it for anything but an Eastern capital. Not even in the European quarter has it taken on the insufferable and debauched disguise with which we are familiar in the hideous streets of Galata and Pera. Its most distinctive features retain an individuality of their own, differing from what I have noticed anywhere else in Central Asia. Jeypore is sometimes extolled as the finest specimen of a native city, European in design, but Oriental in structure and form, that is to be seen in the East. The 'rose-red city' over which Sir Edwin Arnold has poured the copious cataract of a truly Telegraphese vocabulary struck me, when I was in India, as a pretentious plaster fraud. No such impression is produced by the Persian capital. Though often showy, it is something more than gilt gingerbread; and, while surrendering to an influence which the most stolid cannot resist, it has not bartered away an originality of which the most modern would not wish to deprive it.

In the northern part of the new town, but outside the line of the old walls, is situated the principal square or public place of Teheran. This is known as the Tup Meidan or Meidan-i-Tup-Khaneh—i.e. Gun Square or Artillery Square, from the fact that it is surrounded by the artillery barracks, and that it contains a park of rusty cannon, dating from an obsolete past. The length of this fine *meidan*, which is cobble-paved, is 270 yards, its width 120. On the longest, i.e. the northern and southern, sides, it is surrounded by low one-storeyed buildings, where the guns are housed and the men quartered; on the western side is the Arsenal, in front of which some twenty-five venerable smooth-bores, 24-pounders, and wholly useless, rest upon their ancient carriages. The eastern face is entirely occupied by a fine building with an ornamental plaster façade, which is now tenanted by the Imperial Bank of Persia. In the middle of the square is a great tank, fenced round by an iron railing, with some cast-iron statuettes, and with four big guns planted at the corners and covered with tarpaulins.

Its most distinctive features, however, are the gateways by which it is entered or left, and which are regarded by the Persians as triumphs of modern architectural skill. They are certainly, as the accompanying illustration will show, very imposing and original structures, and, with their light arcades and fantastic fronts, present a handsome appearance from a distance, though a closer scrutiny of the coarse tile-work with which they are faced is apt to destroy the illusion. Of these gates the two principal and most striking are those which lead from the two southern angles of the square, opening on to streets which skirt the outer wall of the Ark, or citadel, on either side, the entire intervening space being occupied by its courts and buildings. From the south-east corner the Nasirieh Gate leads down to the eastern entrance to the palace and to the bazaars. From the south-west corner the Dowlet Gate conducts to the Khiaban-i-Almasieh (or Avenue of Diamonds), from which the western or public entrance to the Ark and palace is gained. Upon this gate, when the Shah is in Teheran, floats the royal standard.

Two other *meidans* are worthy of notice. One is the Meidan-i-Mashk, a vast open space, over a quarter of a mile in length, which is used as a Champ de Mars, or parade-ground, for the garrison, and where I witnessed a military display which I shall afterwards describe. This *meidan* is a little to the north-west of the Tup Meidan, and is reached by a gateway opening out of the so-called Street of Ambassadors, which leads from the north-west angle of the Gun Square. The remaining square, called the Meidan-i-Shah, is outside the gardens of the Ministry of War, and the more southerly portion of the palace enclosure. It contains a large tank in the centre, and a colossal brass gun, known as the Tup-i-Murvarid, or Cannon of Pearls, which has always been an especially sacred *bast*, or sanctuary, for the fugitive criminal, a veritable 'horns of the altar', in Teheran. Successive chroniclers of the capital have given different and inconsistent accounts of this monster cannon, some alleging that it was brought by Nadir Shah from Delhi, where it was originally decorated with a string of pearls near the muzzle, others that it was cast by him in Persia. Sir R. K. Porter says that it was the same gun that Chardin saw in the *meidan* at Isfahan; but, as I cannot find that Chardin saw or described any particularly big gun there, I am loth to accept this explanation. Elsewhere I have read that the gun was cast by Kerim Khan Zend at Shiraz, and that, having been kept for some time under cover in an *imamzadeh* there, it acquired a sacred character, which it has retained since its removal to the Kajar capital. Jehangir Khan, the late Minister of Fine Arts, informed me, however, that, according to Persian historians, this cannon is one of the Portuguese ordnance captured by the allied Persians and British at Ormuz in 1622. Whatever be the truth, its semi-sacred character is unimpeachable. An artillery guard is stationed hard by, and barren women make a pilgrimage hither, and pass beneath the gun, in order to promote the object of their desire.

The most distinctive feature, however, of this smaller *meidan* is the great arched gateway leading from it, and used as the Nakkara-Khaneh (or Drum Tower), whence, every evening, at sundown, is discoursed, from prodigious horns, kettle-drums, cornets, and fifes, the appalling music which is an inalienable appurtenance of royalty in Persia, and is always sounded at sunset from some elevated gallery or tower in any city blessed with a royal or princely governor. Over two hundred years ago it used to disturb the slumbers of Tavernier and Chardin at Isfahan, where it was sounded at sunset and at midnight; the truth being, as the former writer sagaciously observed, that 'the musick would never charm a curious ear.' It is commonly supposed that this practice is a relic of the old fire or sun worship, that luminary being saluted both at its rising and setting by respectful strains. Whether this be so or not I cannot say. What is

Nakkara-Khaneh (or Drum Tower), whence, every evening, at sundown, is discoursed, from prodigious horn, kettle-drums, cornets, and fifes, the appalling music which is an inalienable appurtenance of royalty in Persia, and is always sounded at sunset from some elevated gallery or tower in any city blessed with a royal or princely governor.

certain is that it has for long been an Oriental attribute of royalty; and, in a letter from the French traveller, Bernier, written in 1663 from the Court of the Great Mogul at Delhi, where there neither was, nor, so far as we know, ever had been, fire-worship, I have come across the following passage, describing the practice as it prevailed there and then, in terms which exactly fit the sonorous and portentous discord which is evoked every evening by the band of brazen-lunged youths to whom I used to listen with a sort of horrified fascination at Teheran:—

Over the great gate there is a large raised place which is called Nagar Kanay, because that is the place where the Trumpets are, or rather the Hoboys and Timbals that play together in consort at certain hours of the day and night. But this is a very odd consort in the ears of an European that is a new comer, not yet accustomed to it; for sometimes there are ten or twelve of these Hoboys, and as many Timbals that sound all at once together; and there is a Hoboy which is called Karna, a fathom and a half long, and of half a foot aperture below; as there are Timbals of brass or iron that have no less than a fathom in diameter, whence it is easie to judge what a noise they must needs make.

Bernier goes on to say that at first he found this royal music quite insufferable; but that afterwards it was very pleasing in the night time, when it seemed 'to carry with it something that is grave, majestical, and very melodious'. Verily, *de gustibus non est disputandum*. The same practice is still kept up by some of the native princes in India.

From the Tup Meidan, as I have indicated, two streets run in a northerly direction towards the outer walls. These streets or avenues—for they are planted with poplars—are regarded as the crowning glory of modern, being, in fact, the nucleus of European, Teheran. The more westerly of the two, known to Persians as Khiaban-i-Dowlet, has been sometimes described as the Boulevard des Ambassadeurs, from the fact that the representatives of several foreign Powers have acquired residences upon it. Of these, by far the most spacious and imposing is the Legation which shelters the representative of Her Britannic Majesty. At the distance of nearly half a mile from the great square, a fine gateway, upon which Her Majesty's initials are carved in stone, conducts on the left hand into a large wooded enclosure, where nothing at first is visible but a dense growth of trees, interspersed with winding pathways and runnels of water. This delightful grove, which, as the result of only twenty years' growth, shows of what the Persian soil under irrigation is capable, conceals the main building of the Legation, as well as four other substantial detached houses accommodating the various secretaries. The principal structure is a low building occupying three sides of a court, and terminating at one end in a campanile, or clock-tower, of Byzantine design, in which a large clock tells the time after the English fashion and according to the hours of the English day. On one side is the Chancellery; in the centre are the reception-rooms and Minister's quarters; on the other side are the spare rooms. The building opens by a verandah at the back on to a lovely garden, where swans float on brimming tanks of water and peacocks flash amid the flower-beds. The design was the work of Major Pierson, R.E., of the Indo-European Telegraph Department, who may be credited with a very successful result. The coolness and seclusion of the entire enclosure is one of the most agreeable and uncommon features in Teheran. The Turkish Embassy and the Legations of several others of the Great Powers are in the same street, or near at hand. Russia, however, is elsewhere accommodated; the residence of her Minister being, as I have pointed out, in the older portion of the town, near the bazaars. In the same quarter as the British Legation are situated the establishment and chapel of the American missionaries. The Armenian church, where British subjects used to be interred, and which contains the tomb of a son of Sir Walter Scott, was near the former British Mission in the old city.

To a stranger, possibly also to a native, the most interesting portion of Teheran is the great quadrilateral, containing the Ark or Citadel, and occupying a space of probably nearly a quarter of a mile square on the southern side of the Tup Meidan. Since the demolition of the old town there is nothing in the appearance of this enclosure to identify it with a citadel in the ordinary acceptation of the term; for, although it is surrounded by mud walls, it is in no sense fortified, and is now merely a vast collection of courts, gardens, and buildings, the greater part of which appertain to the Royal Palace.

In a country that is always bewailing its lack of money, and which cries aloud for the regeneration that might so easily spring from the construction or repair of roads, bridges, caravanserais, and other elementary public works, it can excite but one feeling to see such impotent wealth piled up in the Royal Museum, secreting beneath a glass case that which should serve to populate entire districts and to enrich great communities. How much worse is it when we know that the treasures here displayed do not stand alone, but are supplemented by hoards of specie and bullion stored in the vaults below, which the lowest estimate values at three millions sterling and the highest I will not say at what figure. Patriotism need not be so very difficult an attribute in royalty, when it is able to stop short of the treasure-house and the money-bags.

Below the Museum are a number of vaults, known as the Chinee-Khaneh, or Porcelain Room, where vast quantities of Sèvres, Dresden, old Worcester, and other porcelain are stored, the gifts of European sovereigns to the present and preceding kings. There is also an Aslaheh-Khaneh, or Armoury, containing curious arms, and the Shah's rifles and fowling-pieces; and a gallery wherein is hung a large collection of the paintings of the late esteemed artist, Abul Hasan Khan Ghaffari, styled the

Sani-el-Mulk. These last-named apartments I did not see.

In a room sometimes called the Council Chamber I was admitted to a private audience by the Shah. It was empty on all the occasions when I saw it, save for an object standing in the corner by the window. This was the Takht-i-Taous or celebrated so-called Peacock Throne, said to have been brought by Nadir Shah from India in 1739–40, and identified by a long consensus of writers (I know of no divergent opinion) with the famous Peacock Throne that stood in the Diwan-i-Khas at Delhi (where its site is still shown) and that was the main ornament of the glittering court of the Great Mogul. From a study of all the extant authorities bearing upon the question, I had come to the conclusion that this claim could not be substantiated, and that the throne at Teheran, exquisite work of art though it be, was a fraudulent pretender to the honour of having supported the majesty of the Great Mogul. Let me deploy the chain of reasoning by which I had arrived at this conclusion. The standard reference to the original Peacock Throne at Delhi is contained in the well-known description of the French jeweller Tavernier, who visited that capital in the year 1665 in the splendid reign of Aurungzebe. He wrote as follows:—

The largest throne, which is set up in the hall of the first court, is in form like one of our field beds, six feet long and four broad. The cushion at the base is round like a bolster; the cushions on the sides are flat. The under part of the canopy is all embroidered with pearls and diamonds, with a fringe of pearls round about. Upon the top of the canopy, which is made like an arch with four panes, stands a peacock with his tail spread, consisting all of saphirs and other proper coloured stones. The body is of beaten gold enchas'd with several jewels, and a great ruby upon his breast, at which hangs a pearl that weighs fifty carats. On each side of the peacock stand two nosegays as high as the bird, consisting of several sorts of flowers, all of beaten gold enamelled. When the king seats himself upon the throne there is a transparent jewel with a diamond appendant of eighty or ninety carats, encompass'd with rubies and emeralds, so hung that it is always in his eye. The twelve pillars also that uphold the canopy are set with rows of fair pearl, round, and of an excellent water, that weigh from six to ten carats apiece. This is the famous throne which Tamerlane began and Cha Jehan finish'd, which is really reported to have cost 160 million and 500,000 livres of our money.[2]

Now contrast this with the Persian claimant to the title. I have purposely caused to be reproduced an engraving of the Takht-i-Taous at Teheran (see page 96), in order to accompany and elucidate my argument. It is certainly a platform, or, as Tavernier calls it, a Field-bed Throne; as were the majority of those employed by the sovereigns of the East. It is further a sumptuous and a beautiful work of art. The entire fabric is overlaid with a plating of gold, which is exquisitely chiselled and enamelled, and is absolutely encrusted with precious stones, among which rubies and emeralds are the most prominent. Seven bejewelled legs sustain the platform, access to which is gained by two steps, decorated with salamanders. An elegant balustrade containing inscriptions in panels runs round, and the lofty back, which is one mass of gems, rises to a point in the centre whereupon is fixed a circular star of diamonds, with scintillating rays, made to revolve by a piece of mechanism at the back. On either side of the star are two bejewelled birds, perched on the edges of the back-frame, and facing each other. Now there is in the fabric thus delineated and reproduced above very little except general shape that tallies with Tavernier's detailed description. There is no trace or sign of a canopy, or of the means by which a vanished canopy could have been added to the existing throne. Above all there is no peacock.[3]

The Persian claimant to the title of Peacock Throne. I have caused to be reproduced this engraving of the Takh-i-Taous at Teheran.

At this stage, however, I felt compelled to remember that Tavernier, while particularly describing the Peacock Throne, had also left on record that 'The Great Mogul has seven thrones, some set all over with diamonds, others with rubies, emeralds, and pearls'; and that Hanway had reported Nadir as carrying off nine other thrones in addition; and it might be therefore that the Teheran throne, though not *the* Peacock Throne, was one of the rifled thrones of the Emperors of Hindustan. Such a theory seemed to find a momentary corroboration in the description given by another Frenchman, Bernier, in the same century, of a throne (clearly not *the* Peacock Throne of Tavernier) at Delhi. The throne that he saw was supported by six high pillars or feet of massive gold, set with rubies, emeralds, and diamonds. Its value was estimated at forty millions of rupees (a rupee at that time was equivalent to half a crown) or to sixty millions of French livres. And yet, to maintain the confusion, this too was a Peacock Throne, for he added:—

The art and workmanship of this throne is not answerable to the matter; that which I find upon it best devised are two peacocks covered with precious stones and pearls, which are the work of a Frenchman called ——— that was an admirable workman.

Nevertheless, this could not be the Teheran throne; for the latter has seven legs; nor was an acute observer like Bernier likely to have committed the error that Morier did, and mistaken its winged supporters for peacocks.

In this dilemma, but with the growing conviction that the modern Takht-i-Taous had a very shadowy connection, if any at all, with the plundered treasures of Delhi, I turned to contemporaneous records. I found in Malcolm that Nadir Shah was so fond of the real Peacock Throne of the Great Mogul that he had an exact duplicate of it made in other jewels. This left two Peacock Thrones to be demolished between his death and the end of the last century, a catastrophe which in the anarchy and violence of those times would have been in itself no unlikely occurrence; but it left the Takht-i-Taous unexplained, as under no circumstances could the latter be described as a duplicate of Tavernier's original. Now, however, I came across a passage in Fraser's 'Khorasan' in which he mentions that an old Kurd told him in 1822, that 'when Nadir Shah was murdered and his camp plundered, the Peacock Throne and the Tent of Pearls fell into our hands, and were torn in pieces and divided on the spot.' Any Kurd might certainly have been trusted to handle such an object as the Peacock Throne in the unceremonious manner here described, and, assuming the veracity of this particular Kurd, I witnessed with some delight the disappearance of the real Peacock Throne, or one of the two, from the scene.

A phrase in Morier's account had now set me thinking that the Takht-i-Taous at Teheran must be a modern structure after all. In the same passage which I have quoted in a footnote, he adds: 'It (i.e. the throne) is said to have cost 100,000 *tomans*' (equivalent at the beginning of the century to about 100,000l.);[4] herein clearly implying that an account or a tradition of its cost prevailed at Teheran, which was far more likely to be the case with a new than with an old fabric, and which was extremely unlikely to have been the case with an object carried off in plunder from a remote country seventy years before. At this stage, accordingly, I referred my doubts for solution to Teheran itself, and after an interval of some weeks was interested and (I may confess) rejoiced to hear, on the authority of the Grand Vizier and the former Minister for Foreign Affairs,[5] that, as I suspected, the Takht-i-Taous is not an Indian throne at all. It was constructed by Mohammed Husein Khan, Sadr (or High Priest) of Isfahan, for Fath Ali Shah when the latter married an Isfahani young lady, whose popular sobriquet, for some unexplained reason, was Taous Khanum or the Peacock Lady. The King is further said to have been so much delighted with the throne, that it was made a remarkably prominent feature in the ceremonies that commonly ensue upon marriage. Here, therefore, at one fell swoop, toppled down the whole of the brilliant hypothesis, which has sustained scores of writers, and provided material for pages of glowing rhetoric. From the same authorities I learned that the original Peacock Throne of Nadir Shah (i.e. the survivor of the two facsimiles) was discovered in a broken-down and piece-meal condition by Agha Mohammed Shah, who extracted it along with many other of the conqueror's jewels by brutal torture from his blind grandson Shah Rukh at Meshed, and then had the recovered portions of it made up into the throne of modern shape and style, which now stands at the end of the new museum in the palace at Teheran, and to which I have alluded in my description of that apartment. In this chair, therefore, are to be found the sole surviving remnants of the Great Mogul's Peacock Throne, and the wedding present of Fath Ali Shah must

(Opposite, above.) Fath Ali Shah never built or occupied a palace anywhere without immortalising himself, and his regiment of sons, and his crown and jewels and throne, and, above all, his wasp-like waist and ambrosial beard, in canvas, upon the walls. Here the monarch is surrounded by his sons and chief ministers of State, seated upon the Takht-i-Taous, and receiving in solemn audience the plenipotentiaries of European Powers. An historical anachronism appears to have been perpetrated here, with a view of representing, not so much a single incident, as the events of an entire period. Accordingly, Sir John Malcolm, Sir Harford Jones, Sir Gore Ouseley, and the French General Gardanne, all figure in the picture, being recognisable both by their uniforms and their features.

descend from the position which it has usurped in the narrative of every writer in this century, without exception, who has alluded to it.

Beyond the room in the palace containing this beautiful impostor, which, with a respectful iconoclasm, permissible, I hope, to the student of history, I have endeavoured to depose from its false pinnacle, extend a series of chambers of some size, but no merit, exhibiting an extravagant and often farcical contrast of the Oriental and European. Illustrations, snipped from the English illustrated newspapers appear side by side upon the walls with photographs of the Shah and his little boy favourite, the Aziz-es-Sultan, and with inferior copies of Italian oil-paintings. Here is a picture of the Paris Exhibition and the Eiffel Tower; there a deplorable oleograph of an Alpine village, both hung in a room adorned with Persian plaster-work and spread with Persian carpets. I noticed here, what I observed in the other palaces that I visited, that the Oriental intellect seems to derive a peculiar gratification from the display of duplicates. Thus, the King's son, the Zil-es-Sultan, has, in his town residence, a long row of facsimile portraits of himself hanging upon a single wall. Similarly, in the royal abode, I noticed in one place two large copies of a semi-nude Venus or Magdalen of the later Italian school, absolutely identical, hanging on either side of a doorway; and the same phenomenon was constantly repeated. The impression left upon me by an inspection of many modern Persian residences of size and magnificence, was this: that whereas the Persian taste, if restricted to its native art or to the employment of native styles, seldom errs, the moment it is turned adrift into a new world, all sense of perspective, proportion, or beauty, all aesthetic perception, in fact, appears to vanish; and in proportion as its choice will have been correct and refined amid native materials, so does it become vulgar and degraded abroad. I am sometimes not sure that our own countrymen can escape the same impeachment, particularly when I observe rich Englishmen triumphantly carrying away from Japan the gaudy embroideries that are made *for them alone*, and which no civilised Japanese gentleman would admit into his house.

The rooms of which I have been speaking look out on to a vast garden court, which is entirely surrounded by the various buildings of the palace, and which I consider to be by far the prettiest and most effective portion of the entire enclosure. This great garden is divided by paved avenues and gravel paths into flower beds, tanks, and extensive lakes. Magnificent pines and cypresses, as well as the more familiar plane and poplar, line its alleys and create a pleasant shade. It is called the Gulistan or Rose Garden. Little iron bridges cross the numerous channels, often lined with blue tiles, down which the water runs in perpetual motion; the pools are alive with fish and decked with swans and waterfowl; elegant kiosques are seen amid the trees. It was in this lovely garden, and under an entrancing sun and sky, that I witnessed a royal Salaam, or Levée of the Shah, to which I may devote a few words in passing. It was the replica, on a smaller scale, of the great ceremonial that takes place at No Ruz.

The theory of the Court Levée in Persia is not that the subjects attend upon, or are introduced to, the sovereign, but that the sovereign displays himself to his awestruck and admiring subjects. Accordingly, the two central and essential attributes of the scene are the monarch being gazed at on the one side, and the audience gazing on the other. Very little else transpires, and not more than half-a-dozen persons play any other part than that of statues during the ceremony. I will describe, however, exactly what takes place. Upon entering the palace I was conducted to a chamber where the regulation coffee and *kalians* were served. Soldiers and officials were pouring pell-mell into the palace on every side. Bands were aimlessly tuning up or playing in different corners. Officers in every variety of uniform were marshalling troops in every variety

(Left.) The best known son of the Shah, Sultan Masud Mirza (Prince Felicitous), more commonly known by the title of the Zil-es-Sultan, or Shadow of the King—a misnomer in this case, seeing that he is very nearly double his father's size. Three years older than the Crown Prince, having been born in 1850, he is yet disqualified from the succession to the throne by reason of his plebeian origin on the maternal side. Though not destined to rule as sovereign, this prince has, from youth upwards, been allowed to ape the part, and to wield the functions of sovereignty with a freedom that could not fail to encourage extravagant pretensions, and that ultimately led to his downfall.

Palace of the Zil-es-Sultan at Teheran.

Persia vol I 418

The palace of the Prince or Zil is one of the finest in Teheran, having an imposing façade, relieved with stucco work, and broad large windows.

of disorder. *Mirzas* (i.e. government clerks) and accountants were hurrying to the scene of action. The royal executioner, clothed in red, was stalking about, while some attendants carried the *fellek*, a red pole about eight feet in length with a double loop or noose of cord attached to the middle, into which are fixed the upturned soles of the culprit condemned to the bastinado. He was the Persian counterpart of the Roman lictor with his axe and rods. The members of the Royal or Kajar tribe were all congregated together, and wore the old court costume, which was obligatory on all alike at the beginning of the century, and which consists of a lofty and voluminous Kashmir (more probably Kerman) turban, big, flowing Kashmir cloaks, and the well-known red leggings, or *chakshurs*, which the English ministers and plenipotentiaries were obliged to pull on over their breeches when attending the audiences of Fath Ali Shah, but of wearing which they were ultimately relieved by treaty. Here I was met by the Lord Chamberlain, or master of the ceremonies, known as the Zahir-ed-Dowleh (Supporter of the Government), a young man of magnificent stature and singularly handsome countenance, who belongs to the Kajar House, and is married to a favourite daughter of the Shah. This gorgeous individual was clothed in a resplendent white frock coat and trousers beneath his Kashmir robe of state; a jewelled sword hung at his side; a portrait of the Shah set in diamonds depended from his neck; and he carried a silver

The Shah appeared in the room adjoining that in which I was placed and took his seat upon a gilded chair in the window.

wand or staff of office. I was conducted to a room next to that in which the Shah was about to appear, the uplifted sashes of both apartments opening on to the garden, where, on the broad, paved pathway running in front and down the central alleys between the tanks and flower beds, were disposed in order the various participators in the ceremonial. A little to the right of the middle spot stood the Naib-es-Sultaneh, the third son of the Shah and Commander-in-Chief of the army, standing at the head of a long line of field-marshals and generals. His bosom blazed with decorations, and was crowned by a light-blue ribbon that might have been mistaken for that of St. Patrick. Next to him, also in field-marshal's uniform and with a tiny sword, stood the

(Opposite, above.) The great twin-towered pavilion called the Shems-el-Imaret, or Sun of the Palace, which is such a conspicuous object from the exterior of the palace on the side of the bazaars. This remarkable structure, which is, in my opinion, a triumph of fanciful architecture, is built in the form of two towers, sloping inwards towards the top, and terminating in two elegant kiosques. A slender clock-tower, with a European clock, rises from the roof between the two. This beautiful pavilion was begun by the Shah twenty-five years ago, and is certainly a very creditable specimen of the fanciful ingenuity that still lingers in modern Persian art.

(Opposite, below.) Eshretabad, a very pretty palace, where the main pavilion is occupied by the Shah, and seventeen smaller pavilions, situated round a lake, by the ladies who accompany him (a creditable reduction from the standards of his great grandfather).

diminutive favourite of the Shah, whose features had become so familiar in Europe during the royal journey of the preceding summer. Next in order, and accentuating the ludicrous contrast, came a tottering veteran, the oldest field-marshal in the Persian army; then a row of full-blown generals; finally, the officers of the so-called Cossack regiments, including two Russians. In front and in the middle stood alone the former Ilkhani of the Kajar tribe, a white-bearded elder, once out of favour with his sovereign but long since reconciled.[6] Behind stood the solid and forbidding figure of the Kawam-ed-Dowleh, Minister of Foreign Affairs; and beyond again the various functionaries, each in his due rank and position. The whole of the assemblage was now arranged, every man stood shoulder to shoulder with eyes fixed in front, and absolute silence prevailed.

Suddenly a cry was raised. The Shah appeared in the room adjoining that in which I was placed and took his seat upon a gilded chair in the window. His principal ministers accompanied him and stood in the background. As the King appeared every head was bowed low, the hands outspread and resting upon the knees. Bands struck up the royal air in different parts of the garden, and guns banged away at a slight distance. The Ilkhani of the Kajars now, acting as spokesman of the entire assembly, exchanged formal compliments with the King, who spoke in short, brusque sentences in reply. Then a *mullah*, standing behind, recited in a loud voice the *Khutbah*, or prayer for the sovereign. This done the Poet Laureate advanced, and, pulling out a sheet of paper, read a complimentary ode. Meanwhile the bands went on playing different tunes in different parts, and the guns boomed noisily outside. When the ode was at an end, the Shah rose from his chair, and slowly stalked from the chamber; the troops, with very little attempt at precision, slouched past the windows; and a waving mass of helmets, plumes, and turbans was seen disappearing through the garden entrance. Such is a Levée as held by H.I.M. Nasr-ed-Din Shah at Teheran.

For a great capital Teheran is singularly destitute of those immense religious edifices, whether mosques or *madressehs*, which tower, too often in a state of utter ruin, above the house-tops of most Oriental towns. The reason is that, only having become a capital, so to speak, in later life, the city has found no patron to endow it with the great structures that have immortalised the seats of government of earlier kings.

The bazaars of Teheran occupy a very considerable space in the old city; although, in common with the rest of the capital, they have experienced a much-needed renovation in the reign of the present king. The main entrance is from the street opposite the Shems-el-Imaret, and conducts, through an open courtyard containing a pool of water, and known as the Meidan-i-Sebz, into the dim, vaulted arcades which are so familiar to the wanderer in Eastern lands. The Teheran bazaars are vaulted throughout with a succession of low brick domes, and open frequently upon small courts or squares. They contain a number of spacious and well-built caravanserais; and there are few objects of Eastern use or consumption—from a saddlehorse to a tea-tray,—which cannot be there procured. European merchandise is exhibited on every other stall, and one of the first and most obvious discoveries is that Persia clothes itself from Europe. Another of the most widely-spread but unintelligible of modern Persian tastes is abundantly illustrated, and can be inexpensively gratified, in the Teheran bazaars. This is the fondness, which seems to permeate all classes, from the Shah downwards, for lustres, candelabra, candle and lamp shades, and glass vases or ornaments of every conceivable description. I never entered a Persian prince's or nobleman's house without encountering a shop's window full of these articles, as a rule proudly stacked, as though they were rare treasures, upon a table; and I imagine that a

The mighty mountain-sentinel *Demavend. The shapely white cone, cutting so keenly and so high into the air, becomes so familiar and cherished a figure in the daily landscape, that on leaving Teheran and losing sight thereof the traveller is conscious of a very perceptible void.*

Persian would have no hesitation in pronouncing the Crystal Palace to be the *maximum opus* of the world's architecture.

One result of the royal partiality for suburban residences has been the construction or the improvement of the roads that lead thereto from the city. A very passable road, planted for the most part with trees, leads to Gulahek on the north; and another such road, affording the solitary carriage-drive of Teheran, conducts between stiff rows of poplars in a straight line north-east, towards yet another villa, known, from the rocky eminence on which it is placed, as Doshan-Tepe (or the Rabbit Hill). The rock is an ugly excrescence from the plain at the distance of three miles from the city; and the palace is from the outside a yet uglier excrescence upon the rock. It is, however, a favourite hunting-lodge of the Shah's when he goes shooting in the neighbouring mountains, which are kept as a royal preserve. At the foot of the rock is a large and shady garden, where, in a long row of cages or dens, are kept the wild beasts of the Shah's menagerie. The animals themselves struck me as fine specimens, but they were badly housed, and their number was small. The popularity of the place, however, as a sort of Iranian Jardin des Plantes, or Zoo, is evidenced by the rent of 500 *krans* per annum extracted by the crown from the lessee of a small coffee-house at the entrance of the garden. In the neighbourhood of Doshan-Tepe are two other royal shooting-boxes, Kasr Firuz to the south and Surkheh Hissar to the north. Further to the east is a more considerable hunting-lodge on the banks of the Jajrud.

The Shah, as I have indicated, is not the sole patron of the slopes of Shimran. His

Cadets of Royal College, Teheran.

Persia vol I 605.

sons and the nobility in general have followed the royal example, and there are many tasteful and beautiful residences perched on the hill-sides or hidden in the valleys. Of these, by no means the least agreeable is the summer residence of the British Legation in the village of Gulahek, about six miles from the northern gate of the capital, and said to be 700 feet higher in elevation. The seignorial rights of this village—the lordship of the manor, in fact—were presented by Mohammed Shah to Sir John Campbell in 1835; the grounds and garden, in which stand the Minister's residence, were the gift of the reigning sovereign. Under the terms of these concessions the villagers of Gulahek, which consists of about 100 houses, enjoy quite peculiar privileges, being exempt from the obligations both of conscription and of the billeting of troops. Their assessment is payable to the British Government, and is levied by the Legation. Petty jurisdiction is exercised among them by a village *kedkhoda* (or headman), who is nominated by the British Minister, and is responsible to the member of the Legation invested with Consular functions. As at Teheran, there is more than one edifice in the enclosure belonging to the Mission; but the main building alone is of any size. This is supplemented by a great Indian durbar-tent, which is pitched outside and serves as a dining and drawing room during the summer months. The surrounding garden is a dense thicket of trees, and, though not comparable with what we style a garden here, is yet far better adapted to the torrid climate, from which its shade in the summer affords an invaluable protection. The recent purchase of a neighbouring garden, with its water-supply (every gallon of the precious fluid having a well-

The Shah set up the Royal College with a European curriculum to open to the youth of Persia the benefits of a European education.

The tower of Rhey, like the tower of Yezids is a great fabric, built of brick, entirely hollow inside, and roofless, from sixty to seventy feet in height and one hundred and twenty feet in exterior circumference. It has a Kufic cincture, which has not been restored.

ascertained and costly market value), has added to the attractions of a residence without which it would be impossible for the staff of a European Legation to remain at the capital during the hot months. Russia is similarly favoured in the possession of the village of Zargandeh, a little to the north-west of Gulahek, for which they claim analogous privileges. The French lease a residence at Tejrish, a mile higher up the mountain, where, in the court of an *imamzadeh*, is what claims to be the largest *chenar* in Persia. The Turks own grounds in the same neighbourhood. The Germans were till recently tenants of the English in Gulahek, and now live at Dizashub. The Austrians are leaseholders at Rustamabad.

Before I quit the northern outskirts of Teheran I must pay the tribute of one more parting paragraph to the mighty mountain-sentinel Demavend. The shapely white cone, cutting so keenly and so high into the air, becomes so familiar and cherished a figure in the daily landscape, that on leaving Teheran and losing sight thereof (which, if he be journeying in a southerly direction, he does not do for 160 miles), the traveller is conscious of a very perceptible void. Demavend is a volcano, not, as some have said, wholly extinct, but rather in a state of suspended animation. There is no record of eruption during the historic period, but columns of smoke are sometimes seen to ascend from the fissures, particularly from the Dud-i-Kuh (or Smoky Peak) on the southern side. It is very strange that no mention is made of the mountain by Chardin, whose keen vision overlooked but little; or by Pietro della Valle, who passed almost at its base. Hanway, in 1744, speaks of it as 'the great mountain Demoan on which the Persians say that the Ark rested'. The first to accomplish the ascent—the Persians having always believed and declared, like the Armenians in the case of Ararat, that it was not to be climbed by mortal man—was Mr., afterwards Sir, W.T. Thomson, in 1836. The French naturalist, Aucher Eloy, met Thomson coming down from the top, and himself ascended a few days later. Since that date Demavend has been frequently ascended by members of the various Legations in Teheran, the climb being neither difficult nor dangerous, but intensely fatiguing.

---

[1] The popular etymology which explains Teheran or Tihran as 'the pure' is false. It is an old Persian word which was formerly written with the two-dotted t, and sometimes also Tirun and Tiran.

[2] *Travels in India* (edit. 1678), book ii. cap. viii. p. 122. Hanway (vol. ii. cap. x) says that the Peacock Throne and nine other thrones, as well as several jewelled weapons and utensils, were valued at nine crores of rupees, or 11,250,000*l*. The *Nadir-Nameh* (History of Nadir) valued the Peacock Throne at 2,000,000*l*.; Scott at 1,000,000*l*.

[3] Morier, who saw Fath Ali Shah seated in audience upon this throne in 1809, described it with no great accuracy. He said, 'On each side of the back are two square pillars, on which are perched birds—probably intended for peacocks—studded with precious stones of every description, and holding each a ruby in their beaks' (*First Journey*, p. 191). Now, no one who really inspected them could possibly mistake the birds for peacocks; nor are there (now at any rate) rubies in their beaks.

[4] I understand, however, that it is now valued at nearly 200,000*l*.

[5] When I was in Teheran I had in vain asked the same questions of the custodian of the treasury, and of every Persian official whom I met, but without eliciting any satisfactory response.

[6] He was the son of the wife of Haji Mirza Aghassi, the eccentric dervish prime-minister of Mohammed Shah, and, as an especial favourite of his step-father, lived in princely style. Upon one occasion the present Shah, then Heir Apparent, was going in pilgrimage to Shah Abdul Azim, when he saw an immense and gorgeous cavalcade approaching, which he took to be that of his royal father. Respectfully dismounting, he awaited the arrival of the cortège on foot. Great was his disgust when he discovered that the central figure was only the Ilkhani of the Kajars. In deference to his complaints, the too sumptuous nobleman was banished to Baghdad.

The Northern Provinces

For the King of the North shall return, and shall set forth a multitude greater than the former, and shall certainly come after certain years with a great army and with much riches.—*Daniel* xi, 13.

IN the last chapter I have shown the newcomer the plain of Teheran, bounded on the north by the stupendous barrier of the Elburz Mountains. But on the far side of those mountains, where their northern skirts descend in wooded flounces to the Caspian, and between Resht and Astrabad, extends a range of country, marked by so strange an individuality, and so unlike anything else that is to be seen in any other part of Persia, that a work professing to treat of that country as a whole would err seriously in omitting any notice of it. Readers who have followed me so far will have pictured, and have justly pictured Persia, at least in the winter months, as for the most part a colourless, waterless, and treeless expanse, where wide deserts, with whose monotony the eye aches, roll their sandy levels to the base of bleak mountains, whose gaunt ribs protrude like the bones of some emaciated skeleton through a scanty covering of soil. And yet within a few miles at the most of this cheerless scene, severed by a single but mighty mountain range, lies another Persia, so rich in water that malarial vapours are bred from the stagnant swamps, so abundantly clothed with trees of the forest, that often a pathway can scarcely be forced through the intricate jungle, so riotous in colour that the traveller can almost awake with the belief that he has been transported in sleep to some tropical clime. These extraordinary characteristics, and this amazing change, are exhibited by the northern maritime provinces of Mazanderan and Gilan. Mazanderan signifies *Maz* (a Pehlevi, or old Persian word for mountains) and *anderun* (within, the inner part, whence its application to the women's quarters in a house), i.e. the hollow between the mountains and the sea. Gilan has been commonly said to be derived from a word signifying mud; and this would certainly be appropriate to a region in which that is the chief tangible commodity, and which an experienced and sympathetic traveller has summed up as 'moist, muggy, villainous Gilan'. But this derivation is disputed by some professors, though I am not aware that they have found anything to suggest in its place. The name is, no doubt, adapted from the Gelæ, who inhabited the south shores of the Caspian, and who bequeathed a title both to the sea, the country, and the principal local manufacture. Marco Polo (cap. iv.) called the Caspian 'Mer de Gheluchelan' (i.e. Ghel ou Ghelan), and the silk 'Ghelle'. The characteristics of these two provinces are so similar, if not identical, a slight difference of latitude being the only serious disparity to which they can lay claim, that I propose to treat them in conjunction. Mazanderan starts in the neighbourhood of Astrabad on the east, and runs for a distance of 220 miles along the coast to an unimportant river, which is the boundary of Gilan. From this point Gilan continues round the south-west curve of the Caspian for a further distance of 150 miles, terminating in the mountain district of Talish.

The staple produce of Mazanderan is rice, cotton, and sugar. The staple produce of Gilan once was silk. As Richard Chenie, one of the factors of the British Moscovy Company, wrote home in 1563, 'The King of Gillan, where as yet you have had no traffique, liveth al by marchandise'. Since it was this silk traffic that brought Persia into mercantile contact with Europe, that prompted the interchange of embassies and

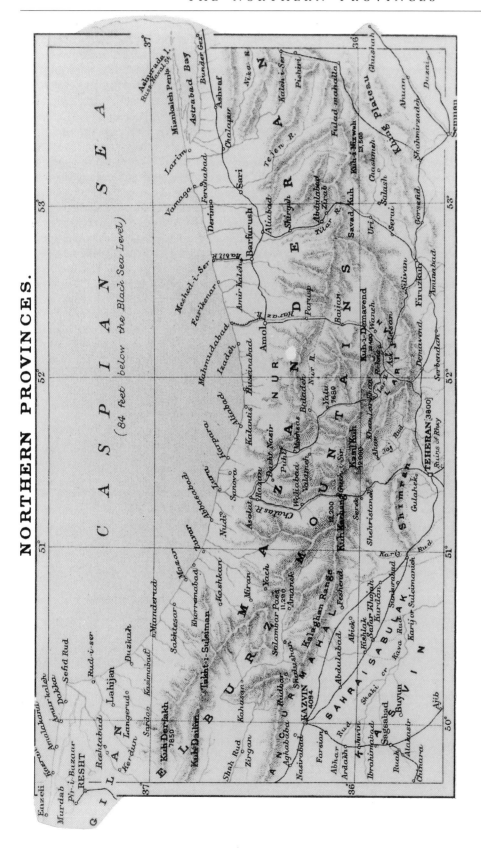

NORTHERN PROVINCES.

the framing of treaties in the sixteenth and later centuries, and that made Persia wealthy and famous; and since, moreover, it is only recently that it may be said to have permanently declined, I shall take advantage of this opportunity to give a short *résumé* of this interesting page of Persian history, only treating of the subject in so far as relates to Gilan and Mazanderan.

The romantic story of the introduction of the silkworm from China into Europe in the reign of the Emperor Justinian, about 550 A.D., is one of the favourite anecdotes of history. The first mention of its cultivation in the northern provinces of Persia that I have come across, is in the pages of the tenth-century pilgrim, El Istakhri, who travelled from Rhey to Sari, the capital of Mazanderan, and spoke of the silk which was produced in great quantity in the province called Taberistan, the ancient name for the Elburz region in these parts. Three centuries later we learn from Marco Polo that the merchants of Genoa, then at the height of its commercial renown, had recently brought the Caspian within the far-reaching sphere of their trade, and had begun to export 'the silk which is called Ghelle'. In the middle of the sixteenth century the Moscovy Company, through its agents, Anthony Jenkinson and others, made that courageous attempt to open up a British Caspian trade through Russia. It was the silk of Gilan in quest of which they came. In the succeeding century the main channel of export of this product was in Dutch hands from the Persian Gulf. Early in the eighteenth century, Peter the Great, who fully understood the part that commerce can be made to play in schemes of imperial aggrandisement in the East, endeavoured to divert the entire northern export into Russia, by an arrangement with the Armenian traders of Baku. After a while this conspiracy broke down and the Russians attempted the business themselves. In 1725 Peter was about to enter into an engagement with a company of English merchants, being willing even to invoke foreign aid in order to gain his end, when he sickened and died. Then ensued the second brief, but gallant, experiment on the part of a small band of English merchants, headed by Elton and Hanway. Since then, no direct endeavour has been made forcibly to divert the traffic into this or that channel, although the conquests of Russia in the early part of the present century have rendered it inevitable that the greater part of the exports of northern Persia should pass through her hands.

Restricting our observations to Gilan alone, in the absence of sufficient data upon which to base any more general conclusions, we notice the lamentable falling off in production between the seventeenth and the eighteenth centuries, consequent upon the anarchy that succeeded the overthrow of the Sefavean kings. In Hanway's time Gilan only furnished one-eighth of the total output in the days of Chardin. At the close of the century, the firm hold of the Kajar family upon the northern provinces re-established security and brought with it a revival of trade. During the first half of the present century the progress continued without intermission. Sir J. Sheil, when British Minister, wrote in about the year 1850, 'Silk is the great staple of Persian commerce, particularly of foreign traffic, which enables it to pay for a portion of its imports from abroad'. He spoke of attempts that had been made by English merchants to introduce improvements in the preparation of the silk, but which the normal supineness of the Persians and their reluctance to abate one jot or tittle of archaic routine, had rendered unavailing. In 1864, the very year in which the climacteric of production was touched, disease appeared for the first time. By the year 1869, its ravages had made such serious inroads that the value of the annual output had sunk to one-fifth of the figure at which it stood five years before. From this attack the silk trade of Gilan has never recovered. Eggs from Khorasan and eggs from Khanikin in Turkey were tried, but with no success. Eggs were brought all the way from Japan, but without much better results. In despair at bad season succeeding bad season, the peasants have turned their attention to other crops. Tobacco was started as an experiment in 1875. An impulse was given to the olive cultivation of Rudbar near Resht. In the central silk-growing districts of Persia, opium has been largely adopted as an alternative, and has produced most gratifying results. But in the northern provinces rice has proved the most popular and remunerative substitute; and in a country where new ideas and improved methods penetrate so slowly as in Persia, it is doubtful whether, at least in Persian hands, the silk industry will ever permanently revive. Under other auspices, a different tale might very likely soon be told; for the disease having been expelled, and the soil and climate remaining what they formerly were, there is no valid reason why so lucrative an industry should either be abandoned or should cease to flourish.

At present the silk-worm is cultivated, in addition to Gilan and Mazanderan, in Azerbaijan (where in 1885 the crop was 32,500 lbs.), in Khorasan (16,250 lbs.), and in the central district of Persia, whose chief marts are Kashan, Isfahan, Yezd, and Kerman (13,000 lbs.). In the two latter cases, the produce is wholly, or almost wholly, required for local consumption, and it is from Gilan and Azerbaijan alone that the export now takes place to Russia, and still more to Marseilles. The native manufactures in which Persian silk is employed are velvets, brocades, satins, and sarsenet, as well as plain silk, and silk mixed with cotton. Since pure silk is forbidden by the Koran, such of the Persians as are sticklers for that somewhat neglected code of precepts, salve their consciences by wearing silk with the slightest admixture of cotton. Of the modern fabrics that I saw in the above-mentioned towns, I admired the velvets of Kashan the most. Old Persian velvets and velvet brocades are superb, but are very difficult to procure in pieces of any size. Silk carpets are still made to order at Kashan and Sultanabad, and are as magnificent and as costly as heretofore; but, unless carefully watched, the manufacturer flies to the use of cheap aniline dyes, and the artistic value and durability of tone of the fabric are irretrievably ruined.

Before I quit the subject let me very briefly describe the manner in which the silk cultivation is conducted in northern Persia. In the month of April the natives, and chiefly the women, take the eggs, attached to a sheet of paper, and expose them to the warmth of the human body by wearing them beneath their clothes, next to the skin. After the lapse of three days the eggs are hatched and the caterpillars appear. They have before them a life of about forty days, which is spent in alternate spasms of excessive gluttony and stupefied repose. The periods of feasting, however, last from seven to ten days, the intervals of torpor not more than two. After the first ten days the worms are transferred to a *tilambar*, or platform, covered with a thatched shanty and reared at a height of about five feet from the ground, where, in the intervals of voracity, they are stuffed to repletion with mulberry leaves. After about forty days they become fat, full, and nearly transparent, in which uncomfortable condition they exhibit a desire to climb up a number of branches placed vertically in the shed, and to spin their cocoons. This goes on for ten days, during which time the *tilambar* is hermetically closed. At the end of that time it is again opened, the boughs are removed, the roof is found to be entirely covered with beautiful cocoons; and while some of these are spared to develop into moths for breeding purposes, the bulk are taken down, the chrysalis is killed by exposure to the sun, or immersion in boiling water, and the silk is unravelled and wound off on reels. The survivors come out as full-blown moths in a fortnight, when the female, having done her duty by laying from 100 to 300 eggs, pines, and incontinently expires.

Editor's Note: For reasons of space, this chapter has had to be greatly abbreviated, but I was anxious to include part of it, particularly the 'romantic story' of the silkworm. The next two pages are taken from Curzon's chapter on the North-West.

The Mar Shimun (Patriarch of the E. Nestorians)

The Blue Mosque is worthy of attention

(Opposite.) The Mar Shimun, leader of the Nestorian Christians. The Nestorian Christians of the Turco-Persian highlands have been variously estimated at figures between 100,000 and 200,000, the higher being in all probability the more correct calculation. Of these by far the greater numbers are Turkish subjects, the Nestorian population of Azerbaijan being, according to the latest report (which nearly doubles all previous estimates), a little over 40,000 persons. There are, at this moment, three branches of Syrian Christians: (1) the Old Nestorians, under Mar Shimun; (2) the Old Chaldaeans, under the Partiarch of Babylon; (3) the New Chaldaeans, under Mar Elia Melus of Mosul. The first named is the most numerous of the three, and is supposed to contain nearly 100,000 members, 40,000 in Persia and 60,000 in Turkey. The Mar Shimun has long resided in the mountain village of Kochannis, near Iulamerk, in Turkish territory, above the famous waters of the Zab. Nominally he unites in his own person the spiritual and temporal functions of government.

Tabriz, the capital city, which occupies much the same position in North-Western as does Meshed in North-Eastern Persia, is the residence of the Heir Apparent, the station of a British Consul-General, and the largest commercial emporium in Persia. Situated at so slight a distance from the frontier, it has fallen the first victim to invading armies, and has been successively held by Arabs, Seljuks, Ottomans, Persians, and Russians. What the rage of conquest or the licence of possession has spared, Nature has interfered to destroy. The city has been desolated by frequent and calamitous earthquakes. Among the monuments of antiquity worthy of any notice is the Kabud Musjid, or Blue Mosque, so called from the magnificent specimens of enamelled faience by which it was once encrusted.

TEHERAN to ISFAHAN.

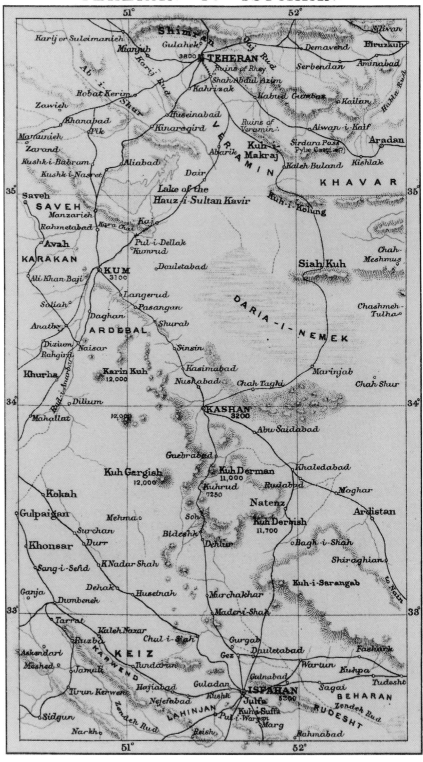

From Teheran to Isfahan

Then pomp and pleasure dwelt within her walls.
The merchants of the East and of the West
    Met in her arched bazaars.
    All day the active poor
Showered a cool comfort o'er her thronging streets.
    Labour was busy in her looms,
    Through all her open gates
Long troops of laden camels lined the roads.

SOUTHEY, Thalaba the Destroyer, bk. v.

AFTER some weeks spent in the enjoyment of the hospitality of the British Legation, and in the interesting and often highly-charged political atmosphere of the capital, it was with no slight reluctance that I again resigned myself to the tender mercies of the *chapar-khaneh* and the Persian post-horse, and started forth on my 800 miles' ride to the Gulf. In justice, however, to a much abused institution and animal, I must observe that along the stretch of road from Teheran to Shiraz, which is the most frequented in Persia, the former is in a better state of repair, and the latter is sprightlier in his movements, than in other parts of the country. Execrable horses and an inhospitable track had been the distinguishing features of my ride from Meshed to Teheran. With a tolerable mount, with the chance of European converse and entertainment in the Telegraph stations, encountered at distances of from sixty to seventy miles along the road, and with the prospect of great cities and world-famed ruins before him, with leisure to rest in the one or to linger over the other, the southward journey soon loses the visionary horrors with which the traveller has credited it, and proves to be deficient neither in comfort nor charm. To the student of works on Persia it will present little novelty. It has been traversed by almost every visitor who has either entered or left the country on the south, and it has on many occasions been excellently and conscientiously described. There remains for me the task of faithfully depicting its features as they now exist, and of doing somewhat fuller justice to the great and historic cities through which it passes than is commonly rendered by the scribe of travel.

Leaving Teheran by the Hamadan Gate, I followed the main caravan-route to the west, to a little beyond the village of Robat Kerim, the single wire to Baghdad, originally erected by English engineers, and afterwards handed over to the Persian Government, taking the same direction. At about sixteen miles from Teheran I crossed the slender stream of the Karij, flowing in a deep fissure between high banks, by a single-arched bridge. Robat Kerim is a straggling village with a filthy ditch running down the main street. Thence the road to Pik is as devoid of interest as it is wholly destitute of life; although running as it does over a level expanse, it is a welcome stage to the *chapar* rider. Low ranges of hills enclose the plain on either side; and towards one of these the track wends, plunging into a series of rolling hollows and undulations about four miles before reaching Pik. Demavend and the Elburz range were always behind me, the one snow-robed, the other snow besprinkled; and with every quarter of an hour they took on a different light, from pink to ashen grey, through all the dwindling gradations of rose and saffron, as the afternoon died down into dusk. At Pik I found a *chapar-khaneh* with two separate towers and *bala-khanehs*, one of which had the usual overplus of open windows and flapping unshut doors. From there the track cuts across the surrounding fields in an easterly direction, and enters a low pass in the surrounding hills, down the further slope of which runs a stream strongly impregnated with salt, on its way to the new lake, which flashed before me in the morning sun, its borders marked by a glittering fringe of saline scum. I may here quote, as a sample of His Persian Majesty's style, the passage in which he described the surrounding scene:—

At this season (April) when most of the camels had brought forth their young, the greenness of the plains, the clearness of the air, the lake and the reflection of the sun on its waters, the vastness of the plain, the many camels and their young, the camel men and their children who were all busily tending the camels, the black tents of the Nomads, the many flocks of sheep, which were grazing in the plain, were wonderful to see.

Skirting the west shore of the lake the carriage-road from Teheran is here first encountered, driven in a bee-line across the valley (which is about sixteen miles in width), and joined by the *chapar* route on the crest of the further hill. On descending from this ridge by an easy pass on the south, we come to the magnificent new cara-vanserai of Manzarieh, with gorgeous tile-covered façade and emblem of the Lion and Sun sculped in stone. Further down, and just before reaching the solitary post-house of Rahmetabad, the river Kara Chai, which flows from Saveh,[1] is crossed by a pro-digious stone bridge, the most solid construction of the kind that I had so far seen. Another low ridge is climbed, another valley opens out, towards the southern end of which extends the belt of mingled brown and green that in the East signifies a large city. Above it the sun flames on the burnished cupolas and the soaring minars of Fatima's mosque. As we approach, the sacred buildings loom larger, and are presently seen to consist of two domes overlaid with gilded plates, and five lofty minarets, disposed in two pairs and a single standing in close proximity to the larger dome. Emerging from small clumps of trees, or standing in solitary prominence are to be seen the conical tiled roofs of scores of *imamzadehs* erected over the remains of famous saints and prophets, whose bones have been transported hither and laid to rest in the con-secrated dust of Kum. There were formerly said to be over 400 of these structures in and around the city. Some of them are in good repair, and contain beautiful panels or lintel-bands of tiles with Kufic inscriptions from the Koran. Others are in a state of shocking ruin, the blue tiles having peeled off their cupolas, upon whose summits repose enormous storks' nests. The landscape is framed on the south by a range of hills of splintered outline and peculiar sterility, whose forbidding aspect is in harmony with the traditional and fanatical superstition of the holy city.[2]

The approach to the town lies through richly-cultivated fields; and at the very end of the road, which supplies a vista thereto, flashes the holy Fatima's dome. Immediately outside the gates flows, in the direction of the new lake, the Rud-i-Anarbar, which is crossed by a substantial bridge of nine arches. Some of the houses on the further bank have two storeys, with windows and balconies overlooking the stream—a more advanced degree of exterior embellishment than is usually attained by Persian domiciles. The remainder of the city, viewed from the outside, consists of a multitude of squat clay domes, the roof of nearly every building being shaped into half a dozen or a dozen of these protuberances. I traversed the entire length of the bazaar on my way to the *chapar-khaneh*, which, having recently been shifted, is now situated in a caravanserai opening out of the bazaar. The latter is vaulted throughout, and consists of one long alley, with a few parallel and transverse aisles. The roadway is broad, the shops large

and well-furnished, and the jostle of human beings, camels, donkeys, horses, and cattle, was greater than I had yet seen in Persia. I subsequently retraced my footsteps to see as much of the mosque as is permissible to a Christian and an unbeliever. Outside its encircling wall extends a vast necropolis, adorned with thousands of stone slabs and crumbling mounds. A conjurer had selected this incongruous spot as his theatre, and was holding spell-bound a large crowd. I rode up to the gateway of the big court of the mosque and, gazing in, not without attracting a large concourse of the curious, could see an immense quadrangle, with arched and tile-faced recesses all round the walls, and a tank for ablutions in the centre. Fraser, in 1821, entered the mosque in disguise, and visited the tomb-chamber. A Dr. Bicknell, who had already been to Mecca, made a similar entry in 1869, disguised as a Haji. Arnold, in 1875, having entered the outer court, remembered that discretion is the better part of valour, and beat a retreat; while any less adventurous Giaour must be content with what he can see through the open gate.

Kum is the site of the second most sacred shrine in Persia, and the Westminster Abbey of many of her kings. I have already spoken of the solicitous regard for the welfare of his devotees that led the Imam Reza to scatter his relatives while living, and their corpses when dead, throughout the country that he loved so well. At Kum are deposited the remains of his sister, Fatima-el-Masuma, i.e. the Immaculate, who, according to one account, lived and died here, having fled from Baghdad to escape the persecution of the Khalifs; according to another, she sickened and died at Kum, on her way to see her brother at Tus. He, for his part, is believed by the pious Shiahs to return the compliment by paying her a visit every Friday from his shrine at Meshed. Kum appears to have existed from an earlier period, although we may be absolved from accepting the legendary Persian foundation by Tahmuras or Kai Kobad. It was not, however, till it became the sepulchre of the illustrious Fatima, nor, after that, until the Shiah faith had become the national religion, that the town attained its reputation for especial sanctity. It was, of course, sacked by Timur, and has been in a state of greater or less ruin ever since. As the quaint Herbert phrased it, 'in the Sable weed she is still apparelled; for great Coom is now onely *magni nominis umbra*'. Nevertheless, under the patronage of the Sefavi sovereigns, the city revived; fine quays adorned the banks of the river; extensive bazaars and handsome caravanserais received or dispensed a considerable trade; and the shrine was added to and adorned by the devout munificence of successive sovereigns. Chardin said that in his day the city contained '15,000 houses,

I followed the main caravan-route to the west.

as the people say'; but a measure, both to our own credulity and to the local hyperbole, is set by the earlier Herbert and the later Le Brun, who unite in crediting it with only 2,000 houses, albeit these were 'wel-built, sweet, and wel-furnished'. In 1722 it found in the Afghans an even more savage enemy than it had experienced in Timur, and was all but destroyed. A century later Fraser still described it as 'a wretched mass of ruins'. Its population was estimated as 4,000 in 1872, and as 7,000 in 1884; and when later lists have returned it as 20,000 to 30,000 persons, I imagine that the discrepancy is to be reconciled by regarding the smaller total as the permanent, and the higher as the fluctuating population, which is much swollen by pilgrims.

From the seventeenth century onwards Kum has been in high favour as the sepulchre of many of the Persian kings. Here repose the bodies of Shah Sefi I, Shah Abbas II, Shah Suleiman, and Shah Sultan Husein of the Sefavi dynasty; and here, among the Kajar monarchs, have been laid the remains of Fath Ali Shah (with two of his sons) in a separate building in the outskirts of the town, and of Mohammed Shah. Other sovereigns must also have been interred in the same spot; for the Persian records speak of the graves of 444 saints and princes, and of ten kings. Over their bodies, enshrined in magnificent sarcophagi of alabaster, of marble and ivory, of ebony, and camphor wood inlaid, which are covered with rich draperies, *mullahs* day and night read passages from the Koran. But of small account, it may be imagined, in the pilgrim's eyes, is even the royal dust, compared with that of the Lady Fatima.

Chardin, Tavernier, Le Brun, and others have given minute descriptions or illus-

From the seventeenth century onwards Kum has been in high favour as the sepulchre of many of the Persian kings—indeed it is the most sacred shrine in Persia—their Westminster Abbey.

Cemetery and Mosque of Fatima at Kum — Persia vol II. 8.

trations of the principal shrine; of which Herbert obscurely remarks that 'the mesquit is of Epirotique form'. It is preceded by several courts, the outermost of which is planted with trees. From the inner or principal quadrangle twelve marble steps lead up to the enclosure containing the saint's tomb. Three doors, one of which is overlaid with silver plates, open into an octagonal chamber beneath the dome. Chardin writes:—

Kum was, of course, sacked by Timur, and has been in a state of greater or less ruin ever since.

In the midst of that chappel stands the tomb of Fatima, overlaid with tiles of China, painted à la Moresca, and overspread with cloth of gold that hangs down to the ground on every side. It is enclosed with a gate of massy silver, ten foot high, distant half a foot from the tomb, and at each corner crowned as it were with large apples of fine gold. Several breadths of velvet, hung about the inside of the gate, hide it from the view of the people, so that only favour or money can procure a sight of it. Over the tomb, about ten foot in height, hang several silver vessels, which they call candil, being a sort of lamp. But they never light up any fire therein, which they are not made to hold, nor any sort of Liquor, as not having any bottom. Upon the grate hang several inscriptions in Letters of gold upon thick velloms, as large as a large sheet of paper, which inscriptions contain the elegies of the saint and her family.

It is when he ascends the twelve marble steps that the pilgrim removes his shoes, and leaves behind his staff or his arms. Then, as he enters, he kneels and kisses the threshold. Again he kisses the silver rails, through which he peers at the shrouded sarcophagus; he breathes the prescribed prayers; and with further genuflection and salutations, and fees to the hovering *mullahs*, he retires. He is one step nearer to heaven.

For its present splendour of golden cupola and tile-encrusted minars the shrine is indebted to the reigning family. In his early life Fath Ali Shah registered a vow that should he ever succeed to the throne, he would enrich Kum, and relieve its people of taxation. It is more than doubtful whether he ever carried out the latter pledge, though he gave the city and district as a private estate to his mother; but his promise as to the shrine was simply redeemed. He stripped off the tiles with which the dome had hitherto been covered, and replaced them with plates of gilt copper; he erected a neighbouring *madresseh* or religious college, with endowments and quarters for 100 students; he built at Kum a hospital and a *mehman-khaneh* or inn; he was said to have spent 100,000 *tomans* annually upon the shrine; when he visited it, he always came on foot; and when he died, hard by his body was by his orders laid to rest. In more recent times a second dome has been gilt; a clock was erected by one of the royal princes, who was Governor of Hamadan; and the glittering elegance of the large court into which I gazed was due, as I heard, to a restoration by the late Amin-es-Sultan. In one of the sanctuaries is an inscription to Ali, the refreshing originality of which entitles it to be quoted. It runs thus: 'Oh, inexpressible man! By thee, in truth, is Nature enriched and adorned! Had not thy perfect self been in the Creator's thought, Eve had remained for ever a virgin, and Adam a bachelor.'

Kum is indeed the possessor of a situation that might appear, at first sight, to recommend it for the capital city of Persia. It stands upon a river; it occupies a very central position; and it is the meeting-point of many important roads, from Teheran, from Kazvin, from Sultanabad and Burujird, from Yezd, and from Isfahan. It contains one of the two only inns or hotels in Persia that are worthy of the name—a fine building standing in close proximity to the mosque. On the other hand, although there is a river, the water-supply is inadequate for a great city; and the heat in summer is excruciating. The city has been famous in past and present times chiefly for its melons and cucumbers, its armourers, its shoemakers, and its long-necked earthenware jars for cooling water. Of the last-named Chardin observed:—

This is peculiar to the white ware which is thence transported, that in the summer it cools the water wonderfully and very suddenly by reason of continual transpiration. So that they who desire to drink cool and deliciously never drink in the same pot above five or six days at most. They wash it with rose water the first time, to take away the ill smell of the Earth; and they hang it in the air full of water, wrapt up in a moist linen cloth. A fourth part of the water transpires in six hours the first time, after that, still less from day to day, till at last the pores are closed up by the thick matter contained in the water which stops in the pores. But so soon as the pores are stopped, the water stinks in the pots, and you must take new ones.

As might be expected from so holy a place, the population contains a large number of *seyids*—fanatics inured to long impunity of conduct—and is much addicted to bigotry and superstition. No Jews or Parsis live here; and English ladies, resident in the Telegraph offices, have usually found it prudent to veil in public. These superstitions are now dying fast throughout the East; but Kum is one of the places where an accidental spark might still be fanned into a disagreeable flame. Its title of Dar-el-Aman or Seat of Safety is an indication that its shrine is a particularly favourite sanctuary for Mussulman refugees; and many is the malefactor who has escaped retribution by a flight to the inviolate asylum of its walls. Apparently, too, the good folk of Kum are without honour in their own country; for there is a Persian proverb that says: 'A dog of Kashan is better than a noble of Kum, albeit a dog is better than a man of Kashan.'

In leaving Kum, it took me three-quarters of an hour to get quit of the maze of intricate streets and alleys of which the greater part of the city outside the bazaar is composed, and to emerge upon the open country. There a fast gallop on an excellent little horse conducted me to the post-house of Pasangun, standing, with a caravanserai, near the base of a range of hills on the south-east. Skirting this range, the track now becomes very stony, then crosses a stream, passes the big caravanserai of Shurab (salt water), which was built about eighty years ago, and winds by a long and arid pass through the range, till it debouches upon another plain, whereon the *chapar-khaneh* and caravanserai of Sinsin (erected by the Amin-ed-Dowleh, a prominent minister of Fath Ali Shah) are situated immediately at the foot of the hills. Sinsin was once a flourishing place, but was ruined by the Turkomans at the end of the last century—to such a distance did those incorrigible freebooters (of the Yomut tribe in this instance) push their marauding expeditions. Malcolm, on his way up to Teheran in 1810, him-self conversed with one of the survivors of the catastrophe. Thence, over a perfectly level expanse, we press forward to Kashan, thin wreaths of smoke in the distance be-traying the existence of the city at the base of what is sometimes called, for want of a general title, the Kuhrud range (from the village of which I shall speak presently), but is in reality a spur of the same mountain system that continues without a break from Kashan to Yezd, and thence to Kerman.

Local tradition ascribes the foundation of Kashan to Zobeideh, the wife of Harun-er-Rashid. But it appears certain that the town existed much earlier; for there is in a native historian a reference both to Kashan and Kum as having contributed a force of 20,000 soldiers to the army of the last Sassanian monarch; and some have seen in the name a contraction from *Kai-ashian*, or King's dwelling. From a very remote period Kashan appears to have been famous for five things: the industrial aptitudes of its inhabitants, its silk manufactures, its brass and copper utensils, its earthenware or *faïence*, and its scorpions. Geoffrey Ducket, one of the English factors who sailed to Persia in the fifth venture of the British Moscovy Company in the sixteenth century, went up to Kashan in 1573 and reported it to be:—

A town that consisteth altogether of merchaundise, and the best trade of all the lande is there, beyng greatly frequented by the merchauntes of India. The towne is much to be commended for the civill and good government that is there used. An idle person is not suffered to live amongst them. The childe that is but five yeeres olde is set to some labour. Playing at dice or cardes is by the lawe present death.

John Cartwright, preacher, in 1600, called it 'the very magazeen and warehouse of all the Persian cities for stuffes'. Sir T. Herbert in 1627 said:—

This noble city is in comparison not less than York or Norwich, about 4,000 families being accounted in her. A more industrious and civil People or a town better governed Persia elsewhere has not. The Carravans-raw, is an unparallel'd fabrick, and precedes all other I saw in Persia.

Chardin also spoke of 'the Royal Inn, built by Abbas the Great,' as 'the finest in all Persia,' and said that in his day the city had a double wall, five gates, 6,500 houses (including the suburbs), forty mosques, three colleges, and 200 sepulchres of Seyids.

The silks, satins, velvets, and brocades of Kashan have long been famous throughout the East. In former times the silkworm was largely cultivated in the neighbourhood, and there was further a considerable import of raw material from Gilan. A number of beautiful silk, and silk with cotton, fabrics are still manufactured here (of which the shawls called Husein Kuli Khani, from the name of some early designer or patron, are perhaps the most artistic textile production of Persia), as well as velvets with a peculiar mottled pattern. The pierced and inlaid brass and copper wares are also remarkable; and Kashan is the great native manufactory of domestic utensils in copper. Formerly the metal was procured from Sivas in Asiatic Turkey, *viá* Erzerum and Tabriz, but it is now imported in bars or sheets from England. The bazaars and busy part of the town are in its southern quarter, where also are the principal buildings, consisting of the Musjid-i-Meidan, which contains a superb *mihrab*, or prayer niche, in embossed and enamelled *faïence*, a tall leaning minaret, and vast caravanserais for the storage or barter of merchandise. In 1870, Colonel Euan Smith reported the city to contain twenty-four caravanserais for the sale of goods, thirty-five for the accommodation of strangers, thirty-four public baths, eighteen larger mosques, and ninety smaller shrines. He returned its population as 90,000—an altogether exorbitant estimate, although General Gasteiger Khan's calculation of 5,000 in 1881 is scarcely less inaccurate at the opposite extreme. In 1885, Schindler reckoned it as 30,000, though where these people are stowed away one is at a loss to imagine after inspecting what is outwardly one of the most dilapidated cities in Persia. A more funereal place I had not yet seen. Scarcely a building was in repair, barely a wall intact. Both the cobbled roadway and the houses that lined it were in an equal state of decay, and it was as melancholy to see the one as it was to ride over the other.

From Kashan, the still surviving name for Persian earthenware, viz. *Kashi-kari*, was derived, and this city, in whose neighbourhood good clay was to be found, as well as colouring materials, was one of the chief centres of the industry. A larger number of the beautiful vases with iridescent lustre, or *reflet métallique*, which are the most cherished among the curios of Persia, have been found at Kashan than elsewhere, but there is no positive proof that they were manufactured here. On the other hand, most of the tiles, so plentifully and effectively employed in the decoration of mosques, were burned in Kashani ovens.

It is, perhaps, to mercantile habits, pursued without a break for centuries, that must be attributed the widespread reputation of the Kashanis for pusillanimity of character. Their fame in this respect has passed into a proverb, even in a country where courage did not appear to me to be popular; and among the many stories to which it has given birth, perhaps the best is that of the 30,000 men of Kashan and Isfahan (a sister-city as regards the same attributes), who, when Nadir Shah disbanded his army on their return from India, applied for an escort of 100 musketeers to conduct them safely to their homes. Possibly a somewhat enervating effect is produced by the great heat in summer, which Chardin ascribed to 'the high mountain on the south, the reverberation of which so furiously heats the place in the dog days that it scalds again'.

Touching the scorpions, the black variety of Kashan has enjoyed a prodigious fame, and was commemorated by El Istakhri as early as the tenth century. So venomous was their bite that one of the familiar forms of expressing hatred was to pray that your enemy might either be stung by a Kashani scorpion or be made Governor of Gilan. John Struys, the Dutchman, declared that, in order to escape these pests, the people slept in hammocks, and took an antidote made of filings of copper tempered with vinegar and honey. But the more popular cure was the homoeopathic application of the oil of the scorpion itself, which was extracted by frying the insect. Olearius, the secretary to the Holstein Embassy in 1637, was bitten by a scorpion at Kashan and derived great relief from this remedy. There is a tradition that still survives that the creatures do not attack strangers, but this modest display of hospitality is hardly likely to induce a longer stay than is possible in so unattractive a spot.

About four miles to the south-west of Kashan, on the slopes of the mountains, is situated the palace of Fin, the springs of which have rendered it a favourite resort of royalty from early times. Shah Abbas built a residence here, but the present structure, now in a state of great decay, is the work of Fath Ali Shah, who made it one of his favourite summer retreats, though originally intended for his brother Husein Kuli Khan. Cypress avenues, water flowing in marble canals, and jets for fountains adorned its gardens; a picture of Fath Ali and his sons and hunting and battle scenes hung upon its walls. Sir J. Malcolm and his escort were accommodated here on their upward march to Teheran in 1810. In later times, a gloomier memory has attached to the palace of Fin; for here, in 1852, Mirza Taki Khan, the first great minister of the reigning Shah, and brother-in-law of the king, was put to death by the Royal order, his veins being opened in a bath. The place is now deserted.

After leaving Kashan, the track runs for a distance of about sixteen miles over a stony expanse, nearly flat, though with a slight rise, to the foot of the mountains, where it turns sharply to the right and plunges into the main range. At a little distance up the pass, in what the foolish Ker Porter described as 'a confined dell of this darkling labyrinth', stands the large dilapidated caravanserai of Guebrabad—a ruined settlement of the Zoroastrians. Here we finally lose sight of the snowy spire of Demavend, which has accompanied us all the way from Teheran, gaining each day in pride and stature as his inferior satellites have sunk from view, and the monarch has stood forth alone with his crowned head in the heavens. The distance, as the crow flies, is a little over 150 miles. Continuing up the pass, the road enters a rocky gorge, which, of course, elicits from Porter the descriptive epithets of 'a tremendous abyss, an insurmountable pass, overwhelmingly grand, vieing with any part of the Caucasus for sublimity in form, hue, and bearing'. The rhodomontade of the worthy baronet proceeds from such inexhaustible wells that he could afford to leave the tap perpetually running. Presently we arrive at the great stone *bund* of Ali Verdi Khan, Commander-in-Chief under Shah Abbas and builder of the famous galleried bridge of Isfahan. This great structure, which completely blocks the valley from side to side, damming up the waters of a mountain stream in spring time, and forming thereby a lake of some depth and size, whose outflow towards the plain of Kashan is regulated by a sluice, still answers to the description of it left by Tavernier:—

The Minaret of Kashan, which is outwardly one of the most dilapidated cities in Persia. A more funereal place I had not yet seen. Scarcely a building was in repair, barely a wall intact.

At the end of the valley you meet a great wall which crosses it and joyns the two mountains together. This wall is above 100 paces long, above thirty foot thick, and fifty high. It was the work of the great Sha Abas, whose design it was to stop the waters that fall from the mountain, and to make a receptacle for water in that place to serve his occasions. At the foot of the wall there is a sluice, which being let down keeps in the water; but is pull'd up to let out the water over all the neighbouring lands to the plains of Cachan.

When I passed in the early winter the bed of the lake was dry, and such water as remained in the stream was frozen, for at this elevation, about 7,000 feet, it was very cold. Other travellers have reported the reservoir as half-full, or full, with the water spilling over the *bund* in a fine cascade. In January and February, after the deep snows have fallen, the pass, which below Kuhrud has an altitude of 7,250, and further on, at its highest point, of 8,750 feet, is sometimes impassable.

Above this point the valley widens somewhat, and, about four miles further on, encloses a succession of charming orchards thickly planted with walnut, pear, plum, and apple trees, for the fruit of which Kuhrud is famous. The sight of a little timber was a welcome relief after the long leagues of bare plain and brown mountain, and Kuhrud is to be congratulated on its snug little inheritance, which in summer-time is considered a terrestrial Paradise by the sentimental sons of Iran. Above the terraced orchards is situated the village—a typical Persian mountain hamlet of rude houses built one above the other in ascending tiers upon the side of the hill, such as I had seen daily in Khorasan, but not before in Central Persia. The people of Kuhrud and Soh speak a dialect or patois of their own, containing many archaic words and idioms, and said by philologists to be closely allied to the Lur dialect, to the Dari of Yezd, and to that of Sivend near Persepolis.

Thence for over twenty miles the track lies amid the spurs and ramifications of the mountain range, climbing one ridge only to reveal another beyond, and wearying the tired traveller with the perpetual new vista of the same mountain maze. At length the caravanserai and imposing Telegraph station of Soh are reached, at a point where the ridge really begins to dip towards the plain of Isfahan. A *farsakh* further are the village and posthouse of Bideshk. A descent among the lower undulations carries us on to the flat, where a canter can be enjoyed for miles, a thin streak of verdure in the distant hollow of the plain marking the village of Murchakhar, near to which, on November 13, 1729, Nadir Shah inflicted a decisive defeat on the Afghans, who were soon expelled root and branch from the country. Here also in 1785 died Ali Murad Khan, who enjoyed a brief reign of four years in the anarchy that succeeded the death of Kerim Khan Zend. A short rise leads past the large Mader-i-Shah caravanserai, built of brick upon a foundation of bluish stone by the mother of Shah Abbas, to the crest of a low ridge that separates the plains of Murchakhar and Isfahan. Thence over the flat we speed in the direction of the Sefavi capital, already indicated by faint blue smoke-wreaths and by the converging lines of innumerable *kanats*. Behind it the panorama is closed by mountains of striking and irregular outline.[3]

As we approach the city the most conspicuous objects in the landscape are a number of large circular towers with smaller turrets projecting from their summits, sometimes

The great stone bund *of Ali Verdi Khan, Commander-in-Chief under Shah Abbas and builder of the famous galleried bridge of Isfahan. This great structure completely blocks the valley from side to side, damming up the waters of a mountain stream in spring time, and forming thereby a lake of some depth and size.*

sixty to seventy feet in total height, planted in the midst of enclosures and gardens, and suggesting to the untutored eye the fortalices of a feudal baronage. The real explanation is deplorably material and deficient in the slenderest element of romance. They are pigeon-towers, erected for the preservation of the dung and for the breeding of those birds, who spend the day afield and return at night to these comfortable quarters. The photograph which I present of a section of the interior will show that the towers contain an infinite number of cells and a well in the middle for collecting the manure, which is spread upon the melon-beds in the surrounding fields. They are opened and cleaned once a year, but I should imagine that the damage inflicted on the grain crops by the depredations of the birds would all but counterbalance the profit accruing from the distribution of their guano. In Chardin's time there were reckoned to be 3,000 of these pigeon-towers outside Isfahan, and we read in the pages of Olearius of the king stationing himself on the summit and anticipating the Hurlingham or the Monte Carlo of the nineteenth century by shooting the birds (which represent two varieties of the genuine 'blue-rock', and are called by the Persians *kabutar*, or 'the blue one') as they bolted from the apertures.

Above the low buildings of the city, as we draw nearer, emerge a blue dome and a single minaret. Presently the road passes between garden walls, and, through the familiar labyrinth of intricate lanes, we enter the former capital of Persia. Traversing the town, but avoiding its principal marts and thoroughfares, I came out on the far side into the Avenue of the Chehar Bagh, crossed the Zendeh Rud by the great bridge of Ali Verdi Khan, and having spent another half-hour in diving in and out of the still more intricate alleys of Julfa, arrived at the house of my host. Here I shall pause to give a detailed account of the past and present of the renowned capital of Shah Abbas.

Isfahan or Ispahan (the former is the commoner pronunciation, the *p* being softened into *f*, as in the case of Fars for Pars [Persia]) is probably the same name as the Aspadana of Ptolemy,[4] and may possibly be derived from the family name of the race of Feraidan, who were called Aspiyan in the Pehlevi dialect, elsewhere Athriyan. Whatever part, however, may have been played by myth in determining the nomenclature of the place, we need not admit the same element into a discussion of its actual history, which we will therefore not pursue into the nebulous period of Jamshid and his successors. Under the Achæmenian kings, a city named Gabal or Gavi seems to have existed on this site, and later to have become the Jai of the Sassanian epoch, which was captured by the conquering Omar in 641 A.D., after the battle of Nihavend. In the early Mohammedan period, about 931 A.D., the city, already known as Isfahan, passed into the hands of the Dilemi or Buyah dynasty, who ruled as petty princes in Fars and Irak, at which time it consisted of two quarters, known as Yehudieh, or Jews' Town, and Shehristan, or Medinah, i.e. the city proper, which were finally united within a single wall by Husein, the Rukn-ed-Dowleh, father of the even more famous Asad-ed-Dowleh, of that line. About this time Isfahan was visited by El Istakhri, who reported it as a very flourishing place, renowned for its silks and fine linen. Early in the eleventh century it was taken by Mahmud of Ghuzni, and next fell under the control of the Seljuks, having been besieged and captured by Togrul Beg. Nasiri Khosru, who was there in 1052 A.D., soon after the siege, found that the city had quite recovered, and occupied a walled space three and a half *farsakhs* in circumference. Benjamin of Tudela, a few years later, corroborates these dimensions, calls Isfahan 'capital of the kingdom of Persia', and says that it contained 15,000 Jews. Jenghiz Khan pillaged it; but was outdone in this instance by Timur, who, in revenge for an attack made by the citizens upon the garrison which he had quartered in the city,

As we approach the city the most conspicuous objects in the landscape are a number of large circular towers with smaller turrets projecting from their summits, sometimes sixty to seventy feet in total height, planted in the midst of enclosures and gardens, and suggesting to the untutored eye the fortalices of a feudal baronage. The real explanation is deplorably material and deficient in the slenderest element of romance. They are pigeon-towers.

ordered a general massacre, the fruits of which, in the shape of 70,000 heads, were piled up in pyramids of skulls. At about the same time that Henry VII was ascending the throne of England, 'Spahaun' was visited by the Venetians, Barbaro and Contarini, who found there installed the court of Uzun Hasan, or Long Hasan, of the White Sheep Dynasty. Thus we are brought down to the period when, always having been a capital city, though of a restricted dominion, Isfahan was promoted to the metropolitan rank of the entire Persian empire by the renowned Shah Abbas.

This great monarch would ill have sustained his own conception of royalty had he not provided for himself, and adorned with all the magnificence that an enlightened taste could suggest, a new seat of residence and power. Some chroniclers have attributed to him inferior or subsidiary motives: the unhealthiness of Kazvin, the distance of Sultanieh, the omens of astrology. Behind the superficial vainglory which he so dearly loved, lurked, however, an idea of true statesmanship. Of the new empire which he had won, and which stretched from Georgia to Afghanistan, Isfahan was the natural geographical centre. The instincts of a prudent centralisation commanded him to fix his capital at a spot where he would be within equal distance of all corners of his huge dominion, and where, in reasonable proximity to the Persian Gulf, he could at once overawe the maritime provinces, control the foreign trade, and enter into easy diplomatic relations with the potentates of Europe. This decision arrived at, he sketched the outlines of a colossal plan. A new city, approached by superb bridges and stately avenues, furnished with public buildings, as beautiful as they were large, and embellished by terraced gardens, and palaces, and pavilions, sprang into existence. The embassies of mighty sovereigns flocked to the new capital from the uttermost parts of Europe, and were received with all the splendour of a court immensely rich and versed in a fanciful and fastidious etiquette. The factors of great trading corporations occupied a position little short of the accredited representatives of royalty; and a life of gorgeous ceremonial, mingled with holiday festivity, rendered Isfahan the most famous and romantic of the cities of the East. It is fortunate that the cosmopolitan tastes of this great monarch—the contemporary of Elizabeth in England, of Henri IV in France, of Gustavus Adolphus in Sweden, and of Akbar in India—and his successors, should have tempted so many intelligent foreigners to the Persian court; for it is to their presence and, in some cases, prolonged residence in the city throughout the seventeenth century, that we owe a minute knowledge of the life and habits, the pomp and parade, the virtues and the vices of the Sefavi kings. Pietro della Valle, Herbert, Olearius, Tavernier, Chardin, Sanson, Daulier-Deslandes, Kaempfer, and Le Brun successively shed the light of an acute and instructed scrutiny upon the scene, and have added to the respective literatures of Italy, Great Britain, Germany, France, and Holland.

In the middle of the seventeenth century we have the estimate of Chardin that within ten leagues of Isfahan were 1,500 villages; that the city itself was 24 miles round; that inside the walls, which were pierced by 12 gates, were 162 mosques, 48 *madressehs*, 1,802 caravanserais, 273 baths, and twelve cemeteries; and that the various computations of the total of inhabitants varied between 600,000 and 1,100,000.[5] The figures of Olearius, viz. 18,000 houses and 500,000 people, do not fall greatly below the lesser total. No wonder that the Oriental hyperbole should have vented itself in the vainglorious boast that 'Isfahan nisf i Jehan,' i.e. 'Isfahan is half the world.' Kaempfer and Struys credited it, the suburbs included, with an even ampler circuit, which they fixed at sixteen *farsakhs*, or forty-eight miles. In the time of Abbas II the king possessed, in addition to his own numerous residences, 137 royal palaces (probably in many cases only private mansions) in different parts of the city, acquired either by inheritance, purchase, or seizure, and devoted to the entertainment of foreign envoys and strangers of consideration. When the former were received in public audience in the Chehel Situn, or Forty Pillars, all business was suspended for the day; a magnificent but tedious ceremonial preceded and delayed the approach of the ambassador to the footstool of royalty; gorgeous banquets, culminating in general intoxication, followed; while in the Great Square the populace were regaled with the exhibitions of wrestlers, fencers, jugglers, and acrobats, with polo-matches and puppet-shows; and with combats of animals, bulls, rams, buffaloes, wolves, and, on great occasions, lions and panthers. When night fell fantastic fireworks illumined and prolonged the festive scene. In one part of the city stood a great tower sixty feet high, and twenty feet thick, called the Kelleh Minar, composed of the horns and skulls of wild animals slain by one of the earlier monarchs in the chase.[6] The favour and the prestige in which foreigners were held, and the latitude allowed by the liberal-minded Abbas and his successors to the Christian religion, were exemplified by the establishments and churches of the principal monastic fraternities of Europe in the city. The Augustines, Carmelites, and

Capuchins were allowed separate quarters belonging to the Crown in Isfahan;[7] the Jesuits and Dominicans had convents in Julfa. Of the various factories, that of the representative of the British East India Company, from 1617 to the Afghan invasion in 1722, was situated in the Bazaar near the Great Meidan. It is perhaps only fair to quote, as a set-off to the doubtless exaggerated descriptions of some of the afore-mentioned travellers when relating the wonders of Isfahan, the cooler and more cynical verdict of the French jeweller Tavernier, who was not to be deluded by surface show or factitious pomp, but who mercilessly stripped the tinsel from the gilt gingerbread. This is what he said:—

Ispahan in general, unless it be the Meydan, and some few arch'd streets, where the merchants live, is more like a great village than a city; the Houses standing at a distance one from the other with every one a garden, but ill look'd after, not having anything in it perchance but only one pitiful tree.... As for the King's Palace, I cannot make any handsome description of it in regard there is nothing of beauty either in the Building or in the Gardens. Excepting only four rooms which they call Divans, I saw nothing but pitiful low galleries and so narrow that hardly two men could pass abrest in 'em.

As for the Christian Missions and monks, he entertained a very poor opinion of their propaganda, for he wrote:—

The number of the Religious Teachers is far greater than the number of hearers, for in all Ispahan and Julfa, take the Franks that come out of Europe, or born in Persia, as well men as women, there are not 600 persons that profess the Catholic Religion.

He further declared that the city was ill laid-out, the walls broken by great gaps, the streets narrow, unequal, and dark, encumbered with heaps of ordure and the carcasses of dead animals, and buried in summer dust or winter mire. We are justified, indeed, in believing that the pomp of Isfahan was limited to outer show, and to the appurtenances of royalty; and that, one grade only below these, were encountered the slovenliness and the filth of the unregenerate East. Such as it was, however—a strange but truly Oriental mixture of splendour and squalor, of dignity and decay— the city continued with little alteration till the first quarter of the eighteenth century, when the virtues of the reigning dynasty having been sapped by an inherited course of debauchery and intoxication, the capital and its monarch both fell a disgraceful prey to the Afghans in 1722. The horrors of the siege—when the Zendeh Rud was choked with corpses, when mothers devoured their children in the extremity of famine, and when the inhuman conqueror, after massacring all the princes and nobles on whom he could lay hands, surrendered the city for fifteen days to an indiscriminate carnage—have been powerfully described by the Polish Jesuit Krusinski, who was himself a resident in the capital at the time. From this shock, and from the brutal savagery of the Afghans, who overturned, and sacked, and defiled out of all recognition, palaces, and avenues, and gardens, whatever of beauty or grandeur met the eye, Isfahan has never recovered. It was patronised by Nadir Shah, but was less esteemed by him than Meshed. Kerim Khan Zend shifted the seat of Government to Shiraz. Agha Mohammed Khan Kajar shifted it again to Teheran, when he dismantled the fortifications of Isfahan. Fath Ali Shah sometimes visited the city, and ultimately died there in 1834. It has only once, in 1851, been favoured by the presence of the reigning monarch. Under the depressing influence of all these circumstances, Isfahan has fallen from its high estate, and now in perpetual sackcloth and ashes—no inapt metaphor to apply to the present appearance of the town—bewails an irrecoverable past.

The method which I shall adopt of describing the city will be to give an indication of its general features, and then, step by step, to visit its most renowned or interesting localities, depicting at each stage the contrast between a past of grandeur and a present of sorrowfulness and decay. The only plan of Isfahan that I know appears among the plates of M. Coste's splendid work, entitled 'Monuments Modernes de la Perse'. Roughly speaking, Isfahan lies to the north of the Zendeh Rud, Julfa to the south. In about the centre of the former is situated the great block of buildings, gardens, and pavilions constituting the Palace enclosure, and abutting on the western side upon the Great Meidan, a parallelogram, whose length is from north to south and width from east to west. South-east of the Meidan is the Ark or Citadel. From the western flank of the palace enclosure runs the Chehar Bagh, or principal avenue to the great bridge of Ali Verdi Khan, conducting to Julfa. Further to the east, a similar avenue leads down to the second storeyed bridge, known as Pul-i-Khaju. Older bridges exist at some little distance both to the east and west of these two structures, while between them a fifth conducts to the palace of Haft Dest.

The centre of Isfahan is the Meidan-i-Shah, or Royal Square, which is undoubtedly one of the most imposing piazzas in the world. It was laid out and surrounded with buildings by Shah Abbas; the king's palace, the principal mosque, and the Great Bazaar opened on to it; and it was both the scene of the principal royal pageants, and the nucleus of city life. This Meidan is of 560 yards in length by 174 in width.[8] It is surrounded by a long low range of brick buildings, divided into two storeys of recessed arches, one above the other. Originally the lower of these were shops, opening on to the Meidan, and communicating at the back with the big Bazaar, while the upper storey consisted of chambers with balconies, that were thronged on festival occasions. They have since been used as barracks, and now present a blank and deserted appearance. A row of trees was planted all round in front of these arcades, and in front of the trees was a stone-edged canal filled with water. In 1809 Morier reported that there was not a single tree in the Meidan and that the canal was empty. A scanty row of *chenars* and poplars has since been planted; but the canal was dry when I saw it, a substitute being provided by occasional fountains of drinking-water. In the centre of the Meidan, in the Sefavi days, stood a mast or maypole, twenty-five feet high, on which was placed, on great occasions, a cup of gold, but on ordinary occasions an apple or melon, to be shot at by archers passing at full gallop below.[9] Its place was afterwards taken by a more sinister object, viz., the *kapuk*, or execution pole, with notches on the side, by which the culprit was hanged up by the heels, and subsequently dashed to the ground, or else had his throat cut. This, too, has disappeared. Two great basins of water with porphyry coping adorned the two ends of the piazza, both of which survive, and are kept full. In front of the Ali Kapi, or Palace Gate, over 100 cannon, the spoils of Ormuz, were planted behind a wooden balustrade. These also have vanished. The only other permanent objects in the Meidan were two marble columns, which served as the goal posts in the game of Pall Mall or Polo, called *chugan*, which was very popular with the old Persian nobility, but has also died a natural death.[10] In the daytime the Meidan was all but filled with booths or tents balanced on poles, under which the petty hucksters displayed their wares upon the ground; but on great occasions all these were cleared away, and in the evenings were ordinarily replaced by the shows of mummers, jugglers, and acrobats, by groups of story-tellers, wrestlers and dervishes, by cock-fights and ram-fights, and by the tents of prostitutes. All these are gone, with the exception of a few stalls at the northern extremity.

Here there still stands in a bay or recess a majestic portico, flanked by arched galleries, and opening into the Kaiserieh or main Bazaar. This lofty and ornamental structure, in the main arch of which is a painting of Shah Ismail or Abbas in combat, is the Nakara-Khaneh or Drum-Tower of Isfahan; for here, in the flanking galleries, is dispensed the appalling music at sundown which indicates the residence of royalty, and of which I have already spoken at Teheran.[11] In the lower galleries, looking out into the square, the people used to smoke and drink their morning coffee; and here the paternally-minded Shah Abbas deputed *mullahs* to entertain them with serious discourse. Above the main arch, in a space still visible, but filled with modern tilework, was fixed a great clock (Tavernier alone calls it a sun-dial) which, according to Olearius, was made by an Englishman named Festy for Shah Abbas; but, the maker having been killed by a Persian, it remained out of order ever afterwards. Above the clock was a big bronze bell, which contained an inscription round the edge: 'Sancta Maria, ora pro nobis mulieribus', and had, in fact, been wrested from a Portuguese nunnery at Ormuz. It was never sounded, and nearly a hundred years ago was taken down and melted for cannon. The clock survived till the beginning of this century, and was seen by Olivier in 1796; but in 1808 it was removed by Haji Mohammed Husein, Amin-ed-Dowleh, and Beglerbeg of Isfahan under Fath Ali Shah, on the pretext of repairing the fresco in the archway.

On the eastern side of the square stood, and still stands, the Mosque of Sheikh Lutfullah, frequently called the Mosque of the Grand Pontiff, i.e. the Sadr or Chief Priest (Chardin wrote it Cèdre) of Isfahan. In modern times it seems to have been less frequented than was once the case; but its dome is still covered by the ancient enamelled tiles, with a flowing, almost Florentine, pattern. A little beyond, or to the south of this, formerly existed a tower, which the French writers called Pavilion des

The centre of Isfahan is the Meidan-i-Shah, or Royal Square, which is undoubtedly one of the most imposing piazzas in the world.

Horloges, or des Machines, and which was built for the amusement of Shah Abbas II by some of his European artificers. It contained a mechanical clock with marionettes and figures of animals that moved. Not a trace of it now remains.

In the centre of the southern or narrow end of the Meidan stands the Musjid-i-Shah or Royal Mosque of Isfahan. Erected on the site of a melon-garden in 1612–13 by Shah Abbas, and originally intended as the Musjid-i-Jama or Friday Mosque, it cost over 175,000*l.*, and was from the beginning one of the noblest fabrics in the city. Shah Sefi I covered its doors with silver plates. Inside were preserved the blood-stained shirt of the martyred Husein, and a Koran written by the Imam Reza. It has been many times restored, notably by Nadir Shah, after the Afghan usurpation, and again by Ali Murad Khan. A lofty archway framed in a recess, embellished with interior honeycomb groining in enamelled faïence, surrounded by tile inscriptions from the Koran, and flanked by two minarets with spiral bands of similar ornamentation, leads from the Meidan through a porch, containing a great vase or font of porphyry, into the inner court. Here the peculiar construction of the Mosque, already visible from the exterior, is fully apparent. The axis of the Meidan being almost due north and south, the architect required to incline the axis of the mosque considerably to the south-west, in order that the *mihrab* or prayer-niche might be turned in the direction of Mecca. This purpose was effected by architectural means that are at once grandiose and simple. The inner court, marble-paved and containing a great tank for ablutions in the centre, is surrounded by a two-storeyed arcade, undecorated save by bands of Kufic inscription in tile-work, white letters upon a blue ground. The arches are kept for the accommodation of priests and attendants. On either side rises a lofty tile-faced *aiwan*, a mighty arch in which opens access to a space covered by a low dome. The only Europeans of whom I know as having penetrated beyond this quadrangle into the mosque itself, were J. S. Buckingham in 1816, and E. Flandin in 1840. Opposite the entrance a third *aiwan*, flanked by minarets, conducts into the mosque proper, which is surmounted by the principal cupola, whose exterior, covered with exquisite tiles containing patterns in dark blue and green arabesque on an azure ground, is one of the principal landmarks in the city. On either side of the shrine are further courts, with basins and porticoes, to which the public are admitted on Fridays. The decorative treatment of this beautiful building, though falling, like all other works of art in Persia, into decay, yet remains a superb sample of the style of the Sefavi kings. The four minarets have never been used by the *muezzin*, the kings being afraid that from their summits too much might be seen of the secrets of the royal seraglio adjoining. Their place for the call to prayer is taken by an ugly and stunted cage on the summit of one of the *aiwans*.

We now pass to the western side of the Meidan, the principal structure in which, near the southern end, is a lofty building in the form of a great archway overlooking the square, and itself crowned in the fore part by an immense open throne-room or verandah supported by wooden columns, while the hinder part is elevated to a height of three storeys higher. This is the *talar* of the royal palace, and the porch below is the celebrated Ali Kapi or Sacred Gate. The name of the latter has been variously explained by different writers, some writing it as Allah Kapi, or the Gate of God, so called because of its extreme sanctity; others as Ali Kapi, the Gate of Ali, there being a tradition that Shah Abbas carried it off in its entirety from the sepulchre of Ali at Nejef (Meshed Ali) near the Euphrates, where he replaced the original by a jewelled substitute. The true meaning would appear, however, to be Ali (i.e. Aali) Kapi or the Sublime Porte. Its sanctity has now fallen into comparative abeyance, although any one sitting under the chain at the back, which is covered with rags as offerings, has

In the centre of the southern or narrow end of the Meidan stands the Musjid-i-Shaha or Royal Mosque of Isfahan. Erected on the site of a melon-garden in 1612–13 by Shah Abbas, and originally intended as the Musjid-i-Jama or Friday Mosque, it cost over 175,000l., and was from the beginning one of the noblest fabrics in the city. Shah Sefi I covered its doors with silver plates. Inside were preserved the blood-stained shirt of the martyred Husein, and a Koran written by the Imam Reza.

bast and cannot be touched; but in the Sefavi days it was great and unquestioned. No one might walk over the threshold; the king never crossed it on horseback; all recipients of the king's favour went and kissed the gate; and it was held an inviolable asylum, from which none but the sovereign could drag a fugitive, and he by starvation only. Tavernier gave still further particulars:—

Tis the custom of all Ambassadors to salute the Gate of Ali by reason of a white marble stone made like an asses back, and which serves for a step; being, as they report, brought anciently out of Arabia, where Ali liv'd. That day that the new King receives his Ensignia of Royalty, he goes to stride over that Stone, and if by negligence he should chance to touch it, there are four guards at the gate that would make a show of thrusting him back again.

From Thévenot it appears that this sacred stone was not situated in the gateway, but at the end of an alley leading from the Ali Kapi.

In the *talar* or open portal above, supported by twelve wooden columns and containing a marble basin in the centre, the king gave audience to the ambassadors at No Ruz; and there he sat to witness the horse races and polo, the wild beast fights and public entertainments below. The building, when I visited it, was unoccupied; and presented a very forlorn and deserted appearance.

This portal is the most advanced portion of the Royal Palace, the various courts and gardens and pavilions of which occupy an immense space, estimated by Chardin as four and a half miles in circuit, along the entire western side of the Meidan, terminating on the far side in the avenue of the Chehar Bagh. In this palace still lives the Zil-es-Sultan as Governor of Isfahan; but some of its courts abutting on the square are surrendered to public officials, and, in the absence of the prince, were crowded by the applicants for ministerial or magisterial favour. A ground plan of the entire block would alone reveal or explain its intricate and bewildering partitions. As is common in Persian buildings, all the beauty was showered upon a few special courts or halls, and there can never have been any general effect, either of art or magnificence. Tavernier, indeed, in a passage already quoted, spoke very contemptuously of its features. A few structures, however, always deserved, and still deserve, admiring attention.

Of these the most famous is the Chehel Situn or Hall of Forty Pillars, which was the principal *talar* or verandahed throne-room in the palace, where the king gave audience to ambassadors, and received his ministers in Levée. About the origin of the name there has been some dispute. As the loggia is supported by twenty columns only, the number of forty has been obtained by some too ingenious spirits by counting their reflections in the basin of water that stretches in front. I myself imagined that there might once have been a similar porch, with twenty more columns, on the back or

The porch below the royal palace is the celebrated Ali Kapi or Sacred Gate. The name of the latter has been variously explained by different writers, some writing it as Allah Kapi, or the Gate of God, so called because of its extreme sanctity.

further side of the central hall; and I have been informed that restorations, carried out in the past year (1891) have revealed traces of such an original addition. At the same time I can find, neither in the letterpress nor in the engravings of the old travellers, any hint of such a structure; and I have very little doubt, therefore, that the designation is merely a numerical title, intended to express size and magnificence. For this purpose the number *chehel* or forty is in common use in Persia. Persepolis is called Chehel Minar, or the Forty Towers; and other familiar appellations are Chehel Chashmeh (Forty Springs), Chehel Dokhteran (Forty Maidens), and Chehel Chiragh (Forty Lamps, commonly applied to a European chandelier).[12] The hall is situated at the end of a large garden, down the centre of which extends a tank which, when I saw it, was empty. A row of wires, stretched round it on tall blue and green poles, was a relic of a recent illumination. The gateways opening on to this garden are adorned with the heads of ibex, mountain-sheep, and similar trophies of the chase. The Chehel Situn was originally built by Shah Abbas; but, according to Krusinski, who was resident in Persia at the time, the greater part of the old fabric was destroyed by fire in the reign of Shah Sultan Husein, 100 years later; the latter monarch, who was childishly super-stitious, declining to interfere with the flames, whose ravages he regarded as a dispen-sation of the divine will. However, when they had fulfilled their mission, he set about rebuilding the edifice; a fact which, though it has passed unnoticed by every writer with scarcely an exception, doubtless accounts for the occasional differences between the present fabric and that described by Chardin, Tavernier, etc., in the days before Shah Sultan Husein.

The building consists of four stages or compartments. Of these the outermost is the pillared verandah. Its roof, which is flat and immensely solid, some of the rafters being composed of the boles of entire *chenars* or planes, seven feet round, and unhewn, is supported upon twenty wooden columns, in four rows of three each, and two rows of four each. The outer rows of these were originally covered with small facets of looking-glass, set diamond-wise in perpendicular bands; the inner rows with glass set in spirals. All these facings had, at the time of my visit, been recently removed, a vulgar resto-ration having apparently been attempted, with the result of irreparable damage to the artistic beauty of the fabric. The interior columns rest on groups of stone lions, each facing outwards, and the four central pillars stood formerly at the angles of a marble basin, into which the lions that look that way spouted water from their mouths. But the basin had been filled in, and the lions, too, had succumbed to a recent daub of paint. The walls of this beautiful loggia, whose effulgence drew from the rhapsodical Ker Porter the following tribute:—

The exhaustless profusion of its splendid materials reflected not merely their own golden or crystal lights on each other, but all the variegated colours of the garden; so that the whole surface seemed formed of polished silver and mother of pearl, set with precious stones,

were formerly covered at the bottom with a wainscoting of white marble, painted and gilt, and above with the beautiful *aineh-kari*, or mirror-work, set in facets in panels, for which the Persian artificers were justly renowned. The bulk of this superb decor-ation, which still remains in the throne-room behind to point the bitter contrast, had, on the walls of the loggia, been ruthlessly obliterated by the brush of the painter, who had left in its place a pale pink wash. Had I caught the pagan, I would gladly have suffocated him in a barrel of his own paint.

Immediately behind the verandah is the *talar*, or throne-room; and from this, but on a rather higher level, opens a deeply recessed compartment or dais, or Shahnishin,

whereon stood the royal throne. The decorations of this chamber, when I saw it, were still intact; and the prismatic flash of the mirror panels and facets on the walls, the painting in gold, blue, red and green on the coffered ceiling, and the honeycomb vaulting of the recess, produced a sumptuous effect. Out of the throne-room small compartments open on either side, that were intended for the king's ministers.

Finally, behind the throne-room, and communicating with it by three doors, is a great hall, extending the entire length of the building (Lumsden gives its dimensions as seventy-five feet by forty-five feet), crowned by three low cupolas, and adorned over almost the entire surface of its walls by six immense oil-paintings, three on either side. Pietro della Valle, speaking of the paintings in the palace at Isfahan in the reign of Shah Abbas, made the remark that they were so badly drawn that he was very apprehensive of losing the European artist whom he had brought out to take private pictures for himself, if the king should become aware of his merit. Notwithstanding this criticism, which is so far just that the ignorance of perspective, the ill proportion, and the angular stiffness apparent in all Persian portraiture might well have shocked a seventeenth-century European, whose vision had been trained in the school of the Italian Renaissance, these pictures of the Chehel Situn are both admirable as works of art and invaluable as historical documents. They transport us straight to the court of

The Chehel Situn or Hall of Forty Pillars was the principal talar or verandahed throne-room in the palace, where the king gave audience to ambassadors, and received his ministers in Levée.

the lordly Abbas and his predecessors or successors on the throne. We see the king engaged in combat, or at some royal festivity, enjoying the pleasures of the bowl. The big moustaches and smooth chins, and abundant turbans, represent a fashion of coiffure that has long expired. The arms and accoutrements of the warriors, the instruments of the musicians, the very gestures of the dancing-girls, open to us the locked doors of the past; and we seem to share in the feasts and fights, in the pomp and dalliance of the Sefavi kings. Whether these pictures are the originals that were painted by order of those sovereigns, or whether the originals were burned in the conflagration under Shah Sultan Husein, and repeated by command of that monarch, is not related. But from their correspondence with the description of Chardin I entertain very little doubt that four of them at least are the identical pictures described by him *circ.* 1670; that of Nadir Shah is, of course, a later addition.

I have found in the explanation of these pictures the same hopeless jumble of mistakes in previous writers that is the inevitable consequence of scant historical knowledge combined with perfunctory observation. On the wall facing the entrance are three of the six panels. One of these represents Shah Ismail engaged in combat with the Janissaries of Sultan Soliman. The redoubtable Shah is slicing the Agha of the Janissaries in twain, a red streak marking the downward passage of the royal blade. Adjoining is the picture of Shah Tahmasp entertaining the refugee Indian prince, Humaiun, at a banquet in 1543. The two kings are kneeling upon a dais; around are disposed the singers and orchestra, the bodyguard and royal falconers with the birds perched on their wrists; while in the foreground two dancing-girls are performing with gestures none too prudish. The figures are not far short of life-size. The third picture on the western wall depicts a scene of even more advanced conviviality, the central figures of which are Abbas the Great and Abdul Mohammed, Khan of the Uzbegs. There is the same background of royal attendants; but the carouse has evidently made considerable progress; for the king is holding out his cup for more wine, while an inebriated guest is lying in a state of extreme intoxication on the floor, with a flask pressed to his lips. This picture is said to contain a likeness of Ali Verdi Khan, the celebrated generalissimo of Shah Abbas, and the especial patron of the Sherleys. On the near wall are three corresponding panels. In one of these Shah Ismail at the head of his cavalry is engaged in conflict with the Uzbeg Tartars. In the second Shah Abbas II is entertaining Khalif Sultan, ambassador from the Great Mogul, with the usual accompaniment of musicians and dancing-girls, the latter performing with tambourines and castanets. The last picture represents the battle between Nadir Shah and Sultan Mahmud (mounted on a white elephant), that decided the fate of Delhi. The colours and the gilding on these pictures retain an extraordinary vividness. A portrait of the reigning Shah has been added on the archway of the roof between two of the ancient panels. The lower portion of this great hall, as well as the walls of the side rooms, have been painted an ugly green. There are four fire-places, two on each of the longer sides. In the past year (1891) the picture-gallery has been turned into a species of conservatory, being filled with flowering plants. Smaller cabinets originally opened out at either end, and were adorned with portraits of European ladies and gentlemen of the days of Shah Abbas. All round the Chehel Situn were, and I dare say still are, hung great curtains of needle-work and brocade, which were let down against the sun. Mounsey in 1866, and Madame Dieulafoy in 1881, found the loggia employed as a workshop for the tent-makers of the Prince-Governor. This particular form of desecration has been abandoned; and quite recently (1891) I hear of the Zil-es-Sultan as sitting in daily audience in one of the cabinets to receive the addresses or complaints of his astonished subjects.

Among the other pavilions or courts in the palace enclosure, which I have not the space more minutely to describe, may be mentioned the Sar Puchideh (of which Coste publishes an engraving), a hall of which the octagonal pillars, encrusted with glass, rest upon the shoulders of female figures in marble, themselves holding lions' heads which spout water into a basin; the Imaret-i-Ashraf, or pavilion built by the Afghan usurper; the Imaret-i-Nau, built for Fath Ali Shah by the Amin-ed-Dowleh, and containing many pictures of the king and his family; and the Talar-i-Tavileh, or Hall of the Stables, a part of the palace now used for official business.

On the extreme western side of the royal precincts, opening on to the Chehar Bagh, are a garden and building that merit a less curt notice. These are the Hasht Behesht, or Eight Paradises, a title which some writers have erroneously ascribed to the eight gardens bordering on either side upon the Chehar Bagh. The name, which appears, like the Chehel Situn, to be a numerical expression indicating size and splendour, was given to the place by Shah Suleiman when, in about 1670, he built this palace in a garden previously called Bagh-i-Bulbul, or Garden of the Nightingale. The chief building is a pavilion standing in the centre of a large enclosure. At its prime this must have been a remarkable structure, for it was thus described in 1677 by the rhetorical Dr. Fryer:—

It is a sweet Place, doubtless, were it cloathed with its glory; but as it is, it is a Rich Piece; the Summer House in the middle is saluted by two Channels, in which are Ships and Boats to represent a Naval scene of War; Swans and Pelicans find here their diversion; the Summer House is built entirely of polished Marble, the Arch of the Cupilo is Inlaid with Massy Gold, upon the Walls are depainted the famous Actions of their Heroes; the Tank in the middle is all of Silver, the Posts are stuck with Looking glasses, reflecting the Posture of the Body, and the Figures of the whole Fabrick; an Hemispherical Turret presses on Four Pillars which are the main supporters.

Even Chardin, enthusiastic but seldom sentimental, was inspired to an unwonted outburst by the charms of the Hasht Behesht.

When one walks in this place expressly made for the delights of love, and when one passes through all these cabinets and niches, one's heart is melted to such an extent that, to speak candidly, one always leaves with a very ill grace. The climate without doubt contributes much towards exciting this amorous disposition; but assuredly these places, although in some respects little more than cardboard castles, are nevertheless more smiling and agreeable than our most sumptuous palaces.

Later on this pavilion fell into decay, but it was rebuilt or restored by Fath Ali Shah, who in the main hall, covered by a dome and surrounded by galleries with small chambers in the angles, caused to be executed frescoes and oil-paintings of himself seated in state with his court, and mounted on horseback spearing a lion. Other contemporary pictures adorn the neighbouring walls, including one of Istarji, or Strachey, the English Adonis. This heptagonal pavilion, which is now neglected and falling to decay, is sometimes placed by the Governor at the disposal of strangers of consideration or officials of foreign governments. It stands in a garden laid out in parterres, planted with fruit-trees, and with avenues bordered with cypresses and *chenars*. Like all Persian gardens, this is no doubt very lovely in spring-time and summer, but at any other season of the year it has an unkempt and bedraggled appearance. Tavernier very truly remarked of the royal gardens of Isfahan, even at the zenith of their splendour, that

The Chehar Bagh, or Four Gardens, recalls the fact that the site was originally occupied by four vineyards which Shah Abbas rented at 9,000 francs a year and converted into a splendid approach to his capital. Of all the sights of Isfahan, this in its present state is the most pathetic in the utter and pitiless decay of its beauty.

You must not imagine that these gardens are so curiously set out nor so well kept as ours in Europe. For they have no such lovely borders, nor such close walks of honey-suckles and jasmin as are to be seen in the Gardens of Europe. They suffer the grass to grow in many places; contented only with a good many great Fruit Trees, tufted atop, and planted in a line, which is all the grace of the Gardens of Persia.

From the palace I now pass to the Great Avenue, already mentioned, that conducts from the centre of the city for a distance of 1,350 yards to the Bridge of Ali Verdi Khan. Its name, the Chehar Bagh, or Four Gardens, is not derived from the gardens that open out of it, but recalls the fact that the site was originally occupied by four vine-yards which Shah Abbas rented at 9,000 *francs* a year and converted into a splendid approach to his capital. Of all the sights of Isfahan, this in its present state is the most pathetic in the utter and pitiless decay of its beauty. Let me indicate what it was and what it is. At the upper extremity, a two-storeyed pavilion, connected by a corridor with the Seraglio of the palace, so as to enable the ladies of the harem to gaze un-observed upon the merry scene below, looked out upon the centre of the avenue. Water, conducted in stone channels, ran down the centre, falling in miniature cascades from terrace to terrace, and was occasionally collected in great square or octagonal basins, where cross roads cut the avenue. On either side of the central channel was a

row of *chenars* and a paved pathway for pedestrians. Then occurred a succession of open parterres, usually planted or sown. Next on either side was a second row of *chenars*, between which and the flanking walls was a raised causeway for horsemen. The total breadth is now 52 yards. At intervals corresponding with the successive terraces and basins, arched doorways with recessed open chambers overhead conducted through these walls into the various royal or noble gardens that stretched on either side, and were known as the Gardens of the Throne, Nightingale, Vines, Mulberries, Dervishes, &c. Some of these pavilions were places of public resort and were used as coffee-houses, where, when the business of the day was over, the good burghers of Isfahan assembled to sip that beverage and to inhale their *kalians*, the while, as Fryer puts it,

Night drawing on, all the Pride of Spahaun was met in the Chaurbaug, and the Grandees were Airing themselves, prancing about with their numerous Trains, striving to outvie each other in Pomp and Generosity.

At the bottom, quays lined the banks of the river, and were bordered with the mansions of the nobility.

Such was the Chehar Bagh in the plenitude of its fame. But now what a tragical contrast! The channels are empty, their stone borders crumbled and shattered, the

The Hasht Behesht, or Eight Paradises, a title which some writers have erroneously ascribed to the eight gardens bordering on either side upon the Chehar Bagh. The name appears, like the Chehel Situn, to be a numerical expression indicating size and splendour.

terraces are broken down, the parterres are unsightly bare patches, the trees, all lopped and pollarded, have been chipped and hollowed out or cut down for fuel by the soldiery of the Zil, the side pavilions are abandoned and tumbling to pieces, and the gardens are wildernesses. Two centuries of decay could never make the Champs Elysées in Paris, the Unter der Linden in Berlin, or Rotten Row in London, look one half as miserable as does the ruined avenue of Shah Abbas. It is in itself an epitome of modern Iran.

Towards the upper end of the Chehar Bagh on the eastern side, is a once splendid covered bazaar, through which one can turn aside to enter the Meidan. It is now empty and forlorn; but a short time ago was turned into stables for his *gholams*, by the Zil-es-Sultan.[13] On the same side is the entrance to the Hasht Behesht. A little further down stands a building that is still one of the spectacles of Isfahan. This is the Madresseh-i-Shah Husein, called also Madresseh-i-Mader-i-Shah, which was built, according to Krusinski, about the year 1710, by that monarch as 'a monastery for the Dervishes'. The Polish Jesuit further says that the chief gate was of solid silver; but he probably alludes to the chased silver plates with which the wooden doors are adorned. Beneath a deeply recessed archway, vaulted with honeycomb decoration, we pass into a dome-covered portico or vestibule, on either side of which petty hucksters sell fruit on stalls, and thence into the main court of the *madresseh*, which contains long basins filled with water, and is planted with flowerbeds and overshadowed by trees. On the right-hand side opens the mosque or prayer-chamber, flanked by two minarets and crowned by a dome. In the centre of the remaining sides are similar arched chambers. Two storeys of arched cells for the students extend all round, and the corners are cut off by recessed arches. But it is in the surface decoration of the walls that this noble building still arrests and compels admiration. A wainscoting of the marble of Yezd runs round the base; and above this the archways and recesses, the lintels and façades, are covered with magnificent tiles and panels of enamelled arabesque. It was one of the stateliest ruins that I saw in Persia. I was informed that though there are 160 chambers or cells, there were only 50 pupils, and that the *vakf* or endowment had seriously dwindled, being for the most part appropriated by the Government.

Before I pass from Isfahan to the southern bank of the river and to Julfa, I may mention a few other buildings of interest. Of these the most considerable is the Musjid-i-Jama, or Friday mosque, said to have been originally raised by Abbas Khalif Al Mansur, in 755 A.D. The successive restorations of Malek Shah the Seljuk, of Shah Tahmasp, and of Abbas II, have deprived it of genuine artistic value, and it fell into the second rank after the erection of the Musjid-i-Shah by Abbas the Great. But it still retains titular pre-eminence as the Town Mosque, though its minarets and quadrangle are in a state of decay. There is also another and older *meidan*, entrance to which is gained through the bazaars.

The bazaars of Isfahan are very fine, stretching for a great distance on the north and east sides of the Meidan-i-Shah. Several of them are unoccupied or but partially occupied; but those where business still centres are, next to Kerim Khan Zend's bazaar at Shiraz, the finest in Asia. All the life of the city throbs in the daytime in their packed and clamorous alleys; here is visible an ever-changing kaleidoscope of the unchanged Orient; and the crush of men and beasts renders locomotion slow and bewildering. From the main avenues open out immense courts or caravanserais, piled high with bales of merchandise; and here the clank of weighing-machines, the jostle of camels and mules, and the noise of human barter, are incessant. The European merchants have their quarters in these caravanserais or in buildings opening out of the main bazaar; and many was the business colloquy, attended with coffee and pipes, and protracted by interminable haggling, at which I assisted as an amused spectator.

In spite of its physical decay Isfahan is still the second largest trading emporium in Persia, yielding supremacy only to Tabriz. The English eye is gratified by the sight of English trade marks or figures on nine out of every ten bales of merchandise that pass on camel, donkey, or mule; and inquiry elicits the satisfactory fact that Manchester is still the universal clothier of Isfahan; and that though this city marks the northern limit of undisputed British commercial predominance, yet that ascendency is both firmly secured and shows signs of increase rather than of diminution. From the fact that the principal European houses of business in Isfahan bear foreign names—I allude to the firms of Ziegler and Hotz—it has been erroneously inferred that British enterprise has supinely allowed the trade of the city to pass into other hands. No more incorrect induction could be made. Both these firms, as well as the Persian Gulf Trading Company, who have a representative in Isfahan, trade almost exclusively in English goods; and the considerable profits accruing from their transactions find their

One of the spectacles of Isfahan is the Madresseh-i-Shah Husein, called also Madresseh-i-Mader-i-Shah, which was built, according to Krusinski, about the year 1710, by that monarch as 'a monastery for the Dervishes'.

way in the last resort as wages into the pockets of Lancashire artisans. It is a further evidence of the importance of British mercantile interests in Isfahan that Lord Salisbury has recently taken the wise step of appointing a British Consul to that place, his choice having fallen upon Mr. J. R. Preece, for many years one of the leading officers of the Indo-European Telegraph, than whom no better selection could possibly have been made.

Formerly Isfahan was famous for its armour; and a certain amount is now manufactured in imitation of the old. A good deal of the local industry appears indeed to be devoted to the reproduction of articles or styles that once won a world-wide renown. Of these, perhaps the most noticeable are the chiselled brass ware, in bowls, vases, trays, lamps, and ornaments (far superior, in my judgment, to the analogous products of Benares or Lucknow), the *kalemdans* or painted pen-cases, the mirror cases, and book-backs similarly painted and varnished; and the pottery and tiles, directly copying old patterns, which may be seen stacked in the curio-shops of Constantinople, or, for the matter of that, of London. Also celebrated are the *kalemkars* or printed calicoes of Isfahan, in which elegant native designs are stamped by hand-dyes on cotton fabrics imported from England, and the *kadaks*, a sort of nankeen, much used in dress.

At different times since the Afghan invasion, and the great fall of Isfahan, exaggerated and conflicting accounts have been given of its population. Amid their own countrymen the Isfahanis enjoy an unenviable reputation alike for cowardice and morals. They are inordinately vain of their city and of themselves, and in a country where lying is a

Musjid-i-Jama, or Friday mosque, said to have been originally raised by Abbas Khalif Al Mansur, in 755 A.D.

Musjid - i - Jama, Isfahan. Persia vol II. 40

fine art, are said to be incomparable artists. Their niggardliness and closeness in business matters are illustrated by a story told by Malcolm, which has been crystallised into the saying that 'The merchant of Isfahan will put his cheese into a bottle, and rub his bread on the outside to give it flavour'. Cowardly though the people are alleged to be, they have also acquired a reputation for petty disorder; and the *lutis* of Isfahan are justly regarded as the biggest blackguards in Persia.

Isfahan is also one of those places where a spirit of religious intolerance prevails or can easily be excited, its victims being as a rule the Jews, who are here treated with great contumely; the Babis, whose numbers are vastly on the increase, and against whom sallies are frequently stimulated by the *mullahs*; and in a less degree the Armenians and other Christian communities, who require to conduct themselves with circumspection. The arrogance of the clerical order has been very much augmented since the fall from high estate of the Zil-es-Sultan, as described in a previous chapter. When at the zenith of his power he maintained a style at Isfahan, and ruled with an autocratic independence that kept these unruly gentry in order; but, in his present contracted state of authority, he courts support or popularity wherever he can get it, and fawns upon those whom he once despised. A greater contrast cannot be imagined than between Isfahan a few years ago, and the same seat of government now. Then it was the capital of a prince who affected the monarch, and resounded with the pomp and circumstance of military rule; now it is the residence of a provincial governor, whose power is precarious, and who is all but destitute of armed men. Such is no uninteresting example of the operation in Persia of the irresponsible authority of the sovereign.

I have elsewhere mentioned that at the height of his power the Zil controlled an army of nearly 21,000 men. He took immense interest in the equipment and proficiency of these troops, whom he clad in a variety of foreign uniforms, and whom he constantly paraded for the edification of foreign visitors. One Kerim Khan, known as the Mir-i-Panj, commanded the Zil's cavalry in those days and still follows the fortunes of his master; but only 400 to 500 horsemen are now available, although in the barracks and stores, which were well built and maintained, are equipments and arms for 1,000 cavalry, and rifles and ammunition, it is said, for 10,000 men. The policy of the Zil, in treacherously slaying the Ilkhani of the Bakhtiari tribes, has permanently alienated from him those potent auxiliaries, upon whom a wise and ambitious governor of the central provinces would have relied for help.

South of Isfahan, and separating it from a number of former suburbs, of which the sole survival is the Armenian colony of Julfa, flows the Zendeh or Zaiendeh Rud. Rapid and rushing in its upper courses, it spreads over a wider bed as it enters the plain of Lahinjan, to the south-west of Isfahan. There its waters are largely drawn off for purposes of irrigation, and by the time the river has reached the storeyed bridges of the capital, though swollen in spring time to a powerful torrent, at other seasons it fills but a contracted channel or lies in detached pools. Below Isfahan it fertilises the districts of Berahan and Rudesht, in which its flow is regulated by the *bunds* or dykes of Ali Kuli Khan and Mervan. Later on its surplus waters are lost in the Gavkhaneh marsh.

In conclusion, let me devote a paragraph to the few sights of interest in the immediate neighbourhood of Isfahan. Of these the best known are the Minari Jumban, or Shaking Minarets, of Kalehdan, or Guladan, a village about six miles to the west of Isfahan. Here there is the tomb of a Sheikh Abdullah, though what particular Abdullah no one appears to know. His sarcophagus, a big rectangular chest, stands in an open, vaulted recess, and upon either side of the façade above the arch rise

(Overleaf, left above.) The famous Bridge of Ali Verdi Khan, the general of Shah Abbas, which is also known as the Bridge of Julfa, and the Pul-i-Chehar Bagh, from the fact that it conducts from the base of that avenue to the southern bank of the river. This beautiful structure, whose main features and proportions the march of decay has been powerless to destroy, is alone worth a visit to Isfahan to see; albeit a priori, one would hardly expect to have to travel to Persia to see what may, in all probability, be termed the stateliest bridge in the world. (Below.) At a slight distance below the Aineh-Khaneh, the Zendeh Rud is spanned by the second of the historic bridges of the Sefavi kings. The structure consists, in fact, of a bridge superimposed upon a dam.

(Overleaf, right above.) The king was in the habit of damming up the river, till it formed a great lake before the talar known as the Aineh-Khaneh, upon which he disported himself in boats with his ladies, and which at night was made the scene of fairy illuminations. (Below.) The Aineh-Khaneh, or Hall of Mirrors, from the glass facets that formerly adorned its pillars and walls, and consists of a great projecting verandah, sustained by twelve wooden columns, the inner of which repose upon the clustered bodies of marble lions.

the two minarets to an additional height of about twenty feet, the entire structure being of brick. A small spiral staircase in the interior of either minaret leads to the summit, which is pierced with open arches. An individual usually ascends the right-hand tower, where, by pressing against the walls and swaying to and fro, he imparts an oscillation to the minaret, which, passing along the intervening platform about thirty feet in length, is communicated to the other tower; so that both of them visibly sway in company with the operator, describing a deviation of several inches from the perpendicular. Writers have exhausted their ingenuity in the attempt to explain this phenomenon, which is, of course, attributed by the Persians to the wonderful properties of the defunct Sheikh. One traveller is convinced that the towers are connected by a chain concealed beneath the platform; another says that from the ground to the summit they are detached from and, so to speak, enclosed in the main building, which experiences and transmits the oscillation easily excited in the separate towers. Mme. Dieulafoy says that each tower has for its vertical axis a wooden framework fixed in the staircase, and can thus, when agitated, describe slight oscillations round its own axis. More probably the elasticity of the bricks and mortar employed have something to do with it, the vibration easily excited in one tower being then communicated along the tympanum of the main arch to the other. Dr. Wills calls them 'a terrible fraud', though for what reason I do not understand. There is no fraud, and

The Minari Jumban, or Shaking Minarets, of Kalehdan, or Guladan, a village about six miles to the west of Isfahan. Both of them visibly sway in company, describing a deviation of several inches from the perpendicular. Writers have exhausted their ingenuity in the attempt to explain this phenomenon.

still less is there any miracle. The only folly is that of the visitor who is in the smallest degree excited by so commonplace, even if uncommon, a manifestation.

At a slight distance from the Shrine of Abdullah rises an isolated rocky hill, the summit of which is crowned by some ruined buildings of mud-brick. This is called the Atesh Gah, from a tradition that a fire-altar was here erected by Ardeshir (Artaxerxes) Longimanus. The tradition may be true, but the present ruins are not old. Immediately to the south of Julfa the red rocky ramparts of the Kuh-i-Suffa (from an Arabic word signifying a house on a high place or terrace) frame the landscape with their gaunt and ragged outlines. In a recess or terrace on their northern front, less than half-way up and overlooking the capital, a pavilion or summer-house was built by Shah Suleiman, and called Takht-i-Suleiman, upon the site of a former hermitage. Only the ruins of the villa now remain, but the climb is repaid by the fine view. A neighbouring rocky height supports some ruins, also of modern date, but bearing the name of Kaleh or Takht-i-Rustam, from a tradition that the national hero built a fortress on this site. At the foot of the Kuh-i-Suffa was situated the famous palace of Ferahabad (Abode of Joy), to which its royal architect and master, Shah Sultan Husein, was so devotedly attached that when the Afghans invaded Persia, he was quite ready to sacrifice his capital if only the barbarians would leave him his palace. The latter was distinguished less for its buildings than for its wonderful terraces, and lakes, and gardens, which were the admiration of observers. The Afghans, it is needless to say, spared neither the scruples nor the person of the accommodating monarch. Ferahabad, having been hastily evacuated by him, was occupied by them and was burned to the ground when, a few years later, they were expelled from Isfahan. Its site is now a wilderness of ruins.

Both the name and the first inhabitants of Julfa were borrowed from the town of the same title on the River Araxes, in Azerbaijan. The main church or cathedral was built under the auspices of Shah Abbas by his imported colonists. Having lately been repaired and decorated with new tiles, it presents a smart appearance.

But little more imposing are the remains of the celebrated castle of Tabarrak, which was the deposit of the Royal Treasure under the Sefavi kings, and whose fortifications were described in such glowing terms by Chardin, Kaempfer, and others. Already, in 1704, Le Brun found them shattered and tottering, and the surviving walls are now little more than heaps of clay.

Truly, as he turns his back on Isfahan after completing the local itinerary, which I have here marked out for him, may the traveller observe, in the words of Shelley—

'Look on my works, ye mighty, and despair!'
Nothing beside remains. Round the decay
Of that colossal wreck, boundless and bare
The lone and level sands stretch far away.

---

[1] Saveh is interesting as being Marco Polo's 'city of Saba, from which the three Magi set out when they went to worship Jesus Christ; and in this city they are buried, in three very large and beautiful monuments, side by side. And above them there is a square building, carefully kept. The bodies are still entire, with the hair and beard remaining' (Yule's *Marco Polo*, vol. i. p. 73). The localisation of the home of the Magi at Saveh arose, no doubt, from a purely arbitrary application of the text in the Psalms (lxxii, 10)—'The kings of Tharsis and of the isles shall give presents; the kings of Arabia and Saba shall bring gifts'—whence it was supposed that one of them came from Tarsia in Eastern Turkestan, the second from Arabia, and the third from Saveh. No trace of either the sepulchres or the legend is found in the pages of any traveller in Persia subsequent to Marco Polo, and he himself said that, when he asked the people many questions, 'no one knew anything except that there were three kings who were buried there in days of old'.

[2] The name Kum is fancifully, but improbably, derived from *Kuh-i-mís*, mountain of copper, a mineral which is undoubtedly found in the adjacent hills. Its ancient name was Kumindan, or Kumidan, and it was one of seven villages which, in the eighth century A.D., were formed into a town, and called Kum.

[3] Dr. Wills mentions a single tower as containing 7,000 cells, giving accommodation, therefore, to 14,000 pigeons. Since Isfahan, however, ceased to be a capital, melons do not fetch so high a price; and, accordingly, the majority of the towers have fallen into ruin.

[4] Dr. Fryer (*Travels into Persia*, 1676, letter v.) is responsible for the statement that the pigeon's dung was used 'to supply the Magazines with Salt-Petre for making gunpowder', a use which is, I confess, novel to me.

[5] In illustration of the immense size of Isfahan, Chardin tells the story of a slave who fled from his master to another part of the city, opened a shop there, and remained undiscovered for years. He did not himself, however, think the population greater than that of London.

[6] Commonly attributed to Shah Ismail or Shah Tahmasp, but doubtless of later origin. Olearius says there were the heads of two thousand stags and gazelles that were all killed at one hunting by Shah Tahmasp. Chardin mentions the popular belief that the architect's head was placed on the apex by the royal sportsman, because he had said that the skull of some peculiar great beast was wanted for the summit. Engravings of the tower occur in the works of Chardin and Sanson. Herbert and Tavernier both declared that a great many of the skulls were human.

[7] Of these the Augustines were the first European monks who ever lived in Isfahan. Their first representative was Antonio di Govea, who in 1598 was sent by the Archbishop of Goa as ambassador for Spain and Portugal. The Carmelites under Père Simon arrived as envoys from Pope Clement VIII to Shah Abbas in 1608. The Capuchins (Père Pacifique de Provins and Père Gabriel) were sent out by Richelieu with letters from Louis XIV in 1628.

[8] Nowhere have I been so bewildered at the confusing and contradictory accounts of previous travellers as in their descriptions of the sights of Isfahan. They differ irreconcilably in their orientation of buildings, in their figures of dimensions, in the number of avenues, pillars, bridges, arches, &c. To correct or even to notice these countless inaccuracies would be a futile task.

[9] Angiolello saw Shah Ismail bring down seven out of ten shots at Tabriz, *circ.* 1510; and Tavernier saw Shah Sefi I, who was a great athlete, strike three cups in five courses at Isfahan.

[10] It was played by numbers varying from five to twenty a side. P. della Valle described a game that he saw at Kazvin in 1618. Abdul Malek of the Samanid dynasty was killed by a fall from his horse while playing *chugan*. Sefi I and Abbas II were both excellent performers. Ouseley has an erudite note on the game (*Travels*, vol. i. app. 6), but is very wide of the mark when he traces to it the Cricket of England and the Golf of Scotland.

[11] Chardin says it sounded at sunset and midnight; Sanson at noon, sunset, and two hours after midnight; and on fête days almost all the day and night. A passage in the *Ghazaliat* of Sadi seems to suggest a morning performance also: 'Till you hear in early morning from the Friday mosque, or from the door of the Atabeg's palace, the noise of the big drum.' Le Brun names the instruments employed, and they have changed but little: 'tambours. trumpets, tymbals, clavecins, hautbois, drums, flutes, harps, cymbals.' Thévenot says the trumpets were over 8 feet long. The custom is referred by Persian MSS. to as far back as the time of Alexander.

[12] To the same class, in all probability, belonged the Hekatompylæ, or Hundred Gates of the Greeks. We may also compare the Forty Thieves of Aladdin.

[13] In the early part of the century, a riot having broken out in this bazaar, the governor planted a cannon at its entrance, and fired straight down the central avenue into the crowd, killing or maiming everyone there—a slight contrast to the methods of Trafalgar Square.

From Isfahan to Shiraz

Out of the ivory palaces whereby they have made thee glad.—*Psalm* xlv. 9.

ALTHOUGH the European traveller will have made Julfa his headquarters during his residence at Isfahan, his post-horses will upon arrival have been obliged to return upon their tracks for a distance of over three miles—paid for as one *farsakh*—to the *chapar-khaneh* in Isfahan, and from there they will have to be ordered beforehand to come out again to Julfa when he is ready to start upon his forward way. Quitting the squalid and dusty precincts of Julfa and leaving the Armenian cemetery, with its shattered gravestones, on the right, the track mounts the slopes of the Kuh-i-Suffa, until we reach a point where, as the road dips into a hollow, we inevitably turn round in the saddle to take a parting look at Isfahan. There, outspread over the wide plain, are the cupolas and minars, the pigeon-towers and terraced bridges, the long avenues and straggling suburbs of the fallen capital. From this distance the pitiless handiwork of decay is blurred and imperceptible, and a certain majesty seems still to hover over the wreck of departed grandeur. I know of no city in the world that has ever struck me with a greater pathos, or whose figure is wrapped in so melancholy a garb of woe. The road descends to the post-station of Marg in a small desolate valley, in which, with the exception of a ruined caravanserai, it is the solitary building. After leaving Marg, the track climbs a steep acclivity, known as the Kotal-i-Urchin, or Pass of the Stairway, from the fact that steps have in places been hewn in the rock. This pass, however, although to the timid vision of Sir R. Ker Porter it seemed 'literally a ladder hewn in the mountain for the surer footing of the horses and beasts of burden, who, as we viewed them indistinctly from below, appeared hanging from the rock in the air', is in no sense remarkable, and is child's play compared with the famous *kotals* of the Shiraz-Bushire route that will be encountered later on. Having crossed the ridge, I cantered gaily along the level plain to Mayar, passing on the way a band of six Russians, who had excited great interest in Julfa by their mysterious movements and by the unexplained character of their mission in these parts. No one knew whether they were traders or Government agents. I entered into conversation with them; their leader told me that they were private travellers, journeying for their own amusement to Bushire, a statement which was belied by their obscure appearance, and was subsequently invalidated by the discovery that they were engaged on a sort of roving expedition to Abyssinia, for which place they ultimately embarked from Bombay. The character and quality of the men whom Russia employs on these semi-political undertakings, disguised under a mask of colonisation, are among the puzzles of the East.

Mayar was once a flourishing and agreeable place, and, in Tavernier's day, 'consisted of above 1,000 houses'. Its walls and towers are now in ruins, and almost the sole relic of the good days gone by is the caravanserai, originally built by the mother of Shah Abbas and afterwards restored by Shah Suleiman. This structure, which is built of brick upon a massive stone foundation, is now in a state of dilapidation, but in the early years of the century it was described by travellers as the finest erection of the kind in Persia. I do not know that Mayar or its surroundings possess any other interest, however faint, although the hills which surround its valley awoke in the bosom of the susceptible Porter a paroxysm of the most profound emotion:—

ISFAHAN TO SHIRAZ.

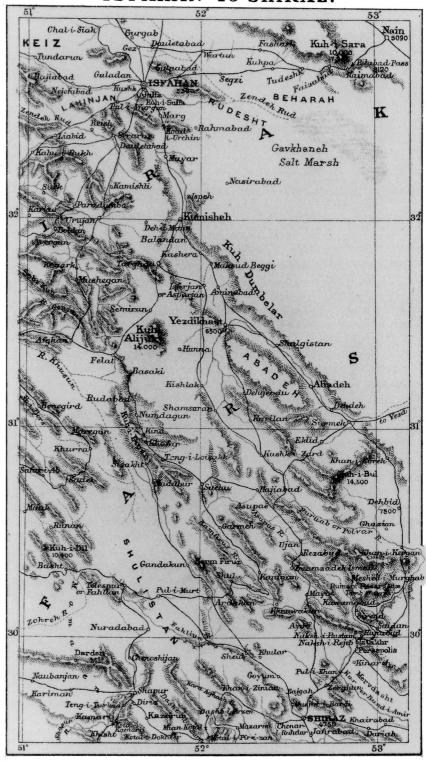

I might have thought myself again amongst the most savage tracks of the Caucasus, climbing the scarred ridges of a shattered, rocky world. The whole seems as if the Titans had really been at war, and this the scene of their tearing up the hills and pitching them against each other, to fall, at any hazard, in the pell-mell heaps in which they stand.

If the transports of the worthy Baronet have never served any other purpose, at least I have often been grateful to them for the relief they have imparted to monotonous sections of my journey.

The road follows the valley, which is barren and without interest, to Kumisheh. A confused vision of big pigeon-towers; of a tattered graveyard, to which a crowd was hurrying a newly-deceased corpse, with the strange mixture of irreverence and mourning that characterises a Mussulman funeral; of a tumble-down city with crumbled walls and mouldering towers; and of a large blue dome surrounded by old *chenars*, and gleaming fitfully through an opaque whirlwind of dust—still remains in my memory as I think of Kumisheh. This place, which is the Komsu of Della Valle and the Comicha of Chardin, was over three miles in circuit in the latter's time, though even then it had fallen greatly from the epoch of its prime under the earlier Sefavi sovereigns. Its present desolation is over a century and a half in age, having been inflicted by the Afghans in their northward march against Isfahan in 1722, a visitation from which the place has never recovered. The blue dome covers the last resting-place of Shah Reza, who is described by Chardin as a grandson of the Imam Reza, but appears more probably to have been his brother and a son of the Imam Musa el Kazim (the Forbearing). In the early part of the century the Persian Shiahs were much less fanatical about the entry of Christians into their mosques and sanctuaries than they now are; and we have records of visits by former travellers to shrines which are now only accessible at a certain risk. Buckingham, who, however, spoke the language and posed as a pilgrim to the Moslem shrines, entered the Mosque of Kumisheh in 1816,[1] and described its interior. The inner court, around which are cells for dervishes and pilgrims, contains two tanks, in one of which have always been kept a number of sacred fish. Two centuries ago the sanctity of these creatures was indicated, as Chardin and Dr. Fryer acquaint us, by 'their Noses and Finns being hung with Gold Rings; besides these here were Ducks devoted to as foppish a Maintenance'. The declining fervour or the more practical temper of modern times may be variously held accountable for the disappearance of these evidences of distinction, but the fish still remain. The tomb of the saint reposes behind a brass trellis or grating beneath the blue-tiled dome.

On the further side of Kumisheh extends a level plain, fringed by mountains on the left or eastern side, which was the scene of a battle fought in 1835 between the army of Mohammed Shah, commanded by Sir H. Lindsay-Bethune, and the combined forces of two of his uncles, the Firman Firma (previously Governor-General of Fars) and his brother, Hasan Ali Mirza (the Shuja-es-Sultaneh), who, upon the death of old Fath Ali Shah, combined to dispute the succession of their nephew to the throne. The royal forces consisted only of two regiments of regular infantry, some cavalry, and twenty guns—less than 4,000 men in all. The pretenders had a much larger army, but were deficient in artillery, in which Lindsay (or Linji, as the Persians called him) had a decided advantage. A mist separated the two forces, who are said to have been unaware of each other's propinquity until the Armenian wife of Colonel Shee, serving in the Shah's army, heard a shot fired in the opposite camp. Bethune then took the enemy by surprise, and aided by his guns, which battered down the walls of a deserted village in which they had stationed themselves, soon put them to flight. Marching rapidly upon Shiraz, he there took prisoner the two claimants and sent them captive to Teheran. The rebellion was thus crushed at the outset.

Several villages are passed in the hollow of the plain on the right hand, and eventually the hamlet of Kishara is reached lying in a depression at a little distance off the road. Here is a village and the *chapar-khaneh*, but the stage takes its name from the walled village of Maksud Beggi (a little further on and nearer the eastern valley-wall), which itself, according to Chardin, was named from 'the late Lord Steward of Persia', to whom it owed its elevation. On the next stage to Yezdikhast, a distance of twenty-five miles, I only passed one place on the way. This was Aminabad, the Abode of Trust or Safety, originally erected as a fortified redoubt against the Bakhtiari freebooters by Daud Khan, brother of Imam Kuli Khan, the celebrated Governor-General of Fars under Shah Abbas. For two centuries the locality continued to attract the hostile notice of those formidable tribesmen, and in about 1815 the whole place was rebuilt for the protection of wayfarers, the walled enclosure including a mud fort, a caravanserai, a mosque, and baths. The members of the early British Embassies to Persia and travellers in the first half of the present century were always instructed to keep a very sharp lookout in the belt of country stretching southwards from his neighbourhood to Dehbid; and in their pages Bakhtiari is a designation almost interchangeable with the name of robber. The nomads are now kept in better order, and Aminabad is no longer a necessary haven of security. Nevertheless, there are but few signs of life or habitation on this part of the southward track, so effectually have the risks and exactions arising from contiguity to the main road driven away a sedentary population. Neither on the road from Isfahan to the Gulf did I observe many signs of through traffic. Caravans of mules and camels are passed, but there is no general stream of wayfarers nor any migration of families similar to those so frequently encountered on the Meshed–Teheran road. If the present extent of traffic between the capital and the cities of Isfahan and Shiraz is of at all a fixed or normal description there would be some difficulty in filling a single railway train *per diem* between those centres. On the plains hereabouts grows the wild plant from which the gum ammoniac, or *ushak*, is derived, and which is more or less common in the hilly country from Kerman to Kermanshah.

A little beyond Aminabad, the administrative frontier between Irak-Ajemi and Fars is crossed; and we enter upon the province which, both in name, in history, and in population, has the best right to be regarded as Persia Proper, and as the central hearthstone of Iran. Fars, or Farisistan, is the same word as the Greek Persis; and, originally the title of a section only of the empire of Iran, has begotten the name which Europeans have, from remote times, applied to the whole. In this province were the capitals of the Achæmenian kings, Pasargadæ, Persepolis, Istakhr; here the Sassanian monarchs, whilst they favoured a more western capital, frequently resided, and have left, in close proximity to the palaces and tombs of their predecessors, the sculptured records of their own majestic rule; and here, in the cradle of the native race, a succession of ambitious soldiers of fortune, springing, as a rule, from a humble stock, found it possible in the early disorganisation and ultimate atrophy of the unwieldy empire of the Khalifs, to carve, with their own swords, the scarcely-disguised reality of an independent kingdom. The first of these was Yakub bin Leith, of Seistan, founder of the Sufari or Coppersmith dynasty, in the latter part of the ninth century, whose earliest conquests were Herat, Kerman, and Fars. In the reign of his brother and successor, the Khalifs recovered their sway, but only to cede it a few years later to the Dilemi, or Al-i-Buyah family, whose founder was a fisherman, and who, nominally as viceroys of the Khalif, ruled with great authority and splendour at Shiraz. Next came the Seljuk invasion. A Turkish general was appointed Governor of Fars, and managed affairs so skilfully as to transmit that office to his son, who again passed it on in like fashion, seven viceroys, whose rule extended from 1066 to 1149 A.D., being thus derived from the same family. Sunkur ibn Modud, a chieftain of the Turkoman tribe of Salghuris, who had been moved by the Seljuks from Khorasan to Fars, threw off the Seljuk yoke and proclaimed his own independence in 1149 A.D. It was during the reign of Abubekr, one of his successors, that Sadi, the poet, lived for thirty years at Shiraz, composed his 'Gulistan' and 'Bostan' and died. At this time Fars was an extensive and powerful kingdom, seeing that it comprised Kerman, Isfahan, the coast-line and islands of the Gulf, and even the opposite or Arab shore. When Jenghiz Khan appeared upon the scene, Abubekr was wise enough to proffer his allegiance to the Mongol, who responded by confirming him in his office, a patronage that was ratified a little later by the marriage of a Salghur princess with the son of Hulaku Khan. Here, however, the independent line of Atabegs terminated; and Fars remained a Mongol province until a fresh principality was created by one Mubariz-ed-Din Mohammed, whose title, El Muzaffer, the Victorious, was transferred to the dynasty of which he was the founder. It was during the reign of the fifth prince of this family that Timur first came to Shiraz (which prudently submitted to his arms), and there enjoyed that friendly interview with the poet Hafiz, that reflected equal credit upon the wit of the bard and the clemency of the sovereign. This was in 1387. A few years later, however, Shah Mansur, taking advantage of the Great Tartar's absence, ventured upon rebellion. Timur knew no mercy. The Persian army was routed, Mansur was slain, and all the princes of his house were put to death. After the break-up of the empire of the conqueror, Fars fell successively into the hands of the Turkoman Black Sheep and White Sheep Dynasties; from whom it passed with the rest of Persia under the sway of Shah Ismail, the founder of the Sefavi royal line; since which time it has remained an appanage of the Persian crown. Few territories have ever succeeded in retaining for so long a period, namely six centuries, the almost continuous reality of an *imperium in imperio*; an achievement largely due to the mountainous barriers by which it is on all sides defended.

In every book upon Persia that I had studied, I had read of Yezdikhast (explained by the old writers as a Pehlevi word, signifying 'God willed it') as a village perched upon a remarkable rock in the centre of a deep valley. Great, therefore, was my surprise, as I drew near the end of my stage, to see what looked like a low line of houses, just emerging above the level of the plain. This, I thought, could never be Yezdikhast; and I must have alighted once more upon the elastic *farsakh* of Khorasan. It was not till I was within 200 yards of the place that I realised my mistake, or that the exact nature of the phenomenon became visible. Yezdikhast is, truly enough, built on the top of a remarkable rock, and this rock does stand in the middle of a deep valley; but the latter, so far from being a valley in the ordinary application of the term, is a deep gash or trench cut down to a depth of over 100 feet, without the slightest warning, in the middle of the plain, the edge being as clearly defined as Shakspeare's Cliff at Dover. One is almost on the brink of the gully before one is aware of its existence. At the bottom flows a swift and dirty stream towards the east; and upon the far side the plain resumes its normal level at the top of the fissure, as though nothing had occurred to break its even expanse. Fraser said the trench was 200 yards in width, Binning half a mile. The former is much nearer the mark, but is somewhat below it. This extraordinary trench has exactly the appearance of the dried-up bed of a great river; and there is a tradition, probably founded on fact, that it was once so filled, and was navigable by boats. Fraser said that a road to Yezd lies for three days in the hollow; while Chardin declared that the latter extended for twenty leagues, seven to the east, and

A village perched on a remarkable rock.

thirteen to the west of Yezdikhast. But I am not aware that any traveller has either traced or surveyed its course; and I would recommend to some future explorer a march across the desert, by this track, to Yezd.

Right in the middle of this strange ditch, which was the old boundary between Fars and Irak, is a long, narrow hump of rock, from 300 to 400 yards in length, severed from the ravine walls on either side, and standing absolutely isolated in the gully bottom. Upon the summit of this rock have been built tiers of cottages, not unlike the man-roost of Lasgird, which I have described in my ride from Meshed to Teheran, to a height of perhaps 120 to 150 feet from the valley bottom; and it was the topmost storey of these edifices, peering above the level of the plain, that had looked, on my approach, like a Persian village of the familiar squat elevation. I own I should never myself have detected any analogy in the rock of Yezdikhast to the hanging gardens of Babylon; but the matter presented itself in a different light two centuries ago to the vision of the excellent Dr. Fryer, who wrote:—

Here, at Esduchos, was truly verified what might be Fabulously delivered of Semiramis's Pendulous Gardens and Summer Houses, there being Tenements made over this Moat out of the ancient Fortifications, barring the Persian Incroachments on their Confines, whose Mouldring Sands have left the jetting Rocks the bare supporters of these hanging Buildings.

Entrance to the village is gained at one spot only, on the south-west (Binning erroneously says north-east) side, by a bridge of wooden rafters thrown across the ravine and leading to a single low doorway pierced in the rock. When this drawbridge is removed or destroyed the place is quite inaccessible, and its inhabitants can laugh at marauding Bakhtiari or soldiers demanding a billet, or tax-collectors unduly extortionate. I entered on foot and made my way down the main street, which is more like a tunnel than a road, inasmuch as the greater part of it is underground or has been so completely built over as to form a veritable subterranean alley. Small vaulted passages diverge from this, and flights of steps lead up to the higher cottages, which have rude projecting balconies with wooden palings on the exterior. From any one of these a fall would mean certain death. I entered without hindrance a decrepit mosque, which is said to be the *imamzadeh* of Seyid Ali, son of the Imam Musa, who is reported to have endowed the world with an offspring numbered at 1,000—a performance that must have greatly stirred the envy of Fath Ali Shah, the philoprogenitive Kajar. The rock, with its strange superstructure, narrows towards the eastern end, where, from below, it looks like the bow of some gigantic ship. This was the spot from which Zeki Khan, the inhuman half-brother of Kerim Khan Zend, who had assumed the real sovereignty on the Vekil's death, while marching northwards in 1779 against his nephew Ali Murad Khan, ordered the leading inhabitants of Yezdikhast, one after the other, to be hurled down, because the villagers declined to satisfy his merciless cupidity. Eighteen had already perished. For his nineteenth victim the monster selected a *seyid*, whose wife and daughter he commanded at the same time to be delivered to the soldiery. This sacrilege proved too much for the tolerance even of his own attendants. That night they cut the ropes of his tent, which collapsed upon him. The villagers rushed in and satisfied a legitimate vengeance by stabbing the brute to death.

At the base of the cliffs are a number of caves hewn in the rocks, which are used as sheep-folds and stables. The *chapar-khaneh* is in the bottom of the ravine on the near side of the stream below the town. On the far side is a caravanserai, originally of the Sefavi age, but restored in the early years of the present century by a governor of Fars. Climbing the reverse side of the gully, I turned my back on Yezdikhast with the reflection that it was one of the most curious places I had ever seen, and continued my ride towards Shulgistan.

In summer an alternative route, lying more to the west and shorter by twenty-five miles than the postal road, is frequently taken from Yezdikhast to Shiraz. It runs *viâ* Dehgerdu, Asupas, Ujan (where Bahram Gur, the sporting Sassanian monarch, lost his life in a quicksand while pursuing the wild ass, from which he was named), and Mayin. But it is not to be recommended to the stranger, seeing that (unless a deviation be made) it misses both Pasargadæ and Persepolis.

Nothing of interest marked my ride over a desolate, gravelly plain, bounded by high hills on the right, to Shulgistan. There are a ruined caravanserai of Shah Abbas, and a dirty *imamzadeh* with a green-tiled cupola, covering the remains of Mohammed, a son of the Imam Zein-el-Abidin. A similar stage conducts to Abadeh, a large walled village, surrounded by numerous gardens, well-watered, and planted with trees. Having galloped on in front of the post-boy, I tried to find my own way to the Telegraph-office by following the wires, but got involved in the stuffy alleys and amid the blank mud-walls of the town. At the time of my visit Abadeh was temporarily celebrated for two young panthers, which had been brought up as pets by the officer of the Telegraph Department stationed there, and which roamed about his house and garden at their own sweet will; although having reached a period of adolescence they were rapidly becoming rather ugly customers. The place has a more abiding fame for the beautifully-carved *kashuks*, or sherbet-spoons, and boxes, which are made from *gulabi*, or pear-wood, and *shimshad*, or boxwood, in the neighbouring villages. The former, though wrought by simple peasants, are veritable works of art; the bowls of the spoons being hollowed out from a single piece of wood till they are almost as thin as paper, and quite transparent; while the handles are models of fragile and delicate filagree-work. The carvings for the box covers and sides are worked on thin slips, which are then glued on to a rustic box.

Continuous villages and evidences of cultivation border on the road, which continues in a south-east direction, from Abadeh to the next post-station of Surmek, whence a well-known caravan route diverges *via* Abarguh to Yezd. For several miles after leaving Surmek, we proceed along the flat, and then commence a steady rise till the sixteenth mile, where a deviation from the track, along the line of the telegraph poles more to the left, may be recommended to the traveller as saving him from a needless détour. The ascent continues by easy inclines to Khan-i-Khoreh, which is merely a post-house and a caravanserai in a bleak desert. Already, since leaving Surmek, we have risen 500 feet; but a further climb of 700 is necessary before we arrive at our next halting-place, which is the highest point on the route between Isfahan and Shiraz. Very desolate and unattractive is this belt of country; nor is Dehbid (lit. Village of the Willow), the place of which I speak, situated in its least unattractive portion. In the middle of a bleak upland plain, surrounded by a network of small watercourses, are seen the post-house, telegraph-station, and one or two huts that constitute the sum total of Dehbid. There is no village, and there are no willows. An artificial mound of earth is attributed by MacGregor to the era of the Fire Worshippers in Persia, and in the first half of the present century was called by the natives Gumbaz-i-Bahur, and explained by them as the site of one of the eight shooting-boxes of Bahram Gur. Dehbid is 7,500 feet above the sea, and though healthy enough from its bracing atmosphere, is considered one of the coldest inhabited places in Persia. A few days before my arrival the thermometer had registered twenty degrees of frost; but a change in the weather had fortunately occurred; and I found travelling very pleasant. The rolling hills and upland plains round Dehbid are the haunts of the Kashkais and other nomad tribes of Fars, who pass to and fro, at regular seasons of the year, driving their flocks to the highlands in the spring, grazing as they go, exchanging milk for bread, and thieving wherever they get the chance.

On leaving Dehbid the track continues to wind over the hills, until, at about the fourteenth mile, it crosses a stream by a very high-backed bridge of five arches, built by a recent Governor of Fars. Close to this is the large ruined caravanserai of Khaneh Kurgan, originally built by Kerim Khan Vekil. The stream is the upper part of the Polvar River, which from this point is almost continually with us, watering successively the plains of Murghab, Hajiabad, and Mervdasht or Persepolis, until it flows into the Kur or Bund-Amir, at the Pul-i-Khan. Following the valley down for a short distance the track then turns abruptly to the right, and climbs a big range of hills by a steep and very stony path. A succession of desolate valleys and ridges follow, until the source of a stream is reached that presently irrigates the villages of Kadarabad and Murghab. Gushing out in great abundance from the hillside it races down the slope, for all the world just like an English trout-stream. At the bottom of the descent, the village of Murghab is seen, clustered against the hillside in an open valley. The distance from Dehbid is reckoned as seven *farsakhs*, but is probably a little more, or about twenty-nine miles. It took me exactly four hours to accomplish, cantering whenever there was fifty yards of possible ground. At Murghab the stream was peopled by a number of wild fowl. I saw several wild duck, a number of snipe, which were quite tame, and

A squared limestone block, 11ft 7in high, whose upper surface formerly displayed the same proud assertion of authorship, while below it is sculpted in low relief—now defaced and indistinct from ill usage and the lapse of time—the famous winged figure that has been variously taken for the fravashi *or genius of Cyrus, and for Cyrus himself.*

The tomb of Cyrus.

a great many plovers. Riding down the valley by the side of a creek infested with these and other water-fowl, I crossed a second small valley containing the tiny hamlet of Deh-i-Nau, and passed over a slight acclivity into a third, which contains the ruins of the famous capital of Cyrus.

Soon after leaving the Musjid-i-Mader-i-Suleiman, the walls of which gleam like a white patch on the sombre landscape, we bid farewell to the plain of Murghab, and enter a lofty range of mountains by a fine gorge, along the base of which rushes the river Polvar. When the water is low, the bed of the stream, or its banks, provide a roadway; for seasons when the channel is full, a path, called Sangbur, has been hewn many centuries ago, for a distance of over fifty yards in the side of the lofty limestone cliff. Twice this dark ravine expands into open valleys, and twice again contracts into narrow defiles, admitting little beyond the track and the noisy river. So we continue for several miles, until, at the far end of one of the valley-windings, we espy the miserable post-house and imposing caravanserai of Kawamabad. This place takes its name from its founder, the Haji Kawam, who was minister at Shiraz fifty years ago. Turning to the left, and pursuing the same ravine, I came, after thirty-five minutes' sharp riding to the village and Telegraph-station of Sivend. The village, which is said to be inhabited by Lurs, is built in ascending tiers on the mountain side, while the valley bottom is thickly planted with vines. From here the track continues in a south-easterly direction, skirting the river, and arrives at the Lur village of Saidan, to which point there is also a shorter track from Murghab than that followed by the postal and telegraph route, running over the hills *via* Kamin. An abrupt turn to the right, or west, then brings us into a valley, bordered on either side by mountains and cut up by watercourses and irrigation channels, which, in the darkness, the sun having set, made riding anything but easy and pleasant, and caused my Persian servant to describe two complete somersaults over the head of his tired and stumbling steed. As we ride down this valley, we are approaching scenes of historic greatness, and on the morrow there lies before us the exciting prospect of a first day amid the ruined palaces and indestructible tombs of Persia's greatest sovereigns. At the end of the cliff wall that borders the valley on the right, or north, are hewn in the face of the rock the sepulchres of Darius and his fellow kings, and the pompous bas-reliefs of Shapur. At the base of the hills on the left lie the vanishing ruins of Istakhr, the capital of Darius. Round the corner of these same hills, but fronting in a westerly direction the wide plain of Mervdasht, into which the valley we have been descending here opens, is built out from the mountain side the great platform that sustains the columns of Persepolis and the shattered halls of Darius and of Xerxes. The *chapar-khaneh*, which the visitor makes his head-quarters while he inspects the monuments of the Achæmenids, is that of Puzeh, situated at the western extremity of the valley of the Polvar, which flows in a deep gully just below and almost on the site of the ancient Istakhr. Here he is within easy distance of all the ruins; and if the blackened walls, the smoky fire-place, the mud flooring, and the crazy, hingeless door of the *bala-khaneh* of the post-house at Puzeh do not constitute an appetising domicile, at least the wayfarer can reflect, with a positive gush of delight, that this is the last *chapar-khaneh* in which he will be called upon to spend the night in Persia.

The plain of Mervdasht, over which the monarchs of the Medes and Persians looked out as they sat in state in their marble halls, is a flat expanse, about fifteen miles in width from north to south, while its south-easterly extension is said to stretch for forty miles. *Kanats* and irrigation ditches, dug from the river, intersect it in every direction, and have always rendered it a fertile spot; though the decline of modern Persia could not be more pertinently illustrated than by the fact that, whereas in Le Brun's day, not two centuries ago, it contained over eight hundred villages, this total has now dwindled to fifty; while so inadequate is the control of the water-supply, that the plain often lies half under water, and is converted into stagnant pools and swamps. As I left Persepolis, after completing my study of its ruins, I was obliged to strike back in a north-westerly direction, in order to escape this network of watery trenches. Passing the village of Kushk, I then kept straight forward in a south-westerly line, towards the Pul-i-Khan, a very lofty bridge, with two main arches of irregular size and shape, which crosses the river Kur (the Araxes of the ancients) a little below its confluence with the Polvar. The conjoint stream formed a deep, wide pool below the bridge, and there was more water in it than in any river that I had yet seen in Persia. From the fact that eight miles further down, this river is crossed by a great dam, upon which stands a bridge of thirteen arches, 120 yards in length, the work of an enlightened ruler of the Al-i-Buyah or Dilemi dynasty, known as the Asad-ed-Dowleh, in about 970 A.D., its lower course has received the name of the Bund-Amir (*lit.* dyke of the Amir), or Bendemeer of Moore, whose rhapsodical description of its charms I shall allow myself, almost alone among modern writers on Persia, the luxury of not quoting.

From here the road continues towards the mountains that fringe the plain of Mervdasht on the south-west side, and, entering a deep bay in these, proceeds for a distance of some miles over an expanse that is occupied, in the rainy season, by a marsh, across which the track is carried for over a mile upon a narrow and irregular causeway. Turning a sharp corner to the left, we presently arrive at the village of Zerghun, famous for its muleteers, built at the base of a rocky chain. From a distance of about three miles from Zerghun, to the very outskirts of Shiraz—for this is the last stage that separates us from the capital of Fars—the post-road is one of the stoniest and most disagreeable in Persia. Its course lies over a succession of mountain ridges, in whose valleys and undulations, and over whose peaks and crests, it is conducted in a line that in many places resembles a torrent-bed rather than a made road. The ground is completely covered with loose stones and boulders, from the size of an orange to the dimensions of a football; and riding over these, particularly at any pace, is one of the most painful of human experiences. Rather more than half-way in a naked mountain-plain, at a spot called Bajgah, or Place of the Tolls, from the fact that there was formerly a station here of *rahdars*, or toll-gatherers upon the *kafilahs* or caravans, is a large, forlorn-looking caravanserai (mentioned by Thévenot in 1666) with a tank of water in front. It is after crossing the subsequent ridge of the Kuh-i-Bamu that we notice, by the roadside, a tiny channel filled with running water that accompanies us for some distance on our march. Lest none should guess it, let me say that this slender rivulet is no less a stream than the Ruknabad, which, rising in the hills twelve miles away, races gaily down to Shiraz, and was celebrated by the patriotic Hafiz in terms that would lead one to expect some less insignificant channel.

It was with no slight relief that, two and three-quarter hours after leaving Zerghun, and while descending the ultimate ridge of this seemingly interminable chain, I caught sight, in the opening of a mountain pass, of a great cluster of solemn cypresses, and, below, the shimmer of mingled smoke and mist that floated above the roofs of a large town, lying in the hollow of a considerable plain. This was Shiraz, which, in the words of its own singer, Sadi, 'turns aside the heart of the traveller from his native land'; Shiraz, the home of poets, and rose-bowers, and nightingales, the haunt of jollity, and the Elysian fields of love, praised in a hundred odes as the fairest gem of Iran. So overwhelmed with astonishment at the beauty of the panorama is the wayfarer expected to be, that even the pass takes its name of Teng-i-Allahu Akbar, the Pass of God is Most Great, from the expression that is supposed to leap to his lips as he gazes upon the entrancing spectacle. I confess that my own gratitude to Providence bore far less relation to the view, in which I saw nothing very wonderful, than to the relief which I experienced at having reached the end of this section of my journey. In the Sefavi days, an aqueduct brought water into Shiraz down this pass, but is now in complete ruin. In the rock on the right-hand side of the road is sculpted here a bas-relief of Fath Ali Shah; smoking a *kalian* with two of his sons; and hard by is another of

The pass takes its name of Teng-i-Allahu Akbar, the Pass of God is Most Great, from the expression that is supposed to leap to his lips as he gazes upon the entrancing spectacle.

159

Rustam transfixing a lion which holds a man in its claws. The end of this pass was formerly fortified and completely filled by an arched gateway, stretching from mountain to mountain. This gateway fell into ruin, but was rebuilt by Zeki Khan, who was Vizier of Shiraz in 1820, in the style and manner apparent in the accompanying photograph. In the upper storey, above the arch, is a chamber, containing, upon a desk surrounded by a wooden rail, a ponderous and monumental Koran. This colossal manuscript, which is said to weigh seventeen *mans*, or eight stone, and of which it is popularly believed that if one leaf were withdrawn, it would equal in weight the entire volume, is variously reported to have been written by the younger Ali of Imam Zein-el-Abidin (Ornament of the Pious), the son of Husein, or by Sultan Ibrahim, the son of Shah Rukh, and grandson of Timur. One may be reconciled to either legend, according as one prefers a sacred or a secular authorship.

In the Sefavean days a species of Chehar Bagh, or broad avenue, planted with cypresses, adorned with marble basins of water in the middle, and lined with rows of walled gardens, entered by arched pavilions, led from the mountain gate to a bridge over the stream that flows outside the city walls. Almost all traces of this approach have disappeared, and the intervening stretch of road is bare and desolate. The stream was all but dry at the time of my visit, though, when the snows melt, it sometimes contains a good deal of water. The panorama of the modern town contains nothing of distinction except three blue domes appearing above a crumbling wall and

A panorama of Shiraz of which the vainglorious saying runs 'When Shiraz was Shiraz, Cairo was one of its suburbs'.

Panorama of Shiraz. from the Haft Tan Garden.

Persia vol II

numerous enclosures thickly planted with cypresses, which seem, in their sable stoles, to mourn like funeral mutes over a vanished past. A low wall of mud, flanked with semicircular towers—both of them in a state of ruin—describes a circumference of between three and four miles, although in the security of modern times the suburbs have encroached upon and obscured the outlines of the earlier city. The valley in which Shiraz lies is about ten miles in width by thirty in length, and is completely surrounded by mountains, whose snows in winter heighten the funereal contrast of the cypress-spires. The population, which stood at 50,000 under Kerim Khan Vekil, 120 years ago, has not greatly fluctuated during the present century, but has usually been reckoned at 20,000 to 30,000; figures which indicate the stationary condition of the modern city.

I find in most histories that Shiraz (variously derived from *shir* = milk, or *shir* = lion, an allusion in the one case to the richness of its pastures, in the other to the prowess of its people) was founded in 694 A.D., i.e. subsequent to the Arab conquest, by Mohammed, son of Yusuf Zekfi. I cannot, however, accept this as a correct version of the earliest foundation, for I regard it as more than probable that there was a city here both of the Achæmenian and Sassanian kings. To a very early and ante-Mussulman origin must be ascribed the castle on the northern mountain and the great well, of which I shall speak presently. Again, there are, within a slight distance of the modern city—which, like all Persian towns, has shifted its site somewhat at different times—remains both of Achæmenian and Sassanian sculptures, which invariably herald the neighbourhood of a royal residence or capital. The former are of the same character and age as the Persepolitan edifices, and are thought by some to have been bodily removed from the Takht-i-Jamshid, while others have been inclined to see in them a later reproduction; the latter are inferior editions of the great bas-reliefs elsewhere encountered and described. I am supported in my belief by the ingenious Herbert, although I cannot say that the evidences of antiquity which he cites would stand the test of the modern scientific school.

Here art magick was first hatched; here Nimrod for some time lived; here Cyrus, the most excellent of Heathen Princes, was born; and here (all but his head, which was sent to Pisigard) intombed. Here the Great Macedonian glutted his avarice and Bacchism. Here the first Sibylla sung our Saviour's incarnation. Hence the Magi are thought to have set out towards Bethlehem, and here a series of 200 Kings have swayed their scepters.

However, no other record that I am aware of, beyond those before mentioned, exists of this ancient Shiraz. The later city was much improved and beautified by the Dilemi rulers, of whom the Samsam-ed-Dowleh, son of the famous Asad-ed-Dowleh, was the first to surround it with a wall, twelve miles in circuit, while the channel of Ruknabad had already been excavated and named by the Rukn-ed-Dowleh, father of the latter prince. The various dynasties of Atabegs, whom I have previously described, and who governed Fars, with Shiraz as their capital, still further adorned the city. Towers were added to the wall by Sherif-ed-Din Mahmud Shah. Ibn Batutah, in about 1330, said that its most celebrated mosque was that of Ahmed ibn Musa, a brother of Imam Reza, in which also was the tomb of Abu Abdullah, who wandered about Ceylon with a sanctity so well established that it was recognised even by the elephants. The mercy of Jenghiz Khan, and the vengeance of Timur have already been recorded. Nevertheless, the city continued to grow in size and importance—as a memory of which, in later days, the vainglorious saying arose, 'When Shiraz was Shiraz, Cairo was one of its suburbs'—until the Venetian Josafa Barbaro, in 1474, represented it as twenty miles in circumference, including the outskirts, while his countryman, Angiolello, said that it contained 200,000 inhabitants, and was larger and more beautiful than the capital of the Mamelukes. With the disappearance of local dynasties, and the centralisation of Persia, that followed upon the accession of the Sefavi line, Shiraz lost much of its importance; although the rule of Imam Kuli Khan, the celebrated Governor of Fars under Shah Abbas, invested it with almost the distinction of a capital; while the subject rivalled his sovereign at Isfahan in the beautification of his seat of government. The old walls, seven miles round, were still standing in 1627, when Herbert passed through the city; but these had disappeared in the time of Tavernier and Chardin; and the march of decay, assisted by a severe inundation in 1668, had made such wholesale inroads that both writers described Shiraz as little better than a ruin. So the town remained for nearly a century, the ferocity of the Afghans, and the anarchy that attended the fall of Nadir, accentuating its decline; until, in the hands of a second powerful and liberal-minded viceroy, it enjoyed a bright spell of rejuvenescence. This was Kerim Khan Zend, who, ruling at Shiraz as Vekil or Regent, on behalf of a Sefavi puppet, from 1751 to 1779, was practically sovereign of all Persia. He rebuilt the walls of stone, with bastions, twenty-eight feet high and ten feet thick, dug a deep fosse outside, and adorned the interior with a citadel and palace, and with beautiful mosques, *madressehs*, caravanserais, and bazaars. Indeed, whatever of stateliness or elegance remains in modern Shiraz, may almost as certainly be attributed to Kerim Khan, as in other Persian cities it must be to Shah Abbas; and the two are among the few monarchs of Iran who have deserved well of their country. After the death of Kerim Khan, there was a brief revival of the halcyon days under the ill-fated Lutf Ali Khan, at which time (1789) Sir Harford Jones, British Resident at Baghdad, was the guest and friend of that unfortunate prince at Shiraz. The triumph of the Kajars and their eunuch chieftain, Agha Mohammed Khan, involved a sure retribution upon the capital of the Zends. Its stone walls were levelled to the ground and replaced by the present mean erections of mud; the ditch was filled up; and Shiraz was degraded from the rank and appearance of a capital to that of a provincial town. Its government, however, remained an appanage of royalty, and has usually been held by a member of the reigning family. Fath Ali Shah was Governor-General of Fars during his uncle's lifetime. When Shah himself, he deputed more than one of his sons to the post, one of these, Husein Ali Mirza, the Firman Firma, utilising the position to embark upon an independent rebellion when the old king died in 1834. The speedy discomfiture of this pretender I have already related. He died, soon after, in Teheran; but three of his sons fled to England, where, for political reasons, they were much fêted, Mr. Baillie Fraser, the Persian traveller, acting as their cicerone, and were ultimately pensioned. In the present reign the office has been filled by various of the Shah's relatives, the most conspicuous of whom was one of his uncles, Ferhad Mirza, who, twenty years ago, earned a widespread reputation for bad government but pitiless severity, and whose son now fills the post with moderation and popularity. Fars was one of the many governments united in the person of the Zil-es-Sultan ten years ago, and was nominally administered by his son, the Jelal-ed-Dowleh, then a mere boy, the leading-strings being committed to the wealthy but extortionate noble known as the Sahib Diwan, who has lately been nominated to Meshed. In his long reign the Shah has never once visited Shiraz.

The interior features of the city are not to be compared for size or splendour with those of the more northern capitals. The Ark or citadel is a fortified enclosure eighty yards square, surrounded by lofty mud walls, with towers at the four corners adorned with bricks arranged in patterns. Its interior is occupied by the courtyards and pavilions of the governor's residence, which struck me as in no sense remarkable. When, upon his courteous initiative, I paid a visit to the Motemed-ed-Dowleh, the present Governor, I passed through two large garden-courts, one of which contained a marble dado of warriors sculped in relief and painted, a relic of the palace of Kerim Khan. The Governor, who is a first cousin of the Shah, is a man of about fifty years of age, tall, urbane, of polished manner and address, speaking French and familiar with European habits and politics, having, as he told me, visited Europe four times, and having accompanied the Shah in 1873. He also possessed a French-speaking secretary. In conversation he showed a thorough acquaintance with the strategical situation in Persia, and very rightly ridiculed a Bushire-Shiraz railway as preposterous. As I have said, he enjoys a good reputation, and is much liked by the English residents at Shiraz. The interests of the latter are officially represented in the city by the Nawab Haider Ali Khan; a member of a distinguished family once prominent in the Deccan, but for many years resident in Persia.

One face of the palace fronts the principal Meidan, which is a desolate expanse containing a number of guns. On its northern side is a large building, now occupied by the Indo-European and Persian Telegraph establishments, but formerly the *diwan-khaneh*, or audience-chamber, of the palace of Kerim Khan. An arched gateway opens from the square on to a fine garden, containing a *hauz* or tank, at whose upper end, on a platform, the face of which is adorned with sculptured bas-reliefs in marble, is the large recessed chamber, now filled with official bureaux and counters, that once held the twisted marble columns and the Takht-i-Marmor, or Marble Throne, previously described as standing in the *talar* or throne-room at Teheran, whither they were removed a hundred years ago by Agha Mohammed.

From the Meidan, access is gained to the Bazaar-i-Vekil, or Regent's Bazaar, an enduring monument of the public-spirited rule of Kerim Khan. This bazaar, which is the finest in Persia, consists of a covered avenue, built of yellow burnt bricks, and arched at the top, about five hundred yards in total length. It is crossed by a shorter transept, 120 yards long, a rotunda or circular domed place marking the point of intersection, where are a cistern and a platform above it, at which the merchants meet for talk or consultation. From the bazaar, gateways lead into extensive caravanserais, the most spacious of which appeared to be that occupied by the Persian Custom-house. In the Bazaar-i-Vekil were all the din and jabber, the crush and jostle, of an Eastern mart, which is the focus of city life in the daytime, and is apt to give to a stranger an exaggerated impression of the volume of business. In the increased activity, however, of the southern trade-routes in Persia in recent years, Shiraz, both as a consuming and as an export market, has borne its share. An immense trade in all European goods has sprung up with Bombay, most of the Persian merchants having agents in that city. The chief imports are cotton fabrics from Manchester; woollen tissues from Austria and Germany; loaf sugar from Marseilles (Russian loaf sugar stopping short at Isfahan); raw sugar from Java and Mauritius; French, German and Austrian cutlery and crockery; copper sheets from England and Holland; tea from India, Java, Ceylon, and China, and candles from Amsterdam. I found the Shirazis very apprehensive of the opening of the new trade route by the Karun, which, without interfering with their local traffic, would, if it superseded the Teheran–Bushire line as the main commercial avenue into Persia from the south, destroy their transit trade altogether. I had myself quite sufficient confidence in the temperate pace at which progress advances in Iran to assure them that there was no immediate ground for alarm. So obstinate is custom in the East, that to kill a caravan track that has been followed for a century is no slight undertaking. I found the chief exports to consist of opium, 10,000 to 15,000 cases of which were said to be despatched yearly from the neighbourhoods of Shiraz and Yezd; cotton, pressed in Bushire and sold in Bombay; dried fruits, especially almonds and apricots; and the famous *tumbaku*, or tobacco of Shiraz, of which the local crops appeared to be, for the most part, locally consumed, the bulk of the export to Syria and Turkey coming from other districts. The wine, for which Shiraz is famous, is also in such extensive local demand as to leave no residue for exportation.

Of the vintage of Shiraz I may here mention that there are two varieties, a red and a white wine, which are stored in jars and sold in glass bottles of curious shape, locally manufactured. I thought that some old Shiraz wine which I tasted was by far the best that I had drunk in Persia, an opinion which has apparently been shared by others before me, seeing that, two centuries ago, John Struys plaintively remarked that it was 'held in such esteem that it was as dear as Canary Sack in the Low Countreys', whilst Dr. Fryer, who may be supposed to have given a more scientific verdict, observed;—

The Wines of the Growth of this Country are esteemed the most Stomachical and Generous in all Persia, and fittest for common drinking, when allayed a little with Water, otherwise too heady for the Brain and heavy for the Stomach, their Passage being retarded for want of that proper Vehicle. It is incredible to see what quantities they drink at a merry meeting, and how unconcerned the next day they appear, and brisk about their Business, and will quaff you thus a whole week together.

Worthy doctor! His genial testamur would have raised a tempest about his ears, and have provoked a fortnight's controversy in the 'Times', had it been proffered in another country nearer home at the latter end of the nineteenth century.

Among the other manufactures of Shiraz which came under my notice, and for which the place is famous, are the enamelled bowls and stems of *kalians* or water-pipes, *repoussé* silver work, of which very elegant frames and salt-cellars with Oriental designs are fabricated for European customers; *khatem bandi*, a species of mosaic work in wood, brass, silver, ivory, and stained bone, small fragments of which are fixed in a bed of glue, and then planed smooth, the strips being fitted together as the sides and lids of very pretty boxes; seals, engraved on cornelians and other stones; and jewellery. Of the natural products I may mention the moss-roses and the *bulbul* or nightingale, which appears to be almost the precise counterpart of the English bird.

Shiraz, like most Persian cities, has its epithet of personal glorification, which is in this case Dar-el-Ilm, or Abode of Science, a pretension for which I should have thought that its notoriously convivial habits would have admittedly disqualified it. Nevertheless, for a city of its present size, it is well supplied with religious edifices, although these, alike by their size and decay, tell the story of a deposed capital rather than of a devout population. The oldest mosque is the Musjid-i-Jama, built in 875 A.D. by Amru bin Leith, brother and successor of the famous Yakub of that name. But little remains of the original structure, the whole being in a shocking state of ruin from earthquakes and the ravages of time; but in the centre of the main court is a small, square, stone building, reported to be a copy of the Kaaba at Mecca, with circular towers at the corners, presenting in blue Kufic inscriptions round their summits the date 1450 A.D. This curious edifice is known as the Khoda-Khaneh, or House of God. In the walls of the main fabric is also inserted a block of porphyry which is looked upon as a sacred stone. Another old building, in spite of its name, viz.

the Musjid-i-No, or New Mosque, an immensely large edifice, is in rather a better state of preservation, having luckily escaped the worst earthquakes. This mosque, which consists of a flat-roofed cloister round a court, is said to have been originally the palace of the Atabegs; but to have been converted to the worship of God by one of those princes named Ali bu Said in 1226 A.D., the *mullahs*, whom he had consulted upon the illness of his son, having instructed him to devote to the service of Allah his most valued possession. The only fabrics, however, in anything approaching repair are those erected by Kerim Khan, the most beautiful of which is the Musjid-i-Vekil near the Meidan, left unfinished by the Regent at his death and never yet completed. A *madresseh* also survives and is still frequently designated by his name; while another, styled the Madresseh-i-Baba Khan, in the vegetable market, is deserted and in ruins, although retaining traces of magnificence. The decorative treatment of Kerim Khan's buildings is less conventional and more secular in type than that of the earlier Mohammedan mosques, bunches of roses and flowers and bright colours being largely employed in the eighteenth century *faïence*, which depended more upon the splendour of polychrome than upon hieratic correctness. The largest of the domes of Shiraz, which are all of a somewhat elongated pattern, that has been irreverently compared to the head of a big asparagus, is that of Shah Chiragh, at no great distance from the Ark. It contains the tomb of one of the sons of Imam Musa, behind a silver grating. Other notable tombs are those of Seyid Mir Ahmed, in a good state of preservation, and of Seyid Allah-ed-Din Husein, another son of Imam Musa, which was described by Buckingham in 1816 as the then finest building in Shiraz. The tomb of Shah Mirza Hamza, outside the walls on the north, which was restored by Kerim Khan, has almost fallen to pieces, and its once conspicuous cupola has collapsed.

The life and beauty of Shiraz were always, however, extra-mural in character and location, and were centred in the umbrageous gardens and beside the poets' graves that have won for it such a place in the realm of song. The superb climate of the southern capital admitted of an almost wholly out-of-door existence; while the vivacious temperament of its people disposed them to jollity and to a life of light-hearted nonchalance and gay carousal. The people of Fars pride themselves upon the purity of their origin, the correctness of their tongue, and the excellence of their wit. No doubt we encounter here a less mixed Iranian type than elsewhere, as is evident from the darker complexions and clear-cut features, the brown hair and blue or grey eyes of the northern provinces being rarely met with in the south. 'In all my life,' said the amiable Herbert, who gleefully welcomed the opportunity of bursting into doggerel, 'I never saw people more jocund and less quarrelsome:—

> They revel all the night, and drink the round
> Till wine and sleep their giddy brains confound.'

A room in the house of the British agent in Shiraz.

Others have been more sceptical about the second attribute; the excitability of the Shirazi being a property that renders him sensitive and irritable, and sometimes prone to outbursts of intolerance. The Babi movement started here, and has always claimed a large number of disciples.

The character of Persian gardens, for its number and quality of which Shiraz has always been renowned, is, as I have explained in other chapters, very different from the European pattern. From the outside, a square or oblong enclosure is visible, enclosed by a high mud wall, over the top of which appears a dense bouquet of trees. The interior is thickly planted with these, or, as Herbert phrased it, 'with lofty pyramidal cypresses, broad spreading chenawrs, tough elm, straight ash, knotty pines, fragrant masticks, kingly oaks, sweet myrtles, useful maples'. They are planted down the sides of long alleys, admitting of no view but a vista, the surrounding plots being a jungle of bushes and shrubs. Water courses along in channels or is conducted into tanks. Sometimes these gardens rise in terraces to a pavilion at the summit, whose reflection in the pool below is regarded as a triumph of landscape gardening. There are no neat walks, or shaped flower-beds, or stretches of sward. All is tangled and untrimmed. Such beauty as arises from shade and the purling of water is all that the Persian requires. Here he comes with a party, or his family, or his friends; they establish themselves under the trees, and, with smoking, and tea-drinking, and singing, wile away the idle hour. Of such a character are the gardens of Shiraz.

The most northerly of these, at a distance of about one and a half mile from the city, is that known as the Bagh-i-Takht, i.e. Garden of the Throne, or Takht-i-Kajar, i.e. Throne of the Kajars. A palace was first built on this site by one of the Salghur Atabegs, named Karajeh, and was called from him Takht-i-Karajieh. Seven hundred years later Agha Mohammed Khan Kajar commenced the rebuilding of a palace on the same site, whose name, by a slight verbal transposition, became Takht-i-Kajarieh. The building was completed by Fath Ali, when Governor of Fars, and was occupied for three months by the Mission of Sir Gore Ouseley, in 1811, when on their way to the Persian capital. It stood, as the name indicates, upon the hillside, the conformation of the latter being utilised to construct seven terraces, one above the other, faced with tiles, with a long *hauz* or tank, called the *dariacheh*, or little sea, at the bottom, and a two-storeyed edifice at the summit. The whole is now in a state of utter ruin. The wall is broken down, the alleys, planted with orange trees, are unkempt and deserted, the pavilion is falling to pieces. In common with many other of the gardens of Shiraz, this is Crown property; but the notorious parsimony of the Shah forbids him from issuing funds adequate for their maintenance; and accordingly decay makes unimpeded progress.

Shiraz is famous for its metal manufacturers in copper and silver.

Copper Bazaar. Shiraz

I also visited the Bagh-i-No, or New Garden, on the right of the Isfahan road, leading down into Shiraz. It was new about seventy years ago, when it was constructed, with the usual features of walks, canals, and cascades, by Husein Ali Mirza, son of Fath Ali Shah. In one of its *imarets*, or pavilions, was a portrait of the latter monarch, seated in state, and receiving the British Mission of Sir John Malcolm. The walled enclosure is still filled with cypress and fruit-trees; but I found the summer palace at the top in a state of complete ruin, the wood-work crumbling away and the painting and stucco peeling off the walls. Water remained in a large circular tank, but was covered with an unsightly scum.

On the other side of the Isfahan road, and a little above the Hafizieh, is the Jehan Nemah, or Displayer of the World, which was known as the Bagh-i-Vekil in the time of Kerim Khan, but changed its name under Fath Ali, who, when Governor of Fars, built a summer-house here. It occupies a walled enclosure, about 200 yards square, but contains little beyond cypresses and ruin. In the early part of the century its central pavilion, or Kolah Feringhi, was in good repair, and was assigned to English travellers of distinction, of whom C. J. Rich, British Resident at Baghdad and the explorer of Kurdistan, died there of cholera, on October 5, 1821, and was buried in the garden.

Higher up, on the same side of the road, is the Dilgusha or Heart's Ease, which was laid out by Haji Ibrahim, when *Kalantar*, over a hundred years ago, and is irrigated by a stream that flows down from the Sadieh, a little above. In 1811 Morier reported it as in a state of ruin; but when I visited it in 1889 it was in better repair than any other garden in the outskirts of Shiraz, having passed into the hands of the Sahib Diwan. Its alleys and trees and tank were in good condition, and a large party of closely-veiled Persian ladies, waddling along like bales of blue cotton set up on end, had been spending an agreeable afternoon under its shade.

But, after all, the chief suburban glory of Shiraz is neither its cypresses, nor its tanks, nor its gardens, but its two poets' graves. The literature of a country never produced two more differently constituted exponents than Sadi and Hafiz, nor two whose opposite temperaments and philosophy appealed more closely to the moralising and the lighter-hearted instincts of their countrymen. Perhaps it is the predominance of the latter ingredient in the composition, at least, of the inhabitants of Fars, that has accounted for Hafiz' greater popularity. Sheikh Maslah-ed-Din, surnamed Sadi, was the elder by a century. Born at Shiraz in 1193 A.D. (some say in 1184), he lived to little short of one hundred years, although his enthusiastic countrymen have sometimes credited him with a considerable excess above the century. He was one of the greatest travellers of the Middle Ages. There were few countries between the Mediterranean and Hindustan that he did not explore in the guise of a dervish, being taken prisoner by the Crusaders in Palestine, making the pilgrimage to Mecca fourteen times, and assuming the religion of Vishnu in India in order to extend his knowledge. Well might he say of himself—and I cannot imagine a better traveller's motto—'I have wandered through many regions of the world, and everywhere have I mingled with the people. In each corner I have gathered something of good. From every sheaf I have gleaned an ear.' Returning from his peregrinations, the poet resided for the last thirty years of his life at his native city, devoting himself to literary production, of which his 'Gulistan', or Rose Garden, and his 'Bostan', or Fruit Garden, are the most famous. Sadi had not been long dead when Hafiz was born; this being the poetical sobriquet worn by Mohammed Shems-ed-Din, also of Shiraz. Of his life we know little, but his mingled vein of gaiety and mysticism, expressed in a hundred odes and sonnets, in praise of wine, women, music, and love, with a higher strain of allegory sometimes lurking behind, have endeared him to his emotional countrymen, while they alternately remind us of the odes of Horace and the Song of Solomon. It is disputed by erudite Persians whether the efforts of Hafiz' more abandoned Muse are to be literally or figuratively interpreted. For my own part, I would not inflict upon the genial memory of the poet the affront of misconstruction that has twisted the beautiful epithalamium of Solomon into an incomprehensible rhapsody about the Church. Hafiz died and was buried at Shiraz in 1388 A.D.

The Sadieh, or enclosure that holds the tomb of Sadi, is at the distance of about one mile from the town in a north-easterly direction, and lies just under the mountains. A garden precedes a building, containing some small rooms in the centre, and an arched *diwan* on either side, in one of which, with plain, whitewashed, unpretentious walls, behind a tall brass lattice or screen, reposes the sarcophagus of the poet. This is an oblong chest of stone, open at the top, and covered with Arabic inscriptions. A friendly green turbaned *seyid* did the honours of the place. A hundred years ago, when Franklin saw it, this tomb, which is the original fabric, was covered with a very ancient wooden case, painted black and inscribed with an ode of Sadi. In 1811, also, Ouseley saw a lid lying near; but I did not observe any such addition. In Tavernier's time (1665) the tomb 'had been very fair; but it runs to ruine'. Kerim Khan restored the building, without altering the sarcophagus; but at the beginning of the present century it had again fallen into such decay that Scott Waring in 1802 and Sir John Malcolm in 1810 offered to repair it at their own expense. It has since been subjected to some sort of restoration, but even now has a forlorn and friendless look. Hard by is a descent by a long flight of steps to a subterranean well, containing fish that are or were regarded as sacred to Sadi, the water proceeding from a *kanat* that subsequently irrigates the garden of Dilgusha.

Above the Sadieh is a place in the mountain known as Gahwareh-i-Div or Demon's Cradle, from a fissure or channel, leading to an arched passage, cut in the rock. A little to the east on the summit of a peak are the few surviving remains of a castle commonly called Kaleh-i-Bander (Ouseley says it is properly Fahender) supposed to have been a Sassanian structure. Here, too, are two wells, whose shafts are hewn to an immense depth in the solid limestone of the mountains. The largest, which is commonly called

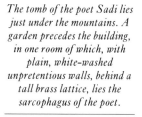

The tomb of the poet Sadi lies just under the mountains. A garden precedes the building, in one room of which, with plain, white-washed unpretentious walls, behind a tall brass lattice, lies the sarcophagus of the poet.

Chah Ali Bunder, is of unknown or uncertain depth. Chardin said he rehearsed a *paternoster* before a stone reached the bottom. Le Brun reported 420 feet and Stack 500 feet, but Morier's servant claimed to have measured a depth of 350 yards, while Dr. Wills let down 600 yards of string and never reached the bottom. I merely mention these conflicting estimates as illustrations of the ambiguity that is found in travellers' descriptions of almost every site or object in Persia. The seventeenth century writers said that in former days women convicted of adultery were pitched down this well; but Dr. Wills speaks of this summary mode of execution as a recent practice. Whatever be the history or origin or these remarkable shafts, for which of course the natives have a miraculous explanation, they undoubtedly appertain to a time long anterior to Mussulman days, when the hill in which they are sunk was occupied by a considerable fortress and used as a place of strength. The third well, which is called Chah-i-Murtaza Ali, is situated in a grotto hewn out of the rock, and is visited by pilgrims who regard its waters as sacred.

Nearer the city, and on the outskirts of its northern suburbs, the tomb of Hafiz stands in a cemetery crowded with Moslem graves. The enclosure, known as the Hafizieh, consists of an upper and a lower part, i.e. the graveyard and a garden, separated by a summer-house. The cemetery is of comparatively modern growth; for ancient authors describe the poet's tomb as surrounded by trees, the last survivor of which, a cypress, said to have been planted by himself at the head of his grave, was cut down about 1814 A.D. The copy of the poet's works that was once chained to the tomb was carried off by Ashraf the Afghan. Nadir Shah, having come here and been opportunely presented with an encouraging *fal* or fortune from the manuscript kept by the *mullahs*, embellished and repaired the tomb. But the original marble slab on which was said to have been sculped a cypress, was taken away by Kerim Khan, who built it into the tank in the Jehan Nemah, and replaced it by the present sarcophagus. This is made of yellow Yezd marble, and has two odes from the Diwan, or collection of the poet's works, beautifully chiselled in relief in a number of elegant panels upon its lid. Of that which is sculped on the centre panels I have made a translation in elegiacs, a metre that seems to me to do least offence to the structure and spirit of the original:—

Tell the glad tidings abroad that my soul may arise in communion,
    I, with celestial wings, rise from the snares of the world.
Didst thou but call me to come and wait as a slave on thy bidding,
    Yet should I rise in esteem over the lords of the world.
Lord, may the cloud of Thy mercy descend in raindrops upon me,
    Now ere my body arise, scattered as dust on the wind.
Sit on my tomb, ye friends, with mirth of minstrel and flagon,
    So shall I rise from the grave dancing, aglow with desire.
Though I be old, one night do thou lie in my loving embraces,
    Then from thy side in the morn fresh in my youth shall I rise.
Image of deeds that are lovely, on high shine forth, that as Hafiz
    I from the grave may arise, soar above life and the world.

A frail iron railing now surrounds the tomb, which is visited by bands of admiring pilgrims, on devotional or festive aim intent; but I confess I think that in any other country in the world a greater distinction would encompass the last resting-place of a national hero and the object of adoration to millions. It is interesting to contrast the grave of the Persian poet with that of his European contemporary, Dante, whose sepulchre is not less an object of pilgrimage at Ravenna.

Adjoining the Hafizieh are two other enclosures, which are also consecrated by much-respected graves. Of these, one is the Chehel Tan, or Forty Bodies, so called from forty dervishes who were there interred, and were, I suppose, very eminent personages in their day. The other is the Haft Tan, or Seven Bodies, built by Kerim Khan over the remains of seven other holy persons, as well, it is said, as of Sultan Shuja, one of the old princes of Fars. The pavilion at the upper end of this garden contains, or contained (for I did not see its interior), a number of paintings of Bible scenes (e.g. Abraham and Isaac, Moses tending Jethro's flocks, etc.), as well as two illustrations of Sadi and Hafiz. These pictures are of no antiquity, nor is there any reason to suppose that they are likenesses. Sadi is depicted as an old man with a white beard, an axe over his shoulder, and a dervish's begging-bowl in his right hand. Hafiz is a much younger man, with an immense pair of black moustaches and a huge club.

Such is a fairly complete summary of the buildings and charms, or shall I not rather say the ruins and mourning, of modern Shiraz. It is, perhaps, difficult for a foreigner to place himself in the precise mental or emotional environment that would enable him to comprehend the extraordinary effect which these have long exercised, and continue to exercise, over the imagination of Persians. I can believe that in spring-time, when the plain is a sea of verdure, and the brooks dispense a welcome coolness as they run beneath the trees, and a brilliant sun shines from the undimmed sky, the gardens of Shiraz may constitute an agreeable retreat. But it is impossible to avoid the conclusion that, in the eyes of the Shirazi, every local goose is a swan, and that there neither is nor has been in the site and surroundings of the city anything to excite such extravagance

The tomb of Hafiz stands in a cemetery crowded with Moslem graves. The copy of the poet's works that was once chained to the tomb was carried off by Ashraf the Afghan.

of laudation. The place is very liable to earthquakes, by one of which in 1855 half the houses are said to have been destroyed, and 10,000 persons to have perished. Some writers, notably Kinneir and Rich (the latter little thinking that he was going to die there), have extolled the climate of Shiraz as among the finest in the world; but this opinion does not appear to be altogether shared by modern European residents. The atmosphere is dry, and certainly far more equable than in the north; but intermittent fever is very rife, and is attributed by some to miasma arising from the abundance of stagnant water.

About seven miles in a south-easterly direction from the city is a swamp called Karabagh, from the mountains by which it is overhung on the south. Here, in the reed-beds and on the marsh, I enjoyed a good day's snipe-shooting, there being a great number of birds. This marsh lies at the upper end of a valley, the lower extremity of which is filled by the salt-lake of Maharlu, some twenty miles in length, into which flows the stream that irrigates the plain of Shiraz. Along its southern shore runs the caravan-track to Sarvistan, Fasa, and Darab. Further to the north-east is the second largest lake in Persia, known as the Daria-i-Niriz, or Bakhtegan, which possesses a very indented and fantastic outline, being almost divided into two lakes by a big projecting promontory or island. Though the chief confluent of this lake is the Bund-Amir, or Kur river, which I have previously traced from Persepolis, its waters, which are fre-quented by flamingoes and wild fowl, are extremely salty, and, in dry seasons, the desiccated bed is found to be covered with a thick saline incrustation. It is doubtful, indeed, whether we ought to describe this expanse of water as a lake, seeing that it is, in reality, only an area under more or less permanent inundation. There is no depth of water, Captain Wells having walked in for a quarter of a mile without getting above his knees. It would appear from the negative evidence of history that the lake cannot be of very ancient origin seeing that it is never mentioned by the ancient writers.

(Overleaf.) Pages from Curzon's photographic album.

Plan of Persepolis.

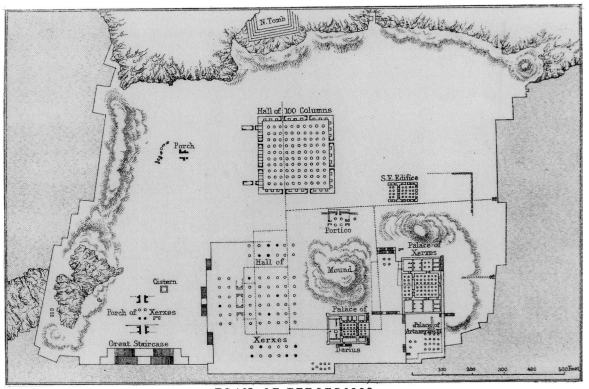

PLAN OF PERSEPOLIS.

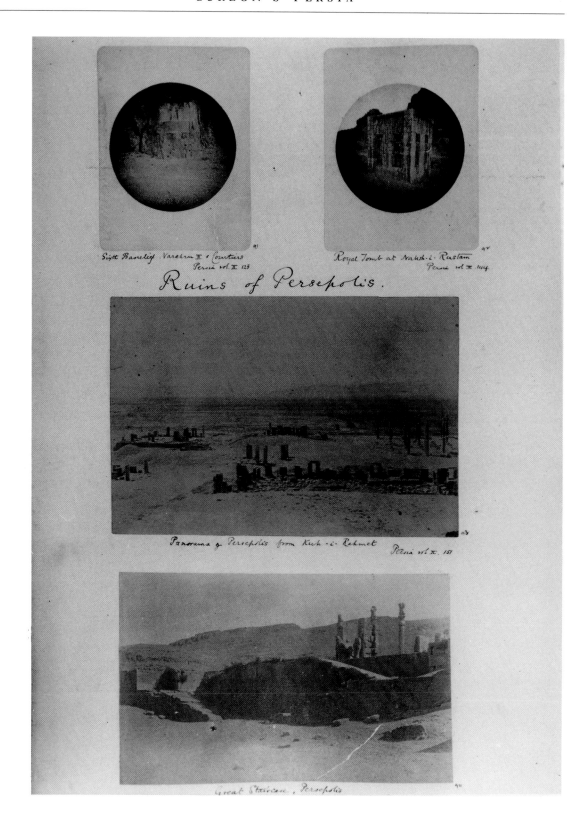

Sixth Baselief. Varahru II & Courtiers
Persia vol II 123

Royal Tomb at Naksh-i-Rustam
Persia vol II 114

Ruins of Persepolis.

Panorama of Persepolis from Kuh-i-Rehmet
Persia vol II 151

Great Staircase, Persepolis

At a distance of forty miles to the north of Shiraz, within easy reach and almost within sight of each other, is grouped in all probability the most considerable collection of important remains, belonging to widely different historical periods, that so circumscribed an area can anywhere display. They belong to two epochs, the Achaemenian and the Sassanian, and they represent three forms of antiquarian art: the structure of palaces, the excavation of rock-tombs, and the chiselling in high relief of sculptures on stone.

(Below.) The palace-platform, which, with its ruins, has for over two centuries been accepted as the Persepolis that Alexander captured and burned, and in the last quarter of that period has been proved, by the inscriptions.

Palace of Xerxes. Persepolis.

wild pinks, mallows, and some flowers of the convolvulus, and other genera which I had never seen before. This being the spring season they were all in blow, and gave an enchanting effect to the scene, which reminded me of a summer's day in England.

The Frenchman, Petis de la Croix, was at Khisht in 1674, and found it so hot that he spent the whole day lying in the river, where he said that he was surrounded by hundreds of fish, who nosed him all over, and were so tame that he caught as many as he pleased with his hands.

For three and a half miles from Konar Takhteh, the track lies across the plain to the south, and then, mounting a slight rise, takes a downward plunge of 1,000 feet, in the Kotal-i-Mallu, or Cursed Pass. The curses are, in all probability, those of the ascending, and not of the descending wayfarer; for it is with the most profound relief that the latter contemplates the approaching exhaustion of the horrors of the Tengistan *kotals*; and tears of joy are far more likely to leap from his eyes than oaths from his lips. Nor is the Kotal-i-Mallu either so precipitous, so stony, or so uncomfortable as those which have preceded it; although the first part is steep, and recalls the definition that was once given a Persian *kotal*, as the kind of mark that would be left by the impression of a gigantic corkscrew on the vertical side of a mountain. A causeway had at some time been built in zigzags up the side of this *kotal*, and was in better preservation than any work of the kind that I had seen in Persia. Its surface, however, was so slippery that it had prudently been abandoned by the caravans, which had worn a tortuous stairway in the rock alongside of it.

From a gorge far down below came the welcome roar of waters; and at a turn in the descent was visible the blue current of the so-called Daliki river, racing merrily towards the south-west. This river rises in the mountains of Fars to the south of Shiraz, runs north-west under different names, the commonest of which it derives from the village of Daliki, which it presently waters, and, having reached the Dashtistan or Plain-land, joins the Shapur river, of which I have already spoken, the two falling into the Gulf to the north of Bushire under the name of Rohillah (Rud-hillah) or Rud-i-Shapur. From the summit of the *kotal* to the banks of the river was an easy walk of one hour and twenty minutes. A light breeze ruffled the stream, which here spreads out into a wide pool, and I observed fish rising everywhere to natural flies. The road now follows, for a little over a mile, the right bank of the river, passing a ruined bridge, all but one or two arches of which have disappeared, and then crosses the stream by a fine stone bridge of six arches, terminating in a causeway on the far side. This bridge and its pavement were both in better preservation than any kindred structure that I had seen in Persia, and were the work of the Mushir-el-Mulk before mentioned. A lofty square tower guards the north entrance to the bridge; and a seedy patrol, armed with a percussion musket, was taking an airing on the parapet. Traffic over the passes is now comparatively safe, although it is not twenty years since no party could proceed without an armed guard; but a few *rahdars* or sentinels are still stationed on the road, their maintenance being a tax on the nearest village; and a few of these apologies for a *gendarmerie* I encountered. The road follows the river down a gorge for nearly two miles further, and then strikes up a lateral ravine, where an evil smell betrays the presence of sulphur in the water that oozes from the ground. In this ravine we continue for some time, until we reach the top of a steep declivity, whence a seemingly endless plain can be discerned stretching away in the direction of the sea, darkened by occasional clumps of date-palms, and terminating in sand hills that hide the waters of the Gulf. The last remaining descent, down an inclined plane formed by a peculiar pitch of the strata—a feeble parody of a *kotal*—alone remains; and we are presently

The Kotal-i-Kamarij, one of three notorious natural stairways between Shiraz and the sea. It takes its name from the place just left, and is the steepest, and, in some respects, most perilous of the four kotals, *there being a sheer drop of 1,200 feet in a distance of less than a mile, and the track being so narrow in parts that an up-coming cannot pass a down-going mule, without itself going over the precipice.*

Shapur bridge, a ruin, all but one or two arches of which have disappeared, then crosses the stream by a fine stone bridge of six arches, terminating in a causeway on the far side. This bridge and its pavement were both in better preservation than any kindred structures that I had seen in Persia, and were the work of the Mushir-el-Mulk.

The Karun river is described in text-books of geography as the only navigable river in Persia. (Below.) The Shushteris are as peculiar in their origin, appearance, and dress as they are in their character and surroundings. Neither pure Arab nor pure Persian in descent, but a hybrid between the two, with a greater admixture of Arab blood, they seem to possess the less attractive features of either race.

on the plain, where, striking the mountain base, we arrive in the course of a mile or two at the village of Daliki. The last stage, which is called four *farsakhs*, and is a good fifteen miles, had taken me five and a quarter hours to accomplish, for the most part on foot.

Around the village of Daliki, which is small and wholly undistinguished, grow a number of plants, known as *ghark*, which also occur, and are called *kalablab*, between Shushter and Dizful. The shrub grows to a height of seven to ten feet, has large greyish leaves, and a flower which I did not see, but which is said to be white and purple in colour. From the fibres surrounding the seeds silk fabrics used to be made; but the material is now used for stuffing cushions. Soon after leaving the village, the road crosses a stream whose waters run an emerald green from the sulphur with which they are impregnated; while on the stagnant pools floats a bituminous scum. Sulphuretted fumes also fill the air and invade the nostrils. The Rev. H. Martyn described the place in 1810 as 'one of Nature's ulcers'; but when the excellent missionary employed it his thermometer was standing at 126°. A little below in the plain is a bitumen pit, from which the natives have long been in the habit of collecting that substance, principally as a prescription for the sore backs of camels, and for the smearing of boat and roof timbers. It was for the working of the petroleum springs suspected to exist here that a concession was procured from the Persian Government, in 1884, by Messrs. Hotz, of Bushire. Their boring was unsuccessful; but the experiment has since been renewed by the Persian Mining Rights Corporation, whose engineers have sunk a bore to a depth of over eight hundred feet, so far without much result, but who are not likely to leave the region until its oleiferous capacities, be they great or small, have been thoroughly tested. Several other streams also flow here from the mountains; and the largest of them meanders down to the plain, and is there lost in a feverish-looking swamp. Beyond, a noble belt of date-palms supplies relief to the eye, and a living to the villagers of Daliki.

The road presently strikes southwards towards a low swell of hilly ground that still separates us from the sea-level; climbs this, alternately rises and sinks in its undulations, and finally emerges on the palm-girdled village of Borazjun (the true name is said to be Gurazdun, or Place of Boars). From a distance one might imagine this to be a place of some military importance; for several miles away can be seen the lofty walls and corner towers of an immense structure, whose other surface is pierced with loopholes only, and presents a decidedly feudal appearance. A longer acquaintance with Persia teaches the wayfarer that it cannot possibly be a fort, because every Persian fort is in ruins, and warns him that he is gazing upon nothing more formidable than a caravanserai; although among the scores that I had seen, this was without exception both the best constructed and the best preserved. It was built in 1875–6 by the same public-spirited official whom I have before eulogised, travellers before that date having bitterly complained of the lack of any similar building. I went in and inspected the interior. It is built of solid stone, well quarried and laid, and contains, in addition to the normal recesses, rooms, and stables, opening out of the central court, a number of upstairs apartments and sleeping-places, designed for the rich and for those travelling with women in their train. The walls of these chambers had been plentifully adorned by the pencils of Persian visitors of an artistic turn; but their imagination had found no higher outlet than the reproduction of steamboats and vessels with all sails spread, the most striking maritime reminiscence, no doubt, to a people possessing an hereditary terror of the sea. From the roof of the caravanserai can be gained an extensive prospect of the plain, of the town below (reputed to contain 6,000 persons), of the site at a little distance where the Persians ignominiously evacuated their position without firing a shot, in the short Anglo-Persian campaign of 1857; and of the long line of mountains, concealing behind their grim ramparts those hideous *kotals* which it was such a profound relief to have quitted, and which I hope never to tread again. The village youths of Borazjun were busily engaged in rustic games, among which hockey and rounders (the precise equivalent to the English game) appeared to be the most popular. Considering that they played on a very rough and stony piece of ground, and with bare feet, the most eager of English schoolboys would have felt little temptation to join in the fun. I noticed at Borazjun that all the men were armed with big pistols, loosely stuck in the belt; and, upon inquiring the reason of this singularly un-Persian habit heard that it is peculiar to Borazjun and a few surrounding places, the inhabitants of which revel in the open profession of robbery, and in the luxury of blood-feuds, still in a comparatively early stage of existence. The only other speciality at the time of my visit was a flight of locusts, which had recently appeared, and was doing irreparable damage to whatever of green was above ground. Not even the prospect of a good dinner cheap—for, like John the Baptist, the natives boil and eat the locusts in the manner of shrimps—could reconcile the Borazjunis to this terrible scourge.

Before bidding a final farewell to the mountain region and the *kotals*, let me here say that it would be paying a most undeserved compliment to the intelligence of the Persian muleteers to suppose that the route which I have described is the easiest or best channel of traffic between Shiraz and the Gulf. It is neither. It is a road that has been selected quite at haphazard, simply because somebody started it, and others followed suit, or because it appeared to take the shortest possible cut for the required destination. Very often it follows the steepest and least practicable of the various available lines; and the continuity with which it has now for more than a century been pursued as the main avenue of commercial entry into, and exit from, Persia on the south, is a combined monument to the apathy and resolution of the Persian character. Bad as it is from the mercantile point of view, from the strategical it is infinitely worse. No field guns in the world could be hauled up those horrible stairways, although a mule battery might negotiate them with success. Similarly they are impracticable for cavalry, except with native mounts; while either cavalry or infantry would frequently require to march in single file. For either commercial or military purposes it may be useful, therefore, to point out that, by a somewhat longer détour, each of the appalling *kotals* above described can be turned and avoided; the general plan to be followed being that of adhering, as closely as possible, to the channels of the rivers, instead of cutting at right angles over the intervening ridges. Thus, the descent to Daliki, the Kotal-i-Mallu, the Kotal-i-Kamarij, and the Teng-i-Turkan, can all be escaped by following up from the coast plains the left bank of the Shapur river to the point where I have traced it as flowing through the gorge with the Sassanian tablets. By still adhering to its course in the plain beyond, we turn the angle of the range that overhangs the Kazerun valley, and emerge into the upper end of the Dasht-i-Barm, or Valley of Oaks, thus avoiding the Kotal-i Dokhter. Finally, the Old Woman can be escaped by striking the mountains at a point two miles east of the present road, where the range dips into the Dasht-i-Arzen. There is also, of course, the more circuitous southern route, from Bushire to Shiraz by Firuzbad, but this is considerably longer, being about 210 to 220 miles. It was down this latter route that the Persians brought their guns in 1857, only incontinently to abandon them as soon as they had reached the plain. The ascent would be a more difficult undertaking, and would require the preparatory labours of a large force of sappers.

About six miles south of Borazjun is the small hamlet of Khushab, which was the scene of the night attack made by the Persians upon the British force under Sir J.

Outram, on February 8, 1857—the sole exploit indulged in by the main Persian army in that short-lived campaign. The British troops had landed south of Bushire in December, had stormed the fort of Reshire, and had shelled and captured Bushire. Then on February 3 they advanced: 2,200 English, 2,000 Indian and Beluch troops, 420 Indian cavalry, 2 light field batteries, and 18 guns. The Persian army, under the Shuja-el-Mulk, consisting of 5,000 infantry, 800 cavalry, and 18 guns, was encamped at Borazjun. Upon the approach of Outram they bolted without firing a shot, leaving their camp, equipments, and ammunition as a prey to the British. Outram blew up their powder magazine, and, conscious that nothing was to be gained, but everything lost, by throwing himself into the *kotals*, began to march back towards Bushire—a movement which the Persians, who are learned in the casuistry of retreat, have always interpreted as a sign of discomfiture. In the night the Persian cavalry attacked the column, while the infantry were found drawn up at Khushab. The cavalry and artillery of the British very soon decided the contest, and by the early morning the Persians were in full flight, leaving 700 killed, as against 16 of the British force. The theatre of war was then transferred to the Karun, where an even less creditable show was made by the *serbaz* of the Shah. It was probably not a very wise step to send a British force to Bushire at all, unless we meant to hold the place. As it was, the war partook of the nature of a series of demonstrations, which were rather summarily cut short by the Treaty of Paris in March.

The ordinary caravan-track from Borazjun to Bushire runs *viá* Ahmedi (where is a caravanserai), and across the low-lying, often swampy ground, called the Mashileh, that connects the peninsula of Bushire with the mainland. The distance is a little under forty miles. For such, however, as are fortunate enough to receive the British Resident's hospitality, and the loan of his steam-launch, a shorter route is available from Borazjun to Shif, a distance of twenty-five miles; whence a short sea passage across the arm of the Gulf that severs Bushire from the coast deposits the delighted traveller at the terminus of his journey. The road to Shif is as smooth as a billiard table, crawling over which at a pace adapted to the movements of tired baggage-mules is slow work. At Khushab the inhabitants were engaged in shaking the locusts from the boughs of the tamarisk trees, and greedily picking them up and stuffing them into sacks for future use at the breakfast table. Here I left the telegraph poles, which take a more southerly line to Ahmedi, and steered a westerly course for Shif. A good many sand-grouse were visible on the way, and, after the fashion of game in general, were as annoyingly tame to the unarmed voyager on horseback as they are wild to the sportsman on foot with a gun. Though the temperature was cool and pleasant, a mirage trembled above the heated soil, and gave frequent glimpses of a sea that ever receded, and of islets that resolved themselves into tiny heaps of sand. The distorting powers of the illusion (called *sirab* by the Persians) seemed to be limited to objects near the surface, but upon that level there was no limit to its achievements; for what appeared at some distance to be the ruins of an extensive marble edifice were converted upon approach into the lank members of an old white horse browsing upon the scrub. At length was visible a square building with a tower, that turned out to be the solitary glory, nay, the sole structure of Shif. It is a dilapidated caravanserai, standing within a few yards of a slimy beach, where a sluggish water laps the sand. Colonel Ross's launch was lying a quarter of a mile off; and a boat was waiting to transfer me to its welcome variety of locomotion. How glad I was to take off the saddle and saddlebags and holsters, to say goodbye to my rickety *yabu*, and to feel that I had without any accident passed through Persia from sea to sea. Shif faces a shallow bay, on the opposite side of which is the small fishing village of Sheikh Saad. Rounding this point, we came out into the open bay, and steered a line straight across for Bushire, whose wind-towers and occasional palms swelled into larger prominence above the waves. Steamers tossing in the offing, quite three miles away, revealed the nature of the anchorage at the first port in Persia. Skirting the eastern face of the town, which, though squalid enough to a new comer, deserves a high rank amongst Persian maritime cities, the launch deposited me at the Governor's Bunder. The Union Jack streaming from the top of a gigantic mast—by far the loftiest object in Bushire—proclaimed the site of the British Residency; and in ten minutes' time I was the guest and inmate of an English home.

Bushire (lit. Abu Shehr) is a town without a history, or at least with only such a history as an existence of 150 years can supply. Originally a small fishing village, it was selected by Nadir Shah in the middle of the last century as his southern port, and as the dockyard of the navy which he aspired to create in the Gulf. A little later, after the collapse of their business at Bunder Abbas, the East India Company transferred their factory to Bushire, where they received *firmans* conferring trading privileges upon them from Kerim Khan Zend. Matters progressed very slowly at the outset, there being only one English merchant in the place when Niebuhr was there in 1765. Gradually, however, as the mercantile marine of the Gulf was developed, and caravans into the interior began to adopt the route of the *kotals*, Bushire grew in size and importance, and at the beginning of the present century had about 6,000–8,000 inhabitants. Under the immense increase in recent years of traffic both by land and sea, the place has swollen to larger dimensions, and now contains a mixed population of 15,000 persons. The town is situated at the northern extremity of a peninsular, eleven miles long by four broad, which is identified with the Mesambria of Arrian, where the fleet of Nearchus cast anchor, and found plantations and gardens. This peninsula has at some period been recovered from the sea, which only a century ago used sometimes to flow across the narrow neck immediately south of the town, converting the latter into an island. Since then the land has steadily risen, and this phenomenon no longer occurs; but the water from the interior or eastern bay occasionally overflows the low-lying flats near the walls, and turns them into a swamp. The town itself has a rather better elevation, being situated upon a ledge of sandy conglomerate stone, which projects above the sea-level, and gives the place from a distance a more imposing appearance than is warranted by a closer inspection.

The people of Bushire, as of all the coast towns in the Dashtistan, were formerly entirely Arabs, ruled by a sheikh of the tribe of Matarish, who had emigrated in the seventeenth century from Oman. In the middle of the last century, Sheikh Nasar (variously reported as being of this family, and of the Nejd tribe of Abu Muheiri), a very remarkable man, raised himself to a position of great authority and wealth, and retained his independence throughout the reign of Kerim Khan. He was master of Bahrein, as well as of Bushire, and much of the Dashtistan, and maintained a large fleet, with which he traded with Muscat and India, and an easily mobilised army of devoted Arabs; he imported Nejd stallions from Arabia, and greatly improved the Gulf breed of horses; and finally, upon his death, bequeathed to his son a fortune of two millions sterling. The latter, bearing the same name, received from his dying father a legacy of fidelity to the cause of the youthful Luft Ali Khan, whom he assisted to place on the throne of Persia, although before long there was disagreement between the pair. At the beginning of the present century, Sheikh Abdur Rasul, grandson of the first, and son of the second, Nasr, was Governor of Bushire; but his sluggish and unwarlike temperament suggested to the government of Fath Ali Shah, already beginning to assert its authority over the outlying portions of the kingdom, the opportunity of interference. The sheikh was seized, by the perfidious violation of an oath upon the

Koran, while the mission of Sir Harford Jones was in Bushire in 1809, and was carried off to Shiraz, where his execution was ordered. Having somehow saved his life, the sheikh, in the alternate ups and downs of Asiatic fortune, found himself again installed a few years later at Bushire, where, from 1816–30, he was continually engaged in conflict, either with a brother named Mohammed on the spot, or with the Persian Governor of Shiraz. A traveller in 1830, while Sir E. Stannus was Resident at Bushire, represented the state of affairs as so critical that guns were planted by the sheikh, and levelled at the Residency, which was barricaded with furniture and lumber, and with a breastwork of water-casks and wine-chests in the courtyard. In 1832, this trouble-some chieftain, whose mischievousness had increased with his years, was murdered in the fort at Borazjun. Another brother, Sheikh Husein, and a son, Sheikh Rasul, continued the family tactics of internal dissension, varied by revolt against the sovereign power, and spent their days either in a state of armed siege at Bushire, or in prison at Shiraz. So matters continued till a little after the middle of the century, when the Government finally asserted its force, and Bushire has ever since received a Persian nominee. At the time of my visit (1889–90) it was under the jurisdiction of the Saad-el-Mulk, a person of low origin, and formerly a *munshi*, or clerk, to the present Governor of Fars, who had been placed by the Amin-es-Sultan as Governor of the Gulf Ports, in charge of the coast-fringe from Bunder Dilam to Jask. The garrison of Bushire consisted of 300 to 400 *serbaz*, and 50 to 60 artillerymen, with some old and rotten guns, lying near the Governor's Bunder, miscalled the Arsenal by the Persians. In the past year (1891) the Saad-el-Mulk was displaced by his elder brother, the Nizam-es-Sultaneh, who was Governor of Arabistan when I was at Shushter.

The change effected in the rulers of Bushire has been reflected in its population. Till the last twenty years the Arab element was largely in the ascendant, although, to a great extent, Persianised both in dress and religion. As trade, however, has increased, and purely maritime occupations have declined, the Persian ingredients have gained the upper hand, and now largely predominate, although the bulk of the people are still of Arab, or mixed Arab and Persian descent. There are about a hundred Armenians in Bushire engaged in trade (fifty years ago, the missionary Dr. J. Wolff founded a school for them here, which subsequently collapsed), and a European contribution of about

Bushire, a town without history, only 150 years in existence.

fifty, supplied by the staff of the Residency and Telegraph department, and by the representatives of business houses, who have much increased in recent years.

The western front of Bushire, facing the open sea, is the most pretentious, for here are the British Residency—a large building with two courts, at whose doorway is always stationed an Indian guard—and the principal European residences or places of business, some of which are lofty and two-storeyed, built of stone, and with verandahs facing the sea. The horizontal lines of the natives' houses at Bushire are broken by frequent *badgirs*, or wind-towers, with narrow slits to admit the air; and on some of the roof-tops may be seen awnings, for sleeping in summer. Considering the size of the town, the bazaars are extensive, though narrow and confined. The bulk of the streets are both narrow and filthy, and in the open spaces on the shore line may be seen encampments of low tents, and *kapars* or huts, made of date-sticks and leaves, the nauseous domiciles of the lower classes of the population. Such pretentiousness of air as the modern town can claim is largely due to the wise expenditure, by Sir L. Pelly, of part of the Mansion House Persian Famine Relief Fund in 1870–1, in the employment of local labour. On the southern side, or along the base of the triangle formed by the apex of the peninsula, the town was formerly fortified by a high wall with twelve towers and bastions and two gates, in front of which stood some old Portuguese guns, brought either from Reshire or Ormuz. The last time that this wall was repaired was in 1838, when Mohammed Shah rebuilt it, to withstand a possible attack from the English, who had occupied Kharak Island in that year. It has since fallen to pieces, and is now a model of nineteenth-century Persian fortification.

The climate of Bushire is trying though not acutely unhealthy. In summer, however, the heat is exhausting, and the thermometer frequently registers over 100° Fahr. in the shade. The average rainfall is about twelve inches in the year. Water is scarce, and most of the neighbouring supplies are brackish. The wells most commonly in use are situated on the plain at the distance of over a mile from the town gate; but the best sources are at five and six miles distant in the direction of Reshire. At the time of my visit the price of the ordinary quality was 5–6 *puls* ($\frac{3}{4}d$.), of the better quality 16 *puls* ($2\frac{1}{4}d$.) per donkey-load. A large reservoir to collect rain-water was built on the sea-front some years ago by a native merchant, and was opened for the public use in April and May; but its contents were found to be infested with the *reshta* or guinea-worm, which 200 years ago was complained of by Chardin and Kaempfer, as tainting the water-supplies along the Gulf coast.

Though Bushire is the main port of Persia, it possesses nothing that could by the wildest exaggeration be described under present conditions as a harbour. The anchorage is in an open and unprotected roadstead at the distance of some three miles from the shore, is much exposed to gales, and in bad weather is inaccessible. Every cargo has to be embarked or disembarked in native buggalows, and the process of lading and unlading is in consequence very slow. The inner bay on the western side is intended by nature, and was formerly used, as a harbour, there being deep water close up to the town. A bar, however, has formed opposite its entrance, and boats drawing over ten feet of water cannot pass. The use of a dredger, and the expenditure of a few hundred pounds, would remedy this, without the need of any costly piers or structure; and the impotence of the Persian Government in this respect lends an additional argument to those who contend that Great Britain should not have evacuated Bushire, for the retention of which the Persians thoroughly expected us to stipulate, in 1857. Of the trade of the port I may here say that in 1889 the customs were sold by the Saad-el-Mulk for 91,000 *tomans*, or 26,000*l.* + 5,000 *tomans*, or 1,400*l.*, *pishkesh*, i.e. present to himself; the farmer also making a large profit, so that the actual amount levied upon imports and exports was greatly in excess of this sum.

About six miles to the south of the town are the ruins of the old Portuguese fort of Reshire. This was no doubt the earliest settlement on the peninsula of Mesambria; for in the mounds here have been found bricks with cuneiform characters, and other remains of a considerable antiquity.[3] The Portuguese established a trading station and built a fort here in the sixteenth century, but were turned out by the Persians after the capture of Ormuz in 1622. The fort was repaired in 1856, and occupied by Persian troops, who made a gallant but ineffectual resistance against the British, the latter losing four officers in the attack. It covers a quadrangular space, 250 yards in diameter, and the ramparts still retain a steep and lofty profile, and the remains of the old ditch. Near here the Indo-European Telegraph department shifted its quarters from Bushire in 1876, to a series of fine buildings, six in number, with a club-room, garden, and lawn-tennis court. Just below, the wires run down into the sea. A little further inland is Sebzabad, the summer quarters of the British Resident, a commodious verandahed building with a pretty garden, and a mud volcano in the grounds. Hither he retires with his staff in the hot months, but it struck me that the place is situated too far from the sea to get the full benefit of whatever breeze may be generated by the Persian Gulf.

The Union Jack fluttering from the summit of the Residency flag-staff is no vain symbol of British ascendency in Bushire. The steamers lying at the anchorage are with scarcely an exception British steamers; the goods that crowd the stalls in the bazaar are British or Indian goods; the rupee is as readily, nay more readily, accepted than the *kran*. There must be many a Persian who has contrasted the smart bodyguard of the British Resident with the slatternly escort of the native Governor. In appearance and structure the English quarter of the town is not unlike an Indian station; while the friendly sentiments of the populace were unmistakably shown by the manner in which was celebrated at Bushire the Jubilee of the British Queen. For nearly twenty years the interests of this country have been in the faithful keeping of Colonel Ross in this distant outpost, not of British power, but of British influence; and he has lately handed over to his successor a position whose unwritten authority is among the many silent monuments to the British name.

---

[1] From my reading I learn that this artificial causeway was first made by the mother of Imam Kuli Khan, Viceroy of Fars under Shah Abbas, at which time Thévenot says it was called Kotal-i-Oshanek, or Pass of the wild marjoram, a name that still survives. At the end of the last century it was reconstructed by Haji Mohammed Husein, a wealthy merchant of Bushire, his motive being variously described as philanthropic, and as strictly mercenary, and having relation only to the losses previously incurred by accidents to his own caravans. About 1820 it was put in thorough repair by Kelb Ali Khan, Governor of Kazerun, and impressed Rich so greatly that he called it the Simplon of Persia! It was again repaired in 1834 by the mother of Timur Mirza, and in about 1870 by the Mushir-el-Mulk, Vizier of Fars; since which date I should imagine that not a penny has been spent upon it.

[2] Would it be believed that the innocent A. Arnold speaks of this clumsy bas-relief as 'some interesting ruins of ancient Persia, where a monarch, heavily bewigged with false hair, in the fashion of Ancient Persia, and as marvellously bearded, is seated with a lion before him, his chair of state encircled by attendants' (*Through Persia by Caravan*, vol. ii. p. 186). And this is how history is written!

[3] The principal of these are a number of old sculptured tombstones, probably of the Arab period (*vide* Morier's *Second Journey*, p. 45); and an immense collection of stone and earthenware vases of rude shape and fabrication, sealed up with earthenware lids or with coverings of talc, sometimes lined inside with a coating of bitumen, and containing human skulls and bones. A great number of these have been found between Bushire and Reshire, at a depth of about two feet below the surface, usually placed horizontally in a long line, one after the other. The jars are about three feet in length and one foot in diameter. They are supposed to have contained the remains of Zoroastrians, after the body had perished by exposure.

PERSIA,
AFGHANISTAN
& BELUCHISTAN.

Compiled under the supervision of Hon. G. Curzon, M.P.

by Wm. Jno. Turner, F.R.G.S.

1891

NATURAL SCALE 1/3,810,000 = 60 MILES TO AN INCH

English Miles